Scale and
Social Organization

Scale and Social Organization

Edited by
FREDRIK BARTH

Universitetsforlaget
Oslo — Bergen — Tromsø

© The Norwegian Research Council for Science and
the Humanities 1978
(Norges almenvitenskapelige forskningsråd)
Section: B.50.30–006T

Cover: Oddvar Wold

ISBN 82–00–01707–9

Printed in Norway by
A/S John Grieg

Distribution offices:
NORWAY
Universitetsforlaget
P.O.Box 2977, Tøyen
Oslo 6

UNITED KINGDOM
Global Book Resources Ltd.
109 Great Russell Street
London WC1B 3Nd

UNITED STATES and CANADA
Columbia University Press
136 South Broadway
Irvington–on–Hudson
New York 10533

Acknowledgements

The meetings which led to the present essays were sponsored by the Wenner-Gren Foundation for Anthropological Research, who also provided a grant for subsequent editorial work. We gratefully acknowledge this support.

Contents

FREDRIK BARTH

Introduction

This symposium seeks to raise and confront analytical problems of scale: the causes and consequences of differences in size and numbers in social systems. How can anthropologists study and describe large-scale social systems without losing sight of real people and their life situations? How can they represent the complexity of complex societies, yet cast their description in an analytical mold which may also serve for simpler societies, thus securing comparability between such diverse forms? How can they delimit a 'convenient area' as an object og study without isolating it from all those events and circumstances outside the area which are major determinants of life within it? How can they relate the actions of a person and his conception of a finite, ego-centred world to the global realities that actually impinge on him?

These rhetorical questions touch on recurrent and troubling themes in much contemporary anthropology, and some other social sciences as well. We generally turn to conceptualizations of *scale* to pose them: small worlds, large-scale organizations, little communities, mass societies, global systems. How can we conceptualize these different levels of system and their interrelations more rigorously — or have we perhaps already, in framing our questions in this way, reified 'levels' and the character of the properties that distinguish them?

The purpose of this symposium is to treat such issues by *investigating* them; concretely by drawing on a wide range of enthographies and comparing forms of local and regional organization, depicting the ethnographically different ways in which persons and social systems are constituted, and giving special attention to the possible effects of size, or the phenomenon of numbers and their consequences.

The papers were originally elicited for a symposium on the theme 'Scale and Social Organization' at Burg Wartenstein, sponsored by the Wenner-Gren Foundation for Anthropological Research.[1] These papers were given a certain unity by a brief pre-conference circular suggesting questions of the kind posed in this brief introduction, together with a reprint of a then-recent article of mine (Barth 1972). They were intensively discussed, and have been variously rewritten to utilize insights developed in these discussions. But the papers clearly also derive from other distinctive sources: the anthropology of each separate author. Herein lies their main value: each treats the topic from a considered and independent perspective. There is consequently no need or place for me to introduce them. What I can more usefully do here is restate their common theme and my intention in taking the initiative in organizing the symposium. A discussion of the major points I learned from the symposium is presented separately in the last chapter of this book.

In the broad comparative writings of earlier soical science, comparative discussions of different societies with reference to such differences in scale, and their correlates, were common. Various sets of concepts were created in this connection, reviewed extensivesively in Berreman's paper in this volume. Such concepts may have reflected their creators' assumptions more than their empirical generalizations (cf. Berreman p. 46) in that they were cast to embody a thesis rather than a discovery procedure; yet they continue to be used by us. The stubborn persistence of the terms *Gemeinschaft*, 'organic solidarity', 'folk culture', and the like must be a measure of the importance of the questions to which they address themselves, and perhaps the light which they shed on these questions. But whereas we have seen a great development in the quality and number of anthropological analyses of social organizations since these terms were coined, we have seen few attempts to utilize this increased range of materials to develop or replace the early, synthesizing terms themselves, and the perspectives they represent. I suggest the time has come to take stock. This does not mean that we need to elaborate a more complex typology of societies, though we certainly want an alternative to the binary simplicity of large vs. small in various terminological disguises; rather, I feel we need to developed ways of conceptualizing which facilitate *discovery* and conceptual *development*. We achieve little, if we simply repeat in unfamiliar words the familiar insight that many features of smallscale societies are conditioned by their smallness, of large-scale societies by their large size: we must become able to use our store of documented and analyzed descriptions of societies to develop our concept of scale so we can show how form is conditioned by scale; specifically for each assertion, and in middle ranges as well as the extremes.

Concretely, our theme concerns such simple questions as this: we recognize that a neighbourhood with 50 residents in the Andaman islands, a Thai village, and New York City differ not just in features such as kinship system, religious organization, or forms of property — they are fundamentally differently constituted internally and in external relations in ways which entail different orders of magnitude of size, numbers and complexity: i.e. different *scale*. Indeed, the fact that they may share the feature of bilaterial kinship organization cannot disguise the feeling that the Andamans may be fundamentally 'more like' a matrilineal South American Indian community than they are 'like' the Thai village or New York City. How do we transform this recognition — not by producing another label for small-scale/large-scale, but by constructing a framework for discovering what in fact are the basic differences in the constitution of men and societies?

Or, if we look at some densely populated areas of the world, we will find that in some places they divide into small, face-to-face community segregates, other places not at all. But how does life differ for the individual in an unsegmented mass of 100,000 from life in a small village community in an area populated by 100,000? What are the forms of social organization capable of giving some shape and order to the life of the 100,000 in the former case, *without* producing a set of primary, small-scale segments? And what are the processes which sustain a seperation into villages in the latter case, yet connect these villages, or their component residents, in certain larger-scale systems?

We should bear in mind that "scale" must not arise as an artifact of analysis, but rather be an empirical property of the things we study. We should not confound our freedom to construct models of any size we choose, by handling factors variously as endogenous and exogenous, with our efforts to discover in what senses the world of the Andamans is smaller than that of New York City people; and how this arises from, and has implications for, respective social organizations.

As a first approach: it is taken for granted that the social institutions of the Andamans simply do not have the capacity to organize large populations — but I am not aware of any methodology whereby this can be demonstrated to be so. Obversely, we are familiar with studies of small and peripheral communities in Western society which seem to function with characteristic difficulties because of their smallness, e.g. in their handling of bureaucratic organizational procedures; but generalizations arising from such materials are few and tentative. We have yet to formulate even the simplest principles and generalizations on the capacity of different forms of social organization to organize populations of different sizes.

Or we might choose to put a rather different question: how do changes in the gross size of the population affect the actual overt form and functioning of groups organized by unchanging social principles? This forces us initially to distinguish features of empirical life which arise from size and numbers of population from those features which reflect cultural values, technological constraints, mode of production, etc. Holding these latter factors constant may prove hypothetical, in that the changing situation generated by population changes leads to individual and collective adaptations of behaviour, and probably in turn to changed principles of social organization. But this perspective on the process reveals precisely those interconnections with which we are concerned, as Colson shows in her paper.

Or we might perform a mental experiment: What would happen if, in the present population of e.g. Bangladesh, an entirely different distribution of skills, rights, and duties could be introduced? Without changing the physical lay-out of villages and residences, we might see an entirely different organization of groups and activities spring to life, with entirely new scale properties in terms of mobilization for joint effort, aggregate production, etc. Perhaps the clearest historical instance of such a transformation occurred when labour was "organized" in many Western countries during the first half of this century — through the simple organizational device of unions, poulation mass was converted into political weight, with varying but profound repercussions for the societies concerned. Yet in these same political systems we also can observe the impression management of pressure groups, the image-making of polls and demonstrations, which show us that not only the awareness, but also the illusions of scale can have consequences.

The essays presented here take up a wide range of aspects and problems connected with this theme. They treat concepts, methods, and empirical materials; they discuss middle-range size as well as the extremes, networks and social persons as well as regions and macro-phenomena, face-to-face interaction as well as ideology. The final chapter attempts to draw together some of the strands of these discussions.

J. A. BARNES

Neither Peasants nor Townsmen: a Critique of a Segment of the Folk-urban Continuum

1. The continuum

Most discussions of 'scale' examine the contrast between small-scale and large-scale societies. However, this contrast makes sense only in terms of some scheme for classifying all societies in terms of a few characteristics. Strictly conceived, the scheme must reduce each society to a single index – the scale of the society – however we may choose to define that characteristic. Contrasting extremes is easy, for at one end there is only one society to examine, the world-wide system in which most people live nowadays, or one or other part of this; there is no room on earth for more than one such giant. At the other end there is a plurality of societies competing for paradigm status: Tikopia, Siriono, the Bushmen, the Baktaman studied by Barth, and several others. Nevertheless the contrast is easy to stage, for whichever small scale society we select, we simply list those many characteristics that differentiate it from Megalopolis and then summarize the differences by labelling the two configurations as small-scale and large-scale. Berreman, in his contribution to this symposium, has dealt comprehensively with the many examples of this dichotomous mode of analysis, so I need not repeat what he has said.

The utility of this procedure can be tested properly only by turning away from the extreme cases and looking at the middle of the range. It is in the middle, and only there, that we can check whether the various characteristics we have lumped together as 'scale' do in fact keep in step with one another and vary concomitantly as we move from one end of the range to the other. Unfortunately this cannot be done directly, for the constituents of scale are still a matter for debate, even at the two extreme points. The word 'scale' has been current for many centuries, but its employment as a summary index of societal differences over the whole observed range dates from 1945, when the Wilsons published their *Analysis of social change*. They do not link their own analysis to earlier typologies of societies; and although they introduce scale as a quality possessed in varying degree by all societies, the Wilsons concentrate their attention on the contemporary plight of Africans living in central

13

and southern Africa. As a first step towards the possible construction of an analytical scheme based on the notion of scale, whether understood in conformity with the Wilsons' definition or not, it may be useful to examine other comparative schemes and see how they handle intermediate societies. In this chapter I attempt to scrutinize one of these schemes, that developed by Robert Redfield, with particular reference to the society he designates as falling exactly at the midpoint of the range, as he perceives it. I round off my discussion by commenting on the relation between Redfield's scheme and an alternative that might be based on the notion of scale.

Redfield developed his ideas of folk society and of the folk-urban continuum in a series of publications stretching from 1930 almost to his death in 1958. He first presented the full range of the continuum in his book on Yucatan (1941) where he contrasted four communities: a tribal village, a peasant village, a town, and a city. In his later writings he continued to give greater attention to the rural or folk half of the continuum, while the urban end remained the domain of his Chicago colleague Louis Wirth (1938). Redfield gave more of his attention to tribesmen than to peasants; but in his Cooper Foundation lectures, delivered in 1955, he set out to delineate peasant communities. He went even further, approximately half-way along his continuum, in describing a community which was 'outside of but not very far away from the cluster of little communities to which I have applied the word "peasant"'. He said, 'We need a basis for comparison on the more modernized side of peasantry as well as on the more primitive side' (Redfield 1956:41).

Redfield's views on folk society have attracted a good deal of comment (Lewis 1951: 432–440; Miner 1952; Foster 1953, 1967; Lopreato 1965; Paine 1966; Pahl 1966, 1967; Lupri 1967; Ortiz 1971), but most of the discussion has understandably been aimed at the rural end of the continuum and has left undisturbed the centre section running between peasant villages and towns. In this chapter I shall leave aside the question of what constitutes a peasant community, a topic on which there is now a growing body of literature (Shanin 1971, 1972, 1973; Powell 1972a, 1972b; Mendras 1972; Claus 1973). Nor shall I examine the intellectual roots of Redfield's perceptions and his notion of towns and cities, except to note that Scandinavian cities differ radically from those cities of the American Middle West of the 19th century (with Chicago as the exemplary case) which provided Robert Ezra Park and his followers, including his son-in-law Redfield, with their urban archetype (Benet 1963). Here I shall look only at the centre section of the continuum, for in his 1955 lectures Redfield's example of a community lying somewhere between a peasant village and a town was the rural district of Bremnes, in western Norway, as described in an article I had published a year earlier. My description was based on fieldwork carried out in 1952–53. I now know a little more about Bremnes than I then did, and in the ensuing twenty years the community has changed radically.

Two topics present themselves for discussion. In the light of additional information, how does Bremnes, as it was in 1952, fit into Redfield's continuum? How do the changes that have occurred in Bremnes since 1952 relate to the changes predicated by Redfield's scheme? Both topics bear on the notion of scale, and of changes in scale, which forms the focus of this symposium. Both topics are legitimate in Redfield's terms, for he presents his continuum as both morphological and developmental. His continuum is a dimension or multi-dimensional field on which communities can be placed, but it is also a sequence showing how communities shift through time in response to external influences, typically emanating from cities, and to internally-generated social pressures.

Redfield does not use any single index such as 'scale' as a metric to specify position on the continuum, but instead supplies descriptive labels for specified areas of the continuum. There are only two basic ways in which labels of this kind can be applied, irrespective of whether we view the continuum synchronically or diachronically. Either the labels are the names for segments or localities within the continuum, thus providing us with a typology by which real communities may be sorted into a small number of pidgeon-holes; or they are names for points on the continuum, giving us a set of ideal or polar reference types, to which real communities approximate or from which they diverge in specifiable ways. On the whole, Redfield adopts the latter alternative (Tambiah 1955: 45–46). He says

We may conceive those societies and cultures in which we are interested as lying scattered about an imaginary field of real societies that differ from and resemble one another in many different ways. The reader might choose one cluster of neighbouring real societies within the field; I might choose another (Redfield 1956: 26).

I interpret this to mean that Redfield sees his continuum as continuous, without natural breaks, and that therefore any labelling or partitioning can be done only arbitrarily. His use of the term 'field' suggests that he sees the continuum as multidimensional. The labels are then an idiosyncratically chosen set of reference points or localities within a multidimensional continuum. Yet Redfield's use

15

of the contrast primitive/modernized indicates that he has a particular direction in mind in locating Bremnes 'outside of but not very far from' his cluster of peasant communities. What criteria indicate position along this direction? In discussing Bremnes and peasant communities, Redfield looks at the basis of subsistence (agriculture and fishing), industrialization, the market, the significance of kinship, the concern with profit, the role of the intelligentsia, the distinction between moral and technical orders, and relations between the countryside and the city. How does the fuller evidence now available match up against Redfield's characterizations?

2. Agriculture, fishing and profit

The territory of Bremnes consists of several islands. In 1952 only a third of the adult men living in Bremnes regarded fishing as their main occupation, but most men in the community gained most of their income from fishing rather than from agriculture. Is it the financial importance of fishing that makes the Bremnes of 1952 not a peasant community? The first people historically to be labelled as 'peasants' gained their livelihood by tilling the soil, and for this reason some modern writers (Wolf 1955: 453; Shanin 1966: 6; cf. Foster 1967) would restrict the sociological use of the term to agricultural producers of a specified type. Redfield appears not to take this view, for he refers approvingly (1956: 26–27) to Firth's use of the term 'peasant' to describe certain fishermen and even hunters and collectors (Firth 1964: 17–18; 1966; 1971; 14, 102; cf. Frankenberg 1967: 53). Unfortunately Redfield decides that 'one cannot do everything at once' and confines his own discussion to agricultural peasants. Hence it is not clear what he has in mind when he states (1956: 44–45) that in about 1800 'only the fishing, not yet industrialized, modified the peasant life' of Bremnes; the social system of dominant importance was based on cultivating the same land from year to year. Some clarification of the possible basis of this 'modification' may come when we examine his views on profit and markets.

Redfield goes on to say that by 1952 Bremnes fishing had become so industrialized that it was an activity fairly independent of peasant life on land. This statement suggests that while fishing may long ago have put the community in a marginal position, Bremnes in 1952 is pulled past the peasant cluster on the continuum because of the presence of industrialization. But again there is some confusion, for Redfield is referring to the industrialization of fishing, not to the arrival in Bremnes of impeccably industrial enterprises like a diesel engine factory and ship repair yard. The hallmarks of 'modern industrial society' are well known but the term 'industry' is applied much more widely, as when ethnographers speak of the useful industries of neolithic peoples, or prehistoric archaeologists of Acheulean and Magdelenian industries. Redfield says little about 'industry' as such, though at one point (1956: 58–59) he draws a contrast between 'industry outside of the indigenous local life, especially capitalistic and highly technological industry' and the 'economic field' found in traditional markets. The presence of markets cannot therefore be diagnostic of industrialization, in Redfield's terms. Yet to argue that Bremnes fishing had by 1952 become independent of peasant-like life on land merely because of technical changes – bigger boats, better nets – would be unconvincing. More plausibly we can argue that Redfield has in mind the capitalistic quality of Bremnes fishing, for it has always been an activity carried on for profit. Redfield argues that peasants 'have, at the least, this in common: their agriculture is a livelihood and a way of life, not a business for profit' (1956: 27), and he contrasts peasants with farmers who 'carry on agriculture for reinvestment and business, looking on the land as capital and commodity'. We might then infer that Redfield is saying that inasmuch as people in Bremnes have always been part-fishermen concerned to make a profit out of the sea they have never been true peasants; and that as fishing became more capitalistic, and hence the urge to make a profit became stronger, they became even less like peasants.

In contrast to farmers, peasants may be innocent of the profit motive; yet it seems that in contrast to members of tribal communities, they are already corrupted. In his Cooper Foundation lectures, where he deals with Bremnes at length, Redfield discusses peasants in relation to farmers, but in his Messenger lectures, delivered only three years earlier, he contrasts peasants with primitive or precivilized societies. Here he writes (1953: 33):

We may summarize the economic character of the peasant village by saying that it combines the primitive brotherhood of the precivilized folk community with the economic nexus characteristic of civilized society. So far as the peasant community faces inward, the relationships that compose it are still personal and familial, but now they are modified by a spirit of pecuniary advantage.

Redfield gives no indication that he consciously shifted his definition of peasant between the two sets of lectures. It seems therefore that we must interpret all his statements rather loosely and infer that he intends to say that while in all peasant societies there are some economic activities determined by considerations of profit, in Bremnes there were already in 1800 significantly more, and by 1952 very many more.

This gloss falls far short of giving us a measure along the traditional-modern dimension from peasant communities to towns, but it might appear at least to fit in with the contrast Redfield makes between 'a way of life' and 'a business for profit'. Agriculture in Bremnes in 1952 was not very profitable; it was directed more towards meeting subsistence needs than to market opportunities, and was partly influenced by the value attached to continuous occupation and cultivation over the generations. But even if Redfield's contrast makes sense in Yucatan, it cannot possibly have cross-cultural validity. Running a business for profit can be a quite traditional 'way of life' and demonstrably is so in the Highlands of New Guinea as much as in Wall Street and Petticoat Lane. It is possible to make the contrast in Bremnes, using emic categories; but, unfortunately for Redfield's formulation, agriculture does not form part of the Bremnes 'way of life' to which considerations of profit are inappropriate. The distinctive way of life is based on ultimate values which have special reference neither to agriculture nor to fishing; both modes of productive activity belong in Bremnes properly to the sphere of rational calculation of economic advantage, and the poor financial return from agriculture is a cause for regret rather than moral approval. The way of life predicated by the dominant pattern of values in Bremnes in 1952 was directed towards eternal life in Heaven rather than to any specific earthly goals.

3. The market

Neither a diminished concern with agriculture, nor increased industrialization, nor a desire to make a profit are satisfactory criteria for locating Bremnes in 1952 somewhere on the continuum on the modern side of peasantry. The other feature that Redfield draws upon in his discussion of Bremnes is the market. Does this provide the yardstick we need? He says:

> This is the second lesson from Barnes's account. It is the market, in one form or another, that pulls out from the compact social relations of self-contained primitive communities some parts of men's doing and puts people into fields of economic activity that are increasingly independent of the rest of what goes on in the local life (1956: 45–46).

Redfield goes on to contrast the local traditional and moral world with the impersonal world of the market, and postulates 'a series of societies in which the separation of the world of the market is progressively greater'. Ignoring the difficulty raised by the traditional morals of Wall Street, we are led to expect that the fishing market in Bremnes would be more independent of the rest of social life than it would be in a truly peasant community. Yet this is not so. It is true that, as Redfield notes, Bremnes fishermen in 1952 participated in a world-wide economy. Many of the fish caught by men from Bremnes were consumed as herring meal by livestock in the USSR and the USA. The price paid to the fishermen depended largely on what the Russians and Americans could be made to pay. The users of the fish were therefore spatially distant from the fishermen and the people of Bremnes had little control over the price they got. In this sense there is a substantial physical separation between Bremnes and its market. But I doubt that this is the kind of separation Redfield had in mind.

There was very little social separation between community life in Bremnes and the external market. The close link between them was demonstrated dramatically at the end of the 1950s, when there was a sudden large drop in the herring catch. The whole economy of the area was depressed, tax revenue fell, public works projects were introduced specifically designed to relieve local unemployment, training courses were arranged so that fishermen and others with related skills could gain alternative technical qualifications, and after a few years new styles of fishing began to spread in response to the new ecological and commercial situation. These social changes were set in motion by a change in the natural rather than in the human order – the failure of the fish to arrive at the right time and in the right place in sufficient numbers to be caught profitably – and were probably not due to overfishing in earlier years (Bakken & Dragesund 1971: 5). It is likely that similar changes might have been triggered off by an act in the human order; suppose that the Americans refused to buy fish. In Redfield's peasant societies, production for the market appears to be a fairly well segregated sector of social activity. By comparison, Bremnes social life in 1952 was much more, not less, closely connected to the world of the market. Indeed, it is misleading to say that 'the rural fishermen is largely separated off from the life on the land, and the fishing field is fluid, competitive, increasing independent of the ties formed in the local life' (Redfield 1956: 49). On the contrary: local life in Bremnes is increasingly dependent on ties formed to further activities emmeshed in the market economy.

4. Complexity and subsistence production

If dependence on markets fails to provide a satisfactory metric for calibrating the rural-urban continuum, what about technological complexity? Is this the aspect of industrialization that Redfield has in mind? This seems doubtful, even though the level of energy utilization does provide us with a scale for classifying communities that reproduces Redfield's order from tribal villages to cities. But Redfield was concerned with values and with symbolic rather than material culture, and for him the complexity of the city lies significantly in its division of labour rather than in its material equipment. It is true that by 1952 fishing in Bremnes had been modernized more than agriculture. Hand milking was general, many pastures were unimproved, there were few silos, hay was cut with short-handled scythes, and mechanization was present only in the drilling machines used for making holes for explosive charges set to blast rocks and so clear the land for cultivation. At the same time, fishing vessels were all powered with diesel engines, and the larger vessels, carrying crews of up to twenty men, were equipped with radio transmitters, echo sounders, and other modern equipment. But if fishing had, as Redfield suggests, already begun to modify peasant life 150 years ago, this cannot have been due to diesel engines and electronic gadgetry. Even with crews of up to twenty, the level of social complexity in Bremnes fishing vessels was not sufficiently higher than is found in many collective economic activities in peasant and tribal communities.

It is more fruitful to treat industrialization as referring to the contrast between production for domestic needs and production for the market. Redfield (1953: 31) explicitly makes the appearance of cities a precondition for the emergence of peasantry; 'There were no peasants before the first cities'. The peasants, in this scheme, produce a surplus which is used to sustain the city. Here Redfield's view is similar to Wolf's, in which the distinguishing feature of the peasant community is that it pays rent to a dominant group of rulers (Wolf 1966: 10). The remark already quoted about peasant activities being 'modified' by a spirit of pecuniary advantage suggests that Redfield envisages production for domestic or community needs as the dominant form of peasant activity, with production to meet the needs of the elite, or of the city, as subsidiary. Nevertheless he admits that in Chan Kom, his type specimen of a peasant village, half the staple crop of maize is sold in the market (Redfield 1941: 163, 1956: 47–48). Likewise, in Tepoztlan, a community with 'its nearest analogues in the peasant communities of the more backward parts of Europe, of the Near East, and of the

Orient' (Redfield 1930: 217, cf. 1956: 23–24), most of the produce is sold outside the village (Lewis 1951: 1970). Yet despite the reluctance of the ethnographic facts to fit the mould provided for them by the model, it seems reasonable to make a distinction between an economy principally oriented to local needs but producing a surplus which goes elsewhere, and one principally oriented to a distant market but producing some products for local use as well. This is the distinction made by Sturt (1912), whom Redfield cites, for a village in Surrey, England, before and after the enclosure of its common in 1861. Prior to enclosure, the villagers were principally engaged in subsistence agriculture. After enclosure, they became day labourers, mainly in tertiary industries, but they kept their gardens. In Bremnes, there has been commercial sale of fish to distant markets for at least a thousand years, but presumably in Viking times most of the fish caught was eaten locally. During the German occupation of Norway during World War II, domestic fishing was the main source of subsistence, and even in the most prosperous times there has always been a good deal of small-scale fishing, mainly of demersal fish, for home consumption. It is the herring fishery that Redfield refers to. Herring swim in vast shoals and when caught are usually available in quantities greatly in excess of local demand. Herring fishing, as carried out in western Norway for hundreds of years, is commercial fishing and cannot be anything else. But this does not mean that the inhabitants have never been peasants. In 1800 food, clothing, and building materials were mainly produced locally and used locally; and it is in these sectors of the economy, rather than in herring fishing, that the significant changes took place during the following 150 years. Well before 1952 the balance between subsistence and commercial production and consumption – however this may be measured, provided non-agricultural items are also included – had shifted in favour of commerce. It is in this sense that the people of Bremnes in 1952, like Sturt's Surrey villagers after enclosure, were no longer peasants.

5. The intelligentsia

If Bremnes in 1952 was not a peasant community because its economy was commercial rather than subsistence, how does its culture fit into Redfield's continuum? Did it have a peasant-like culture or was its culture significantly closer to the culture of a town? In delineating the culture of the typical peasant community Redfield assigns a special role to the intelligentsia. They are marginal persons, who learn the culture of the city and who then provide something the peasants can recognize as better than themselves (Redfield 1953: 44; 1956: 61–62). The intelligentsia mediate to the peasants the great tradition, so that it can blend with the indigenous little tradition of the locality. Redfield provides illustrations of this state of affairs from Mexico, Bulgaria, and French Canada, and he refers to former peasant conditions in Bremnes when the local minister was the sole resident representative of the national civil service.

We need not concern ourselves with the authenticity of the peasant credentials of Bremnes in 1800, when Norway was still a Danish colony and when the established clergy, among their other tasks, played the role of agricultural extension officers. For our present inquiry it is more relevant to ask where the intelligentsia was in 1952. During the latter half of the 19th century, local schoolteachers played the part of Redfield's intelligentsia much more effectively than their 18th century clerical forerunners, bringing the inhabitants into touch with the world of politics that centred on Bergen, Oslo, Stockholm, and Copenhagen, and with religious controversies that raged throughout northern Lutheran Europe. But by 1952 schoolteachers, as a social category, were no longer leaders in social and political life, though some individual teachers were prominent. The demands of teaching were greater than in the days of the 19th century ambulatory school system, leaving less time for participation in other activities. More alternative careers were open to ambitious local boys and girls than had been available in the 19th century, so that qualities of leadership were already far from being a monopoly of the teaching profession. The first generation of lay teachers, who began work in 1820, may well have had a better grasp of a 'great tradition' than the parents of the children they taught. The success of their efforts in school, combined with the widespread interest in literacy as the key to the Bible which flourished throughout the region during the 19th century, reduced the gap between the professional teachers and other members of the community. In 1952 it was members of the population as a whole, and not merely schoolteachers, who organized support for Christian missions, who attempted to defend the Pietist way of life against secular influences, and who argued about local and national politics. Other specialists, such as the two or three doctors and dentists, were mainly over-worked outsiders busy at their jobs and likely to move on after a few years. The one or two clergy exerted a great deal of influence during their terms of office, but being career civil servants, part of a national bureaucracy, they tended not to remain long in Bremnes.

6. The great tradition

It is difficult to look upon the clergy in 1952 as mediating a great tradition to a parochially and traditionally oriented rural population, and it is impossible to identify such a great tradition with the culture of the city, as required in Redfield's scheme. On the other hand it is easy to show that the dominant local pattern of values was not an indigenous little tradition, as Redfield also requires. The moral order of the Bremnes community in 1952 was predominantly Pietist, with a strong emphasis on the laity rather than the clergy as the guardians of the faith, and on the importance of missions to the heathen (Barnes 1971). It seems that 150 years ago, when Bremnes had much better claims on other grounds to peasant status, the inhabitants brewed beer, exchanged their fish for brandy, did not stress the need for personal salvation, and knew nothing of foreign missions. If the movement from 1800 to 1952 was from peasantry towards urban culture, it was in this instance also a movement towards religion, not away from it. The radical change in the value pattern of Bremnes that occurred gradually during the 19th century came about, at least in part, by the efforts of itinerant preachers who were in touch, either directly or at several removes, with national figures such as Hans Nielsen Hauge, Gisle Johnson, and Søren Kierkegaard. A second ideological source of social change was the nationalist movement which, having broken the centuries-old domination of Denmark in 1814, continued to grow in the face of attempts by Sweden to take the place of Denmark. One offshoot of this movement which greatly affected Bremnes was the attempt to create what was to be a 'truly Norwegian' language, free from Danish influence – an attempt in which schoolteachers were particularly active.

In Redfield's dichotomy, these elements constitute a great tradition of the reflective few, not a little tradition of the largely unreflective many. He remarks:

> If we enter a village within a civilization we see at once that the culture there has been flowing into it from teachers and exemplars who never saw that village, who did their work in intellectual circles perhaps far away in space and time (Redfield 1956: 70).

These remarks apply to a peasant village. Bremnes is a community of dispersed settlements, with no traditional villages, and the influence of outside teachers and exemplars is seen most clearly in the prayer houses and in the council chamber. But if we are to call this influence a tradition, it is a tradition of very junior standing. In the form in which this influence reached Bremnes, it was the product of contemporary 19th century movements, creatures of their own time in European history. Furthermore, the association of this tradition with the city is very weak. Indeed, the newly constructed language, *landsmaal* (later renamed *nynorsk*), was based on a conscious attempt to revive and rescue the forms of speech descended from Viking times which had persisted in the countryside during the long years of Danish dominance in the towns. Hans Nielsen Hauge, the most prominent teacher of Pietist doctrines in Norway, was a farmer's son, and although much of his preaching was done in towns he also travelled extensively throughout the countryside. He is said to have behaved like a countryman, walking along the roads knitting as he went, ready to help on the farm whenever he found shelter for the night (Molland 1951: 17). Even the national movement itself cannot be regarded as primarily associated with the towns. Thus the distinctive great tradition found in Bremnes in 1952 – the dominant culture as I have called it – was Pietism, nationalism, and support for *nynorsk*. The latter had been adopted in Bremnes in response to outside influences rather than evolved within the area, but had been mediated by an intelligentsia of school teachers which by 1952 had lost its elite status. The tradition, or at least one strand of it, represented not the influence of the city, but an attempt to fight back against that influence.

Given these departures from Redfield's paradigm, it is not surprising that in Bremnes the distinction he draws between the knowledge possessed by the laity and by members of the hierarch is absent. Redfield argues that whereas among primitive peoples like the Andaman Islanders and the Tiv there is little specialization of knowledge, in some other societies, such as the Maori, Dogon, and Dahomey, there is diversity in modes of thought and symbolism. 'The content of knowledge comes to be double, one content for the layman, another for the hierarchy' (Redfield 1956: 74). In Bremnes there is, as we would expect, a differential distribution of technical knowledge, whether in agriculture, fishing, house building, engineering, even cooking; indeed the notion of specialized, technical knowledge, *fagkunnskap*, seems to be more prominent than in other Western societies I have lived in. However, Redfield is not referring to technical knowledge, but to knowledge of sacred myths and moral ideas. In Bremnes, knowledge of the dominant culture was also differentially distributed; but this differentiation was not between a laity and a hierarchy, nor between ordinary people and experts, *fagfolk*, but between 'children of the world' and 'children of God'. It was the latter who knew their Bible well, although in ecclesiastical terms they were identified with the laity, as contrasted with the hierarchy, whose members were always liable to be suspected of 'liberalism', 'modernism', and other deviations from the word of God. The dominant secular ideology was egalitarian, while the religious ideology was explicitly anti-hierarchical. There was, as we would expect, considerable difference between one individual and another in Bremnes as to knowledge of the doctrines of Pietism and of Lutheran Christianity generally, just as there was in knowledge of secular specialisms. Many men and women from Bremnes have attended Bible schools and similar institutions where the content of religious belief is examined systematically. But these people were never referred to as 'experts'. The place of the technical expert was in secular matters, not in matters of faith. Theology, in contrast to Bible study, was seen as a spurious product of would-be technicians, a man-made corpus of technical casuistry threatening the direct relation between the believer and the word of God set forth plainly for all to read in the Bible. In so far as, regrettably, there was a distinction between the faithful laity and certain members of the ecclesiastical hierarchy, the laity was quite sure that God was on its side. In this respect, Redfield's scheme is quite inapplicable to Bremnes.

7. Moral or technical order

Redfield's distinction between the intelligentsia and the laity cut across the contrast he draws between the technical and moral orders. The moral orders covers 'all the binding together of men through implicit convictions as to what is right, through explicit ideals, or through similarities or conscience', while the technical order 'results from mutual usefulness, from deliberate coercion, or from the mere utilization of the same means' (Redfield 1953: 20, 21) When he says that in peasant societies agriculture is a way of life rather than a business for profit, he implies that agriculture is governed by the moral rather than the technical order. In Bremnes agriculture and fishing belonged to the technical order. In the factory where many Bremnes men worked, either permanently or from time to time, the need for specialist qualifications had always been recognized, and there were the usual arrangements for apprenticeship and trade tests. Similarly, schoolteachers were formally trained, and even the traditional fields of agriculture and fishing had been invaded by courses and diplomas. Occupations were often evaluated by reference to the duration of the appropriate qualifying course; the longer the course, the cleverer and more diligent must be those who complete it.

In general, people in Bremnes were ready to admit the superiority

25

of expert knowledge, and for the most part this technical expertise was seen as coming from outside the local community, from the university and technical institutes rather than from the experience of earlier generations of local residents. This attitude showed itself in a readiness to contemplate – though not necessarily to execute – change in a wide range of activities. Agriculture and fishing did not, for Bremnes men and women, constitute a 'way of life', in Redfield's sense, any more than did working in a factory or going to sea in an oil tanker. The 'way of life' that could be contrasted with a 'business for profit' was to live as a child of God. This was seen as a traditional way of life, though it was a tradition that had become established only during the last 150 years. It was an egalitarian tradition in which all men were equal in the sight of God and which rejected the need for experts and intermediaries. Here we can see that Redfield mistook for a general principle the contingent association he observed in Middle America between religion and hierarchy.

In Bremnes, gaining a living from the land or from the sea was not perceived as an end in itself. Inevitably much that was done on the land and to a lesser extent at sea was done because it was customary, because it was difficult to think what else to do, rather than because a rational calculus of profit and loss indicated that a certain course of action was the most profitable (cf. Barth 1966: 6–10). There was still in 1952 some feeling, in some families, that a son, or failing a son a daughter, ought to take over the parental small holding when ready to do so. A man with land that his sons did not want might regret that they would not benefit from the improvements he had made, though he would not condemn them for seeking their living elsewhere. The moral order impinged at a few points on the technically determined processes of fishing and farming, as for instance in the attitude towards work on Saturday afternoons and Sundays, or towards taking certain fish out of season; but these points of contact were marginal to the organiza- tion of productive activities. The whole field of social relations within the productive process – the obligations of reciprocity be- tween cooperating farmers, the duties of crew members towards one another, and so on – was morally evaluated, but by the application of principles couched in general terms, without specific reference to agriculture or fishing.

In Bremnes the highly valued way of life was defined in general terms that did not link it with any particular mode of livelihood. A carpenter, a house painter, a mechanic, a draftsman, any of these could be as good a Christian as a fisherman or farmer. A few occu- pations, such as publican and professional actor, were incompatible with Pietism, while others, such as missionary and itinerant lay preacher, were particularly associated with commitment to God. Yet individuals who devoted themselves full-time to preaching the word of God were not regarded as necessarily more godly than devoted laymen. In general the good 'way of life' was defined in universalistic rather than particularistic terms.

Thus the contrast Redfield draws between the moral and technical orders cannot readily be applied to Bremnes in 1952. Redfield admits 'In civilization the relations between the two orders are varying and complex' (1953: 24), but his basic assumption seems to be that under the influence of the city, the immutable moral order of folk societies is replaced by a more flexible and autonomous moral order. In Bremnes the moral order, based on the Bible as understood in the Lutheran tradition, was perceived as inflexible and unchanging, though the universality of its specification enabled it to accommodate a changing technical order. The source of the moral order was not the city.

8. The city and the countryside

Yet if the great tradition of Pietism did not come to Bremnes from 'the city', there were other influences that did. Here again we find wide discrepances between Bremnes in 1952 and Redfield's notions of a peasant community and a city. 'The city', realized in Bergen and Oslo, did not provide the people of Bremnes with a higher tradition which they might admire but could not hope to emulate. On the contrary, these cities represented a way of life which Bremnes people were more inclined to condemn and fear. True, Redfield senses something of this state of affairs when he writes that 'The peasant has made a workable adjustment; he is within civilization, but he is wary; he would rather keep the city at a distance' (Redfield 1953: 57). But wariness is inadequate to explain why many people in Bremnes in 1952 believed, for instance, that Stalin and the Pope were united in a conspiracy to stamp out Christianity throughout the world (cf. Valen-Sendstad 1952), or that a certain Norwegian cabinet minister was trying to undermine Christian family life. Many people used to draw a sad contrast between the ungodly leadership of the Norwegian Labour Party, then in power, and the Christian leadership enjoyed by Britain under Churchill, whose speeches included frequent references to God.

Throughout Norway there exist many organizations which actively seek to advance the interests and values of the countryside against those of the city. There are associations for promoting support for nynorsk, for encouraging an interest in local history, and one political party in 1952 specifically stood for the rights of farmers (though not of fishermen-farmers). Country organizations run temperance hotels where the countryman can stay, safe from the dangers of city life, when he has to visit the city. The secondary and continuation schools run by Christian organizations draw most of their pupils from the countryside, and the one explicitly Christian political party is well supported in rural districts in western Norway, including Bremnes. Thus there has been not only a consciousness of difference between the Christian countryside and the secular city but also a conscious effort by countrymen to defend and cultivate their own way of life in the face of pressure from the city.

In Bremnes in 1952 people were more concerned with supporting Christian missions overseas than with helping on the home front in the struggle between the values of the countryside and the city. This may perhaps be explained by the fact that the threat to the Pietist way of life was at that time much less in Bremnes than in many other country districts where city values had gained greater acceptance, or where the Pietist tradition had never gained so firm a hold. A contributory factor may have been the orientation of Bremnes seaward rather than to the mainland of Norway; a Bremnes sailor once remarked to me, 'I know the streets of Bombay better than those of Bergen'. When Bremnes people said of a man that he was 'on the west coast' they meant not that he was on the west coast of Norway but that he was working somewhere between Vancouver and Los Angeles.

Thus if in Redfield's terms we look for a link or hinge between local life and national life (Redfield 1956: 43) we shall not expect to find a few elite members who acted as exemplars to the rest of the community. Rather we find a conscious attempt to defend the cultural autonomy of the countryside, and efforts to invade the territory of the urban enemy. On the national level, the most striking example of this active policy is probably the ascendancy over the State Church which has been gradually established by the Pietists and those ideologically near to them. The residents of Bremnes watched this process with approval, even though no-one from Bremnes seems to have been directly involved. As far as Bremnes itself was concerned, the conscious opposition to urban values led the inhabitants to view the local members of parliament as if they were missionaries to the heathen. Those elected to the national parliament were, as one would expect, already prominent in local affairs. During the period following 1945, the rector, the sheriff, the chairman of the board of directors of the factory, and the secretary of the factory were all elected, each on a different political party list. The rector, who belonged to the Labour Party, was a comparative stranger to the district, but the other three were all born in Bremnes and were the children of men who worked small farms along with their other activities. They were all identified with the country way of life and, in varying degrees, specifically with Pietism and the use of the country language; and these were values which, among others, they were expected to advance in parliament.

Thus Redfield's model situation was reversed. It is not that the way of life of the city had a few adherents in the village; rather, the way of life of the countryside had a few emissaries at the national capital. Instead of the peasant being wary and on the defensive we had the countryman ambitious and ready to attack.

Indeed the bearers of the city way of life who came to Bremnes were not an elite at all. Many people who had been born in the district and who had gone away to work and live in the towns returned from time to time on holiday, bringing their spouses and children with them. Choirs from the cities and towns came to Bremnes to sing. Travelling salesmen visited the factories and shops, bringing samples of new goods and, more insidiously, glossy literature about retailer–consumer relations written in the style of Rotary and the *Readers' Digest*. The radio, newspapers, and weekly magazines all attempted in varying degrees to impose city values. This onslaught did not go unchallenged. Missionary and temperance journals circulated widely in Bremnes, a daily paper published in the city of Bergen and which has many Bremnes readers was specifically Christian and evangelical in its outlook, and the lipstick and the urban accents of visitors were suitably deprecated.

It is perhaps only in what Redfield calls the world of the market that there was no effective counter-attack. The growing dependency on factory-made consumer goods had even by 1952 decreased the material difference between the life of the countryman and that of the city-dweller. The diesel engine factory preserved many features of rural life in its internal organization, but it had to sell its engines in the face of international competition, and in its dealings with its customers and potential customers in, say, Brazil and South Africa, it used the same language as its competitors. The daily prayer-meeting at the factory during the lunch hour was not mentioned in its sales literature. Here, much more than in the fishing fleet, there was a conflict of two worlds.

Redfield states, 'The peasant style of life is a balanced adjustment between moral order and technical order. . . . The necessary condition of peasant life is that the system of values of the peasant be consistent, in the main, with those of the city people who constitute, so to speak, its other dimension of existence' (Redfield 1953: 39–40).

It could well be argued that 'in the main' there was no great difference between the values held by Bremnes and those prevailing in Oslo: culturally, Bremnes was nearer to Bergen and Oslo than to Paris or Rangoon. But there was nevertheless a recognized difference and opposition between the countryside and the town, and the people of Bremnes were quite confident that their way of life was best. Redfield recognizes that something like this state of affairs may exist in peasant societies when he writes of the peasant:

> He sees himself as low with regard to the common culture but nevertheless with a way of life morally superior to that of the townsman (Redfield 1956: 65).

Bremnes people were ready to admit that they were not like the 'fine people' or 'great people' who inhabited the towns, but they had no desire to emulate them.

9. The good life

Redfield devotes a great deal of space to determining what view, if any, of the good life is common to all peasants. After discussing the contrast between the high value put on productive labour by peasants in 19th-century England and elsewhere with the high value put on not working at all by peasants in southern Italy, he comes rather tentatively to the conclusion that where the peasants have been in a long-standing and stable relationship to limited land ment of agricultural labour with

> 'traditional, often reverential, sentiments about the land; the connexion of that labour with ideals as to personal worth; the inculcation in the young of endurance and hard work rather than a disposition to take risks and to perform personal exploits; the acceptance of arduous labour, yet with great enjoyment of its surcease' (Redfield 1953: 69–70).

This statement is then qualified by noting that the peasant's view of the good life cannot be understood in isolation from the view of the townsman.

> The townsman or the gentry form an aspect of the local moral life – form it by reflection, by the presence of example, by the model these outsiders offer, whether that model be one the peasant seeks to imitate or to avoid, or whether he merely recognizes both its likeness to and its difference from its own ideals (Redfield 1953: 75).

30

In Bremnes in 1952 some of these typical peasant attitudes were found: the acceptance of hard work, the importance of decorum and decency, the desire to have a large healthy family, the strong disapproval of adultery. Yet others were lacking. As noted aobve, the land was only residually the object of special moral sentiments, and agricultural labour not at all. I do not think that endurance and hard work were stressed rather than the disposition to take risks or to perform personal exploits. In part the discrepancy here may arise from the nature of fishing, which is a form of hunting and collecting, necessarily involving risks and quick decisions on inadequate evidence, as contrasted with agriculture with its fixed routine. Indeed it is on the fishing grounds that we find institutionalized the most prominent type of individual competitive exploit in the economic sphere. In purse seine fishing the netboss behaved like a prima donna and was in competition with all other netbosses for the highest cumulative catch of the season (cf. Barth 1966: 8). The same phenomenon has been reported from the Norwegian whale fisheries in the Antarctic, involving harpooneers. During the German occupation, when Bremnes became one of the main points of illegal entry and exit in Norway, the local inhabitants demonstrated magnificently their ability to take risks and perform personal exploits (cf. Howarth 1951).

Thus it becomes clear that the Bremnes view of the good life was a long way from that postulated for peasants by Redfield. Despite their disapproval of Vikings as pagans, these modern countrymen still continued to cherish some of the qualities of their Viking forbears which Redfield explicitly contrasts with those appropriate to peasants. Redfield's views on the quality of interpersonal relations in peasant societies have been criticized by Foster (1960–61); but even if we accept Foster's arguments, Bremnes men and women in 1952 still seem not to have had a peasant view of life.

The citizen in Bergen and Oslo often regards the countryfolk of western Norway as parochially minded and out of touch with the modern world. In fact the sea-faring way of life directly linked the men and women of Bremnes with the oceans of the world, and their interest in foreign missions provided them with another set of reference points overseas. In making choices men had to decide not merely between selling a heifer and keeping it to milk, but whether to work in the factory, to sign on for a voyage between Curacão and Rotterdam, or to stay with relatives while looking for a job in Seattle. It is this kind of world of possibilities and experience, and not the circumscribed world of a peasant, that was interpreted in terms of a great tradition, a tradition not of the new secularism but of 19th-century Pietism.

10. The factory in the countryside

It might be thought that the strongest argument for not regarding the people of Bremnes as peasants is that a substantial proportion of them depended on a diesel engine factory and other smaller industrial enterprises for their livelihood. Yet Foster points out that at least in what he calls pre-industrial cities many elements of the distinctively folk or peasant view of life can still be found (Foster 1953: 169–170). He argues that these characteristics disappear with the rise of an industrialized economy. The diesel engine factory in Bremnes in 1952 was different in many respects from factories typical of an industrial economy, but it did have a labour force organized with principally technological considerations in mind. The profits of the enterprise were distributed according to the usual principles of joint-stock ownership, and considerations of kinship and local affiliation did not enter formally into the organization. The industrial characteristics did not entail any significant change in style of life between the factory workers and the rest of the Bremnes population.

They were in fact the same people, for a man who spent from Christmas to Easter fishing and who divided his time between the land and the sea during the summer might well spend the last few months of the year working in the factory, when the demand for labour was greatest. Many of the permanent employees in the factory had small farm holdings which they ran with the help of their families. The annual holiday when the factory closed was arranged to occur at the hay harvest when the demand for labour in the fields was greatest. Many of the factory workers had come to work in Bremnes from other parts of Norway and were not closely related genealogically to the local community. Hence it was less often that a man worked in the factory alongside his kinsmen and lifelong friends, whereas in agricultural work he invariably did so, and in fishing often so, through the operation of what Redfield calls the 'countrywide network' for recruiting crews. Yet many of the men who came to Bremnes to work in the factory settled down and married local girls, or became connected to the local community through the marriages of their children. The factory grew out of a partnership between a local man, part farmer and part blacksmith, and his son; it is now controlled by a board of directors, all of whom are agnatic descendants of the blacksmith. In 1952 many of the leading executives were related affinally or cognatically to the founder of the firm. The ethos of the factory was characterized by an emphasis on Pietism and hard work.

The hierarchical organization of the factory, and of similar but smaller enterprises in the district, might seem to have been at odds with the ambient culture, with its stress on egalitarianism. Yet there seems never to have been any suggestion that the factory ought to have been run by a workers' soviet. Indeed belief in the equality of all men before God, though it led to an assumption that all men are entitled to mutual respect, did not lead to a simple egalitarianism in any economic enterprise in Bremnes, whether in engineering, carpentry, fishing, or farming. In the traditional agricultural system, formal procedures were followed to ensure that access to natural resources should be enjoyed in fair proportions by the peasants entitled to use them. If a farm holding was to be divided into two equal portions, each field separately was divided equally and the assignment of the two ostensibly equal portions was then decided by lot. If a hay field could not easily be divided, it was used by each part-owner in alternate years. Devices such as these merely ensured that all those who had nominally equal shares in the resources of the hamlet had shares which as far as possible were equal in fact, but there was no suggestion that all peasants should have equal shares. Within a hamlet some men might own large shares, some small shares, and others no shares at all. These arrangements had ceased to be so significant following the consolidation of holdings at the end of the 19th century (cf. Barnes 1957), but the same principles continue to apply in fishing. All fishermen receive an equal share of the proceeds of the catch; but the owners of the nets, and the owners of the fishing vessel, as well as the skipper and the netboss, receive separately calculated shares (cf. Wadel 1971). A man may own part of one vessel, and part of the net in a second vessel, and serve as a fisherman in a third vessel. Hence the income from all maritime sources received at the end of a season may vary greatly from one crew member to another. In economic affairs egalitarianism finds its expression not in the simple statement that all should be equal, but in that equal participation should bring equal reward.

In the factory, wage rates were controlled by nation-wide agreements between trade unions and employers' associations, and varied from one task to another. Orders were given and accepted within the recognized technical sphere of operation of the factory, but outside the context of factory production, the hierarchical arrangement largely disappeared. A considerable proportion of the work force lived in the hamlet round the factory, and in the social life of this hamlet it was hard, though not always impossible, to detect signs of the gradations within the factory. All the children went to the same school; the various social, religious, and missionary societies were run in the same way as in any other hamlet; and a well-paid position in the factory did not automatically imply a position of leadership in social life outside it. Naturally the men who had been ambitious and industrious in working their way to positions of responsibility in the factory tended to behave in similar fashion outside it, and hence to find themselves elected to committees and councils. But there was little of the air of patronage which is often found in other countries on occasions when management make an attempt to mix with workers in some welfare activity. Many of the workers, some in quite lowly positions, had remained in the employ of the factory for twenty-five years or more, and their houses and small-holdings were intermingled with those of the managers and of the more newly arrived workers. Some differences in interior furnishings might be interpreted as symbols of differential economic status, but this did not extent to clothing, architecture, or accent.

Thus the factory hamlet did not differ radically from purely agricultural and fishing hamlets elsewhere in Bremnes. Those who worked in the factory but lived away in other hamlets could not be differentiated from their fishing and farming neighbours. There was no distinctively factory version of the good life. The bonds of kinship and life-long association did not run as profusely in the factory hamlet as in the others where there were far fewer immigrants, but there was still a similarity of outlook, for most of those who had come to work in the factory came from areas broadly similar in culture to Bremnes. There were a considerable number who had moved to the factory after living in towns for many years, but there was little to suggest that these people represented an alien way of life in Bremnes.

The modern rural society of Bremnes in 1952 would appear to be one which included within itself a sizeable industrial enterprise without radically altering its character. This seems to differentiate it clearly from the peasant category outlined by Redfield. The technical order, which in Bremnes was paramount in agriculture and fishing, readily claimed engineering as part of its province. The Pietist moral order, defined in general non-occupational terms, continued to operate with this level of industrialization.

11. Diversification

The changes that had occurred in the culture of the factory prior to 1952 might have suggested that the Pietist dominance would not be maintained indefinitely. When the factory started at the time of World War I, pressures on factory workers to conform to the local way of life were much stronger than they were in 1952. Apprentices

were then treated more like members of the family and were
expected to submit to the quasi-parental authority of the head of
the factory. There was no road linking the factory with the rest of
the district, and all communication was by sea. No alcohol was
allowed in the factory hamlet and anyone attempting to introduce
alcohol was likely to be dismissed from employment (cf. Barnes
1971: 13). By 1952 this degree of paternalism had disappeared.
Communications with Bergen had become much easier, the work
force was larger, and the influence of the Bremnes-born long service
employees less. More significantly, the second and third generation
descendants of the founders of the factory of the original employees
had been exposed to many more outside influences than had their
forebears. One of the items of expenditure which in 1952 had
already begun to differentiate the comparatively rich from the
comparatively poor in Bremnes was secondary education. Those
who had prospered materially by long association with the factory
tended to have children who had spent much of their formative
years away from Bremnes in schools and colleges. Many of these
young adults could be seen as at best reluctant conformists to the
traditional dominant way of life.

Following fieldwork in Bremnes in 1955 I predicted, luckily not
in print, that while changes bringing increasing similarity with
urban life styles were likely to occur in the factory hamlet, the
dominant culture, characterized by adherence to the Pietist version
of Lutheranism and exemplified by attendance at the prayer house
and by the prohibition of alcohol and dancing, would continue for
years to come in the other hamlets where fishing and agriculture
remained the main sources of livelihood. I thought that, in Redfield's terms, the rural community had found a stable adaptation
to urban pressure, though in a more agressive stance than he had
suggested, and that further changes were unlikely outside the
factory hamlet. I assumed that, as throughout the last hundred
years, those who were ambitious or dissatisfied with local condition
would leave Bremnes, leaving behind a community content with its
distinctive style of life.

In fact changes since 1952 have been much more drastic than I
had expected. The decline in small-scale agriculture, particularly
in outlying areas, noticeable in Norway generally since 1945, began
to affect Bremnes in the early 1960s. By 1971, many small holdings
which were prosperous in 1952 had been completely abandoned.
In the late 1950s the herring fishing declined dramatically, and
those who wished to remain fishermen found themselves forced to
re-equip with larger vessels which could hunt for fish farther afield
(Bakken & Dragesund 1971: 23–26). In some other coastal districts,

35

a conversion to larger vessels was made successfully; in these areas the combined fisherman-farmer has disappeared, for the larger vessels have to be used all the year round to be profitable (cf. Brox 1966; Wadel 1971). In Bremnes the decline in herring fishing happened to occur just after adequate electric power had become available from the mainland, and was followed fairly quickly by the development of other forms of industry (mammoth ship-building and aluminium refining) in nearby districts. Consequently, the number of men in Bremnes combining fishing, agriculture, and factory work as sources of livelihood declined, while the number of those dependent on only one mode increased. Competition for skilled labour from neighbouring districts has caused a labour shortage in Bremnes. There has been a renewed flow of workers and their families from farther afield to the factory hamlet. These immigrants have been encouraged to come by the prospect of facilities for house building, and by the advantages of living in a rural maritime environment. The growth of a technical school in the same hamlet has also brought strangers, some with no intention or wish to remain after their course of instruction has ended. Throughout the district the newly-introduced television has pre-sented a range of styles of life very different from the traditional dominant culture, and has heightened the awareness among traditionalist supporters of their position as a minority within the nation.

Given these economic and occupational changes, it is perhaps scarcely surprising that the traditional Pietist culture is no longer dominant. The first public dance in the factory hamlet was held in 1971. In 1952 the only films shown in Bremnes were films of missionary activities and other good works; by 1971 commercial films were being shown at regular intervals. Wine-making equip-ment is now openly on sale, and the scandal of public adolescent drunkenness is overshadowed by the knowledge that even worse social problems, drugs and 'sniffing', are to be found only a couple of hours away in the city. New public buildings take the form of council offices, old people's homes, shops and factories, rather than prayer houses. The visitors who come on holiday during the summer are no longer only kinsfolk recruited for the haymaking, but include urban dwellers escaping from the dirt and noise of cities, some of whom lack any kinship links with Bremnes.

At first sight, these changes seem to confirm Redfield's view of the type of change likely to occur in peasant societies. The city seems to have won the battle with the countryside, despite the bouyant hopes of the countrymen in 1952. In a sense this is right, for the city is certainly the source of television and films and, more importantly, of capital for investment in rural industry. Yet I doubt that these changes are quite what Redfield had in mind. In his sketch of the way in which 'Civilization and the moral order' are related (Redfield 1953: Chapter 3), he appears to see the city developing loftier ideas in response to the pressures of developing technology. What has occurred in Bremnes in the last twenty years is the break-up of the local consensus based on the Pietist way of life, and the growth of a more pluralist community in which the existence of alternative life styles is tolerated, albeit often reluctantly. The city, on closer examination, proves to be the source neither of a great tradition, nor simply of the spirit of commercialism, but rather of financial resources, technical innovations, and a variety of life-styles among which the individual can choose. The increased division of labour characteristic of the city, which Redfield recognized, is paralleled by increasing diversity of moral codes, at least some of which can be adopted in the countryside even though the range of occupations available in rural areas remains comparatively restricted. The occupational alternatives open to Bremnes men which do not entail movement away from the district are still comparatively few, and to women even fewer. Even the factory hamlet fails to meet Wirth's first two tests, size and density, for urban status, and it scores only moderately well in terms of occupational heterogeneity, his third index. Nevertheless in styles of recreation, patterns of expenditure, intellectual interests, and moral commitments, the range of choice throughout Bremnes is much greater than it was even twenty years ago. The trend towards 'choice as a way of life', as Pahl (1966: 306–310) puts it, is unmistakable (cf. Dewey 1960).

Redfield (1956: 57) remarks that in talking about Bremnes he may perhaps have extended and generalized my field data beyond my meaning and intention. Likewise I must note that Redfield was professedly a humanist and might well have resisted my attempt to transform his schemes into firm typologies or testable propositions. Nevertheless it is only by putting his ideas to the test, rather than by accepting them merely as imaginative perspectives or orienting statements, that we can decide whether they are worth retaining in any form (Hauser 1965). The rationale behind Redfield's work was the wish to see cultural or social anthropology break out of the isolated primitive world in which it had – regrettably and unnecessarily, in my view – become trapped (Redfield 1955). The ending of colonialism in its classic form has been a far more powerful stimulus towards the restructuring of anthropology than any pleading by Redfield. Nevertheless, until quite recently the study of peasant societies tended to flounder between the ill-assorted tradi-

tions of rural sociology, the analysis of agrarian unrest, and the
ruins of nineteenth-century *Volkskunde* and *Ethnologie*. The architects
of the new peasantology have chosen to define their specialism
partly in terms of a distinctive way of life, thus far following in
Redfield's footsteps, but they diverge from him with their other
criteria. In particular, the subordinate position of the peasantry
which Redfield discusses in symbolic and cultural terms is now
defined primarily in terms of political power and economic exploitation (Shanin 1971: 296).

12. Scale

Redfield does not make use of the concept of scale and does not
refer to the Wilsons' work. Likewise the Wilsons, in their *Analysis of
social change*, do not refer to Redfield. Their uncompromisingly
sociological formal definition of scale (Wilson & Wilson 1945: 25),
however much it may be compromised when applied to specific
instances, cannot be fitted unmodified into Redfield's cultural-
cum-sociological scheme. The sociological emphasis of the new
peasantology might appear to open the way for a revival of interest
in the Wilson's concept. In fact this has not occurred, partly because
of the inevitable concentration in the new specialism on the distinctive features of peasant communities, at the expense of a broader
comparative approach, and perhaps partly because the Platonic-
Christian assumptions of the Wilsons are seen as incompatible with
a dialectical and neo-Marxist orientation, though Redfield's own
civilized humanism is surely no less incompatible. Barth's revival
of the concept of scale frees it from its Central African origins and
from its religious associations, while retaining the Wilson's sociological rather than cultural viewpoint.

Nevertheless, the choice of label is undeniably unfortunate.
'Scale' for the Wilsons belongs to the same semantic domain as
words like 'size', 'density', 'population'; each society has a discoverable scale, ranging from large to small; so that, for instance,
'Bemba society was likewise larger in scale than Nyakyusa society'
(Wilson & Wilson 1945: 37). Thirty years later, 'scale' in lay
language still probably belongs to this domain, but for most social
scientists the word has been moved to a more abstract semantic
domain, where words like 'dimension', 'metric', and 'continuum'
belong. Following the lead of Stevens (1946), there is now a widely
used and well understood hierarchy of scales: nominal, ordinal,
interval, and ratio (Torgerson 1958). Furthermore, one particular
type of ordinal scale, developed by Guttman (Stouffer et al. 1950:
Chapters 1 and 3), has given rise to neologisms like 'scalogram' and

'scalability', and even to a verb, 'to scale'; in many contexts 'the items scale' means specifically that the items may be arranged in a strict order so that responses to them form a Guttman scale. Divergent connotations of 'scale' are therefore likely to obscure the meaning of statements about Wilson-Barth type scale, unless these are phrased with great care and clarity.

Barth's first analytic use of 'scale' (1972: 216–217) makes the term merely a synonym for size of population, but his empirical starting-point has now shifted to the first-order star and zone (Barnes 1972: 8–11) of the individual member of society, embedded in a network of social relations. Like the Wilsons, he perceives scale as a quality displayed by societies rather than by individuals. The scale of a society, so I understand him to imply, is determined primarily by the number and strandedness of the direct contacts experienced by the typical member of the society concerned. Baktaman society is characterized by small total population, high network density, first-order zones with only two clusters each of maximal density, and high probability of zonal overlap between any two individuals. At the other end of the scale range (we cannot say 'the scale of scale') we have modern Norway, where, as in most industrial societies, first-order zones characteristically contain several clusters of relatively high, but not maximally high, density, plus a substantial number of unclustered single-stranded links; there is a low probability of zonal overlap between any two individuals, and a very low probability of overlap in more than one cluster; the total number of members is very large. This revised version of the differences between extreme types follows from the realization that everywhere along the range of societies we find individuals interacting for a substantial part of their social lives within one or other relatively dense clusters, between whose fellow members there are multiplex relations (cf. Martin 1970).

There is no difficulty in equating the two extreme societal types with Redfield's tribal community and city. The difficulties arise when we consider intermediate positions, for in terms of scale these must presumably be characterized by, typically, first-order zones with an intermediate number of discrete clusters, each relatively dense; intermediate probability of substantial zonal overlap between individuals; intermediate total numbers of significally interacting individual members. Peasant villages, small towns, and Bremnes-like dispersed rural communities all fall somewhere in the middle of the range; but it has, I think, still to be demonstrated that they form a regular sequence in the middle of the scale range. The rate of acquisition of new direct contacts may well be greater in towns than among proper peasants. Likewise the urge to convert new single-stranded relations into multiplex ones, as well as the possibility of achieving this goal, is likely to be greater in peasant communities than in towns. Yet any attempt to substantiate these suggestions with empirical evidence is certain to run up against the difficult problems of cross-culturally valid measurement to which Barth refers in his chapter.

The basic dilemma is familiar enough. We have to simplify reality radically even to describe it; to fit it into any typological or developmental scheme we have to simplify it even further. Yet without drastic simplification we cannot see the wood for the trees. Simplest of all is the single index, the point on the one-dimensional continuum. Once each society or community has been reduced to a single point, the way is open for a limitless variety of testable propositions and cross-cultural generalizations. Yet concentration on a single index is unlikely to lead to interesting and insightful propositions about multi-dimensional entities like communities and societies unless the diverse characteristics that go to make up the index are in fact closely correlated with one another. The notion of 'scale' suffers from the fundamental weakness that its constituents – size of network, number of clusters, overlap of cluster membership, rate of formation and decay of relations, rate of conversion of single-stranded relations to multi-stranded, and perhaps other characteristics – have not been shown to correlate closely. At this stage in our inquiry it seems only prudent to look at the various characteristics separately, and to discover what invariant relations, if any, there exist between them. Likewise it would be rash to discard the qualitative contrasts – for example between the laity and the intelligentsia, and between the technical and moral orders – to which Redfield drew attention, even if we query many of his generalizations about them. Perhaps the most persuasive feature of Redfield's folk-urban continuum is that it is multi-dimensional.

GERALD D. BERREMAN

Scale and Social Relations : Thoughts and Three Examples *)

1. Introduction

The subject of scale or size as a variable in social organization had not received my attention in any explicit way until I was invited to participate in the symposium which led to this volume. When the topic was thus thrust before me I set to thinking about what I had read and what my own research suggested about it. My thoughts turned first to Godfrey and Monica Wilson's discussions of scale (1945, 1971), then to a wide variety of theorists' societal typologies and contrasts which, if not explicitly based on scale, have depended at least partly upon variation in the sizes of the societies discussed. I thought also of the literature on urban society, notable among which are Wirth's discussion of 'urbanism' (Wirth 1938), and Sjoberg's work on the pre-industrial city (Sjoberg 1960). I compared these to what I know of the ethnographic literature, in an attempt to judge critically the cross-cultural validity and relevance of the typologies and contrasts, and to assess the contributions they might make to clarification of the concept 'scale', and its application to the comparative analysis of social organization. Finally, I thought about my own field research, first on social integration, cohesion and change among the Aleuts of Alaska's western-most islands (Berreman 1955, 1964), later on culture and social organization (with emphasis on caste) in the lower Himalayas of northern India (Berreman 1962c, 1972a), and most recently on social and ethnic relations in a North Indian city (Berreman 1972b). Each of the studies was undertaken from a theoretical perspective which is in part structural-functionalist, and in part one which has been described as 'symbolic interactionism' or 'ethnomethodology', but which I prefer to call simply 'interactionist' (cf. Blumer 1969; Cicourel 1964, 1968, 1973; J. Douglas 1970; Dreitzel 1970; Garfinkel 1967; Goffman 1959, 1963, 1967, 1969, 1971, 1974; Schutz 1962; Roy Turner 1974). (For an account of ethnomethodology as a 'theoretical break' from traditional sociology, advocated and enacted by a 'coherent group' of sociologists, see Griffith & Mullins, 1972.) The interactionist perspective became increasingly

) Essentially this same paper is published, with CA treatment, in Current Anthropology Vol. 19 No. 3, September 1978.

explicit from the first to the last of my studies. It entails an approach which utilizes detailed observation and inquiry regarding how people behave in face-to-face and indirect interaction, in order to discover how they choose among alternative behaviors in terms of their own definitions of the situations in which they act, i.e. the meanings they attach to the persons, actions, circumstances, tasks, and goals which are the substance and context of their daily lives. Cognitive worlds – the understandings, definitions, perceptions, and systems of relevance – which underlie behavioral choices are the subject of study. Garfinkel (1967: 11, 35) calls them 'the routine grounds of everyday activities'.

I realized that I had previously made three empirical comparisons in my research reports which were in part comparisons of scale and were therefore relevant to this discussion: (1) comparison between the small-scale society of the Aleuts before European contact and during 200 years of post-contact incorporation into the large-scale networks of Russian and American societies (Berreman 1955, 1964); (2) comparison between the small-scale, relatively isolated villages of the Indian Himalayas and the larger-scale village society of the densely populated Indo-Gangetic plain of North India (Berreman 1960a, 1972a); (3) comparison between social relations in the contemporary North Indian city of Dehra Dun and those in the mountain and plains villages of its hinterland (Berreman 1971, 1972b).

On the basis of these ruminations, I came to the conclusion that my most useful contribution would come directly from my own field research with its interactionist bias and its concern with the dynamics of stratification and pluralism and how they are experienced by people.

I shall begin with some preliminary remarks on scale as it is reflected in a variety of concepts from the literature of anthropology and related disciplines. The purpose of this discussion will be to draw attention to the complexity and diversity of the concept, without undertaking to analyze that complexity in any definitive way. I then turn to the rather disparate inferences I have drawn in my own research that seem germane to scale and social relations. – I say that my thoughts on scale are disparate because I have no theory of scale. It has not, hitherto, loomed important in my mind. I have not attempted to investigate it systematically. In fact, I doubt that so gross a concept can be very useful in social analysis. At best, I have a few specific, empirically derived intuitions about some of the limits imposed and the possibilities offered people in their relationships with one another as a result of the scale of the societies in which they live.

42

2. Abstract oppositions: folk-urban and the like

My interactionist predilections impel me to ask: how does scale affect the nature and quality of social interaction in societies? This question is relevant here because social organization is inevitably expressed in interaction, and analysts discover it by observing interaction, or by listening to statements about interaction. It does not preclude inferences about structure, for structure too is an abstraction deriving from interaction. Thus, for example, social stratification (the ranking of categories of people so that they have differential access to valued things, and exhibit hierarchical patterns of interaction, cf. Berreman 1967a, 1968, 1972c: 401), does not occur in the smallest societies. In fact, it is often described as a product of the urban revolution with the occupational diversification, specialized manufacture, and external trade which accompany it, and is based on the agricultural, food-producing revolution with its resultant capability for supporting populations larger than are required to produce their food (Childe 1946, 1965; cf. Braidwood 1964). This does not mean that stratification is inevitable in large societies or even in urban or agricultural ones; only that it is common among them and is not found among hunters and gatherers except where, as on the Pacific Northwest Coast of North America, the hunting and gathering is uncommonly productive and the society is commensurately more complex and larger in scale. There is thus an empirical association among size, specialization and hierarchy. In addition, the characteristic kinds of interaction and the characteristic structural arrangements of stratified societies are inseparable and mutually reinforcing (cf. Berreman 1967a, 1967b, 1972c, 1973), and both are evidently influenced by scale.

2.1 *Bipolar characterizations*

Social science and social philosophy have produced an abundance of concepts, mostly taking the form of bipolar ideal-types, which describe differences between small and large, simple and complex, societies. Here we immediately confront a difficulty inherent in the concept of scale: is it a matter of *size* alone, as Barth seemed to imply in the invitation to the symposium for which this paper was written (if so, is it a matter of total population in a society, and if that is so, where and how does one draw boundaries)? Is it a matter of *size and intensity* or closeness or pervasiveness of interaction, as the Wilsons suggest (if so, how does one weight the two)? Is density of settlement in a population a crucial component (if so, is this simply a pre-condition for intense interaction, or is it a distinct variable)? Is scale a matter of *size and complexity* (if so, how does one weight the two; if not, how does one separate the two)? Is it a matter of *size, density, and heterogeneity* of population, as Wirth (1938) maintained that urbanism entailed (if so, how are they to be calculated and weighted)? Is it a matter of *extensiveness of networks* of communication or of political, economic, and social organization (if so, how does this relate to population density and interactional intensity)? Are time-depth or people's ideas about their past factors in scale?

Obviously size and complexity are analytically distinguishable but practically inseparable. Thus we all know Tönnies' contrast between *Gemeinschaft* and *Gesellschaft* (Tönnies 1940), Maine's status and contract (Maine 1861), Durkheim's mechanical and organic solidarity (Durkheim 1933). We are familiar with efforts of social commentators since the classical Greeks to identify the distinguishing characteristics of 'civilized' or 'complex' societies as compared with 'primitive' ones – in anthropology the unilineal evolutionists come to mind, as do the names of such relatively recent figures as Goldenweiser (1922), Childe (1950, 1965), Kroeber (1948), Redfield (1953), Kluckhohn (1949), Steward (1955), White (1959), and the historian Toynbee (1947). More recently, some of these issues have been addressed, with insight, by Wolf (1966), Service (1966), Sahlins (1968), and Krader (1968), among others. Wirth (1938) drew upon Simmel (1950), Weber (1958), and Park (1925), among others, when he set forth his classic definition and description of urbanism as a way of life associated with, but not restricted to, cities. His own summary bears quotation (some of its shortcomings will be mentioned shortly):

. . . While the city is the characteristic locus of urbanism, the urban mode of life is not confined to cities. For sociological purposes a city is a relatively large, dense, and permanent settlement of heterogeneous individuals. *Large numbers* account for individual variability, the relative absence of intimate personal acquaintanceship, the segmentalization of human relations which are largely anonymous, superficial, and transitory, and associated characteristics. *Density* involves diversification, and specialization, the coincidence of close physical contact and distant social relations, glaring contrasts, a complex pattern of segregation, the predominance of formal social control, and accentuated friction, among other phenomena. *Heterogeneity* tends to break down rigid social structures and to produce increased mobility, instability, and insecurity, and the affiliation of the

44

individuals with a variety of intersecting and tangential social groups with a high rate of membership turnover. The pecuniary nexus tends to displace personal relations, and institutions tend to cater to mass rather than to individual requirements (Wirth, 1938: 1, emphases added).

Perhaps the best-known and most widely debated anthropological attempt to deal with scale is Redfield's characterization of the folk-urban continuum, originally summarized by its author as follows: 'The ideal type of primitive or folk society', as contrasted with 'modern urbanized society',

is small, isolated, nonliterate, and homogeneous, with a strong sense of group solidarity. The ways of living are conventionalized into that coherent system which we call 'a culture'. Behaviour is traditional, spontaneous, uncritical, and personal; there is no legislation or habit or experiment and reflection for intellectual ends. Kinship, its relationships and institutions, are the type categories of experience and the familial group is the unit of action. The sacred prevails over the secular; the economy is one of status rather than of the market. These and related characteristics may be restated in terms of 'folk mentality' (Redfield 1947: 293).

'The principal conclusion [of the comparison of some communities in Yucatan] is that the less isolated and more heterogeneous communities . . . are the more secular and individualistic and the more characterized by disorganization of culture' (ibid: 307). This formulation of the continuum has been revised, refined, and expanded by the addition of the intermediate 'peasant' category (Redfield 1953), but the original statement is a concise version of the central features of the dimensions with which Redfield was concerned. Clearly, scale is closely associated with the characteristics listed above, and no consideration of scale can afford to overlook them.

One might go through the literature and identify a broad spectrum of descriptive terms, generalizations, and characterizations which have been or can be treated as bipolar oppositions describing social and political organization, culture or aspects and attributes thereof, which apply more or less to the poles of the continuum described by Redfield, and which therefore imply differences in scale. I have done so very roughly in Fig. 1, simply to call them to mind. I have hedged on use of a general term by labeling them 'Type I' and 'Type II' societies, but the first are obviously small and simple, the latter larger and more complex. Anyone who looks at the listing will dispute, delete from, add to, and refine the contrasts presented; and this is as it should be if we are to think critically and constructively about the concept of scale. I do not defend the inclusion of each and every pair of concepts, but I do believe that the overall listing is illuminating. It is important to note that in the Figure, many kinds of concepts have been forced into the bipolar scheme which are not so-defined by their authors or advocates. They vary greatly in scope and degree of contrast. Many (e.g. Douglas' group and grid) are not mutually exclusive pairs nor even points on a single continuum. Most reflect their creators' assumptions, impressions, and convictions more than they do empirically derived generalizations. Most have been disputed, for critics delight in the anthropological and sociological game of citing exceptions, as Redfield and Wirth quickly discovered (cf. Sjoberg 1960: 14ff.). Nevertheless, it is remarkable the extent to which the terms in fact group together in their usage along the lines suggested in the listing – lines approximating extremes of scale.

Figure 1

	Type I Societies (simple – small scale?)	Type II Societies (complex – large scale)
Sources	*Analytical terms:*	
Redfield (1947)	folk	urban
Firth (1938)	folk society	urbanism
	rural-folk	urban-industrial
Tönnies (1940)	*Gemeinschaft*	*Gesellschaft*
Maine (1861)	status	contract
Durkheim (1933)	mechanical solidarity	organic solidarity
Durkheim (1954)	sacred	profane
Durkheim (1951)	[normative integration]	anomie
Steward (1955)	band	complex society
Goldenweiser (1922) ⎫ Kroeber (1948) ⎪ Kluckhohn (1949) ⎬ Toynbee (1947) ⎪ Braidwood (1964) ⎭	primitive; precivilized	civilized, complex
Childe (1950, 1965)	pre-urban (food gatherers, neolithic food producers)	urban (food producers, traders, manufacturers, ultimately industrialists)
Sjoberg (1960)	pre-industrial	industrial
Sapir (1949)	genuine culture	spurious culture
Marx (1964)	realization (humanization)	alienation (dehumaniza-tion, self-estrangement)
Mannheim (1940)	substantial rationality	functional rationality
Henry (1963)	personal community	[impersonal community]

Figure 1 (cont.)

	Type I Societies (simple – small scale?)	Type II Societies (complex – large scale?)
Sources	*Analytical terms:*	
Merton & Kitt Ralph Turner (1956) }	reference and membership groups are congruent	reference and membership groups are disparate
Riesman (1950)	tradition-directed	other-directed

Parsons & Shils (1951) {	expressive action
	pattern variables:
	  affectivity
	  collectivity
	  orientation
	  particularism
	  ascription (?)
	  diffuseness
		instrumental action
		
		  affective neutrality
		  self orientation
		
		  universalism
		  achievement (?)
		  specificity

Douglas (1970)	group	grid
Wallace (1961)	replication of uniformity	articulation of diversity
Faris (1932)	primary relationships	secondary relationships
Barth (1960)	involute statuses	[disparate, fragmented, inconsistent statuses]
Garfinkel (1967) Husserl (See Farber 1943) }	indexical behavior	objective behavior
Schutz (1962)	biographical factors crucial in interaction	objective factors crucial in interaction
Victor Turner (1969)	communitas (anti-structure)	structure

Figure 1 (cont.)

Type I Societies	Type II Societies
Miscellaneous characteristics	
small population	large population
sparsely settled	densely settled
isolated	incorporated into vast networks
homogeneous	heterogeneous
simple	complex
equalitarian	stratified
simply stratified	complexly stratified
communalistic	individualistic
stable, slow-changing	fast changing
self-sufficient	dependent upon other units
total-society	part-societies
culture	sub-cultures, contra-cultures (Yinger 1960)
consensus-based conformity	power-based conformity
total society	part-societies
total visibility of persons	fragmented visibility of persons
total social knowledge	specialized, fragmented social knowledge
total accountability	situational accountability

Figure 1 (cont.)

Type I Societies	Type II Societies
traditional	modern
personal	impersonal or depersonalized
close social contacts	distant social contacts
primary relationships	secondary relationships
individual relations	mass or group relations
sacred	secular (cf. Barnes & Becker 1938)
little-traditional	great-traditional
'authentic'	'plastic'
family and kin	status and territory
non-literate	literate
role integration	role segmentation
status summation	status fragmentation
generalized roles	specialized roles
uniform distribution of social knowledge	uneven distribution of social knowledge
power diffuse	power concentrated
social integration	social disorganization (cf. Bloch 1952)
personal integration	personal disorganization
cooperation	conflict
intensive interaction	extensive interaction
mutual knowledge	anonymity
conformity	diversity
rigidity	mobility
structure	ambiguity
informal controls and sanctions	formal (bureaucratic) controls and sanctions

I will not here undertake a critical evaluation of these contrasting concepts. There is already a vast literature on some of them. But anyone hoping to look into scale definitively would have to do that, for otherwise one would be likely to simply reproduce the errors and insights of others and to overlook important data and ideas. To improve upon the work of others, one would have to test, systematically and cross-culturally, each of the criteria postulated as varying directly or indirectly with scale. A modest attempt at such testing was that by Freeman & Winch (1957), who tried, by Guttman scale analysis of Human Relations Area File data, to find out whether the phenomenon described by Tönnies, Redfield and others, and identified by Freeman & Winch as 'complexity', was in fact unidimensional. They came to the conclusion that it was, based on the scaleability of six criteria – in order of increasing correlation with complexity: presence of (1) money, (2) governmental punishment for crime, (3) full-time priests, (4) full-time teachers, (5) full-time bureaucrats, (6) written language. We might debate the adequacy of the test, but it is suggestive of the kind of test that might be applied. How the dimension Freeman & Winch identified as 'complexity' relates to scale would depend, of course, upon the definition of scale – a matter to which I now belatedly turn.

2.2 *Scale itself*

I have mentioned that scale was identified with size in Barth's invitation to the symposium for which this paper was written, and it has been defined by the Wilsons as being a function of the number of people interacting and the closeness or intensity of interaction. The problems in operationalizing such definitions are many. If size alone is the criterion, then we are presumably dealing with the maximal networks in which people are involved, and the concept is so broad and general as to be of little analytical utility. As Firth has reminded us, 'the isolation of any community nowadays is only relative, and even remote Tikopia is not completely self-contained' (Firth, 1951: 50). How, then would one calculate the scale of an Indian village which is incorporated significantly into networks including well over half a billion people, and yet is to a large degree self-contained (cf. Opler 1956; Singh 1956). How would one compare the scale of such a village with, for example, Tokyo? How does one compare the scale of two very different kinds of cities (i.e. Benares and Cleveland), or of a small contemporary American town with a large pre-industrial city? If closeness or intensity of interaction is added to size as a criterion of scale, how is independent variation in the two to be handled? If, as usually seems to be the case, increased size of the interactional network is associated with diminishing intensity of interaction, is this an increase in scale? If so, what is the point of including intensity of interaction in the definition? Are the 1200 Aleuts of today, in half a dozen isolated villages which are loosely but indisputably incorporated on the periphery of mainland, mainstream American society, 'larger-scale' than the 20,000 who populated the shores of their islands 200 years ago in relative isolation? I would think so; but again extent of the network is correlated with diffuseness of interaction, and scale seems to vary inversely with intensity of interaction, as it does also in the comparison of pre-industrial and industrial cities (cf. Sjoberg 1960). The question here is whether size and interactional intensity are distinct criteria, and if so whether separately or together they comprise a manageable, defensible, or useful axis along which to measure social organization. I am not here judging the answer, only raising the question.

The characteristics listed as typifying Type I Societies and

Type II Societies make it clear that size and interactional intensity are only two of many criteria of scale postulated by social scientists. Yet if we take *any* characteristic of Type I Society at random, we will find that it contrasts not only with its designated polar opposite, but almost equally well with *any* characteristic of Type II Society chosen at random. Similarly, any number or combination of characteristics in *either* column contrasts equally well with *any* or *all* combinations of those in the other column. That is, within each column each term is roughly definable in terms of the others – is to a significant extent redundant of the others – and is contrastive to those in the opposite column. Therefore, it would appear that Freeman and Winch were on the right track in identifying folk-urban and *Gemeinschaft-Gesellschaft* as describing a single dimension, and some such descriptive terms as the ones they investigated ('folk-urban' or 'complexity') may prove to be preferable to the more ambiguous term 'scale'.

With these reservations in mind, we can nevertheless agree, I think, that: (1) there is some residual consistency, legitimacy, and analytical utility in the kind of bipolar, ideal-type categorization represented in the figure as Type I Societies contrasted with Type II Societies; (2) although many of the putative characteristics are debatable, stereotypic, and perhaps wrong, social complexity is a major dimension which underlies them; (3) size is a major correlate and enabling condition for such complexity; (4) 'scale' can be used to refer roughly to the size of a society as size influences the nature of social organization (including its complexity). If we wish to determine precisely how scale affects social structure and social relations, we will have to first agree upon a consistent and opera-tionalizable definition of scale, and then undertake detailed comparative, empirical ethnographic study of the kinds of variables indicated by the terms in Fig. 1, constituting possible concomitants of scale. That, presumably, is one of the ultimate goals toward which this volume is an early step, should the goal itself be deemed worthwhile.

3. Empirical generalizations

I will now beat a hasty but strategic retreat from these rather cosmic and sketchily presented considerations, and advance in another direction: toward modest suggestions and inferences about the effects of scale on social organization, based on my own comparative field research. I use 'scale' to mean the maximal size of the social, political, economic, and ideological-communication networks which significantly involve and affect the members of a social entity. That my suggestions and inferences are rather miscellaneous will be emphasized rather than concealed by the format of my discussion, for there is little logical progression to my remarks. They represent simply a variety of ideas about scale which come out of my fieldwork. In each instance (Aleuts, Indian villages, Indian city) I will present summary data, followed by the inferences I draw from them.

4.1 Change and scale in the Aleutians

I have elsewhere reviewed the history of the Aleuts with special attention to the 200 years since first European contact (Berreman 1955). Suffice it to say here that the Aleuts were a maritime hunting people of Eskimo stock whose 16–20,000 population, until the middle of the 18th century, had known and interacted primarily with one another, although they had casual contacts with neighboring and culturally similar Southwestern Alaskan Eskimos and occasional contacts with sea-going parties of Northwest Coast Indians. In the mid-18th century, they were first contacted and then overrun by Russian commercial fur-seekers who massacred many of them and introduced devastating diseases which together reduced their population at once to one-third of its total before contact, and within seventy years to one-twentieth of that number. At the same time, their skill and labor were exploited by the entrepreneurs who took most of the men far from their homes for all but the winter months. The total effect was devastating, a fact I do not want to gloss over. But it is also true that by the early 19th century, sea mammal trapping had ceased to be profitable; the Russian commercial interests had left; the violence, exploitation, and the most deadly of the epidemics were over; and Aleut lifeways persisted to a remarkable extent among the meagre population remaining. A few Russians lived among them, and a famous and respected priest (Bishop Ivan Veniaminov) converted them to Orthodox Christianity, as his less perceptive and empathetic predecessors had failed to do, but the Aleuts were not forced to become Europeanized in their social organization, family life, language, socialization or economy. The few who had survived, managed to do so as Aleuts, self-sufficient in their homeland.

The United States took over the Aleutians with the purchase of Alaska in 1867, but largely ignored the region until the turn of the century. Then, as furs of the plentiful foxes became valuable and livestock raising seemed promising, the Aleuts found themselves again the objects of outsiders' greedy attention. There followed a period of increasingly rapid 'Americanization' of the Aleuts and their homeland: introduction of wage labor and consumer goods which before long replaced the traditional subsistence economy; introduction of compulsory education in English up to the eighth grade (and the possibility of further education in mainland boarding schools for the best and most acquiescent pupils); takeover of virtually all land, including village sites, by outside ranching interests whose only feed-back to the Aleuts was a small number of unreliable jobs at low pay; confiscation of fishing rights and depletion of fishing resources, including the areas adjacent to Aleut villages, by outside commercial interests whose only input to the Aleuts, again, was a few jobs; supervision of all kinds of village and individual activities, and enforcement of alien codes, by poorly informed and often unsympathetic US government agents. There had been a brief period of relative prosperity for Aleuts in the 1920s when they were able to trap foxes profitably, but this ended abruptly when the great depression combined with changes in women's fashions to destroy the market for fox furs. During World War II the Aleuts were removed by the government, under the threat of Japanese invasion, to the alien safety of the Alaskan mainland. Many did not return (due to an unprecedentedly high death-rate and to emigration), while others were returned unhappily, after the war, to consolidated villages which included many strangers and which for many were located on unfamiliar islands. Still others found their villages a shambles as a result of off-duty looting and vandalism by soldiers. All found it hard to return to life in the Aleutians with their numbers depleted, their livelihood largely destroyed, their lives dominated by outsiders, and their lifeways forgotten, despised, or rendered inappropriate by changed circumstances. Since that time the islands have been dominated by the US military and a few alien ranchers, the seas by commercial fishermen, and life for the Aleuts has been a living Hell of want, frustration, and social and personal disorganization (cf. Berreman 1964; Jones 1969). Some have sought escape through emigration; those who have not succeeded in this have sought it through alcohol.

Thus, in the initial 50 years of contact, Aleuts were killed and exploited; in the next 100 years they were Christianized but otherwise left largely alone to heal their wounds and forge a self-sufficient kind of life analagous to that they had known before contact. In the most recent 70 years they have been shorn of their independence, their livelihood, and their way of life, with the result that they have either left their homeland or remained in misery.

4.2 Incorporation into alien networks

In the context of this history, a discussion of scale seems academic at best. However, some observations and questions relating to scale can be derived from the tragedy of the Aleuts' experience, and I will attempt to point them out.

Although cultural change can occur without a change in scale, and therefore the two must not be confused or treated as synonymous, change in scale seems inevitably to entail cultural changes. One reason is simply that, as contrasted to the small-scale situation, interaction among more and different people increases the number of potential innovators, the number of novel situations, and the likelihood of the 'conjunction of differences' which leads to innovation (Barnett 1953: 46–56). Another, broader, reason is that increased size and density of population, and greater territory over which interaction occurs, entail adjustments and changes in social structures and social processes.

It is clear that with European contact and with increasing incorporation into the dominant American society (albeit as peripheral and exploited members), the Aleuts experienced changes which included a drastic change in scale. They entered a vast economic and political network wherein they were acutely vulnerable to remote but fateful events in Europe and the United States. It is also clear that different aspects of Aleut life were affected differently by the various components of the change in scale. Aleuts' incorporation in the epidemeological network of the foreigners was physically devastating (as was the fact that they were subjected to the aliens' violence and greed). The imposition of Orthodox Christianity seems to have been quite thorough but remarkably benign in its effect, partly because of the humanity and wisdom of the priest who introduced it, and his skill in adapting it to Aleut conditions. The imposition, after 1900, of a money economy, schooling and governmental control by the United States – in each case utilizing alien values and offering rewards derivable only from outsiders – did more than the previous 150 years of outside contact to change the Aleuts' ways of life and their aspirations.

4.3 Vulnerability and dependence

One consequence of incorporation into networks of vastly increased scale is likely to be the acquisition of material, political, and or psychic dependence upon, and vulnerability to, institutions and resources outside of the small-scale community and beyond its control or understanding. People become subject to the definitions of themselves held by remote others, and to the needs, aspirations, and values of people they do not know or understand. Their new dependence and vulnerability are often without reciprocal influence, without effective recourse, without choice, without knowledge of the fact, nature or extent of their dependency or vulnerability, and without awareness of the motives or morality of those who deeply influence their lives. Traditional methods of ensuring predictability or coping with unpredictability are rendered inoperative; social control, together with the traditional values it enforces and the traditional rewards those values offer, is likely to be undermined.

This is the experience not only of the Aleuts, but of rural people confronted by city life wherever it occurs. Social disintegration, personal disorganization, and emigration have been the common results, for rarely are the rewards of the large-scale society available in the isolated, rural small-scale milieu. Often these conditions carry over to the city where, as in the case of most Aleuts, the racism and ethnic or class prejudice of the dominant-group urbanites combine with lack of employment opportunities in the city and lack of economic sufficiency, education, job training, and social skills on the part of the immigrants, to preclude the possibility of integrating successfully into the urban milieu or of deriving the rewards thought to inhere in urban life.

4.4 Deprivation, relative and otherwise

A related aspect of change in scale exhibited by the Aleuts is the acquisition of new aspirations and new standards of value compounding their new dependencies. In part this takes the form of acquisition of alien reference groups (Berreman 1964a; cf. Merton & Kitt 1950; Ralph Turner 1956). 'In the process of judging themselves by White men's standards, Aleuts are led to adopt many of the White men's values, perspectives and behaviors' (Berreman 1964: 233). They are led as well to aspire to the rewards those values, perspectives, and behaviors appear to bring to Whites. But they are prevented from reaping the rewards, because they are ineligible for membership in their reference group – it proves to be an ascribed group. This disparity between valued reference group and membership group is frustrating and disheartening. It results in both the feeling and the actuality of deprivation – in some cases *relative* deprivation, since the standard by which it is judged is based on the example of outsiders, while traditional rewards are presumably still available even though they are undesired. But since traditional rewards and values are commonly relinquished, and the means to achieve them are removed or discarded at the same time that new ones are embraced, the deprivation is likely (as in the case of the Aleuts) to soon become absolute.

The process is a familiar one: incorporation into a larger, and especially an alien, network of interdependence brings with it knowledge of different ways of doing things – ways which become preferred because they seem to bring new and highly valued rewards. This is especially common when the increase in scale entails an educational system controlled from outside, and when mass media tout the values and rewards of the large-scale society at the expense of traditional ones. If the rewards are not available in the small-scale context, emigration (especially of the young) is the common result, as the experience of tribal peoples, peasants, villagers, ruralites, and small town people in many societies confirms. If people are thwarted in such mobility, they are likely to seek solace or escape in behavior which is disruptive of the life-style they seek to escape, and yet which is not rewarding to them in itself. Thus it must not be overlooked that the human costs of these changes have been enormous. The Aleuts have become alienated from both their traditional culture and from the imposed culture as they have experienced it. They are personally frustrated and disorganized, as well as socially disorganized and anomic (Berreman 1964a; Jones 1969; cf. Horton 1964; Bloch 1952; Blumer 1937).

4.5 *Exploitation, independence and alien control*

That the first 150 years of contact with the alien large-scale societies did not have these consequences for the Aleuts is a result of the fact that during that time they remained relatively independent; the outsiders did not control nor interfere in Aleut socialization, social organization, political organization, or subsistence economy in such a way as to render these traditional ways inappropriate or unproductive, or to render traditional rewards irrelevant. They exploited the people, they killed many of them, but they did not destroy their independent way of life. After 1900, it was precisely in this regard that the situation changed. Aleuts were placed in a position where control was in alien hands: the rewards offered were alien ones, their attainment was contingent upon behavior alien to their traditions. And even then, once the commitment to change had been made, the rewards proved to be unavailable. The sacrifice had been for nothing; the old ways had been forsaken for new ways which did not work; the Aleuts had been betrayed.

This, again, was in part a result of change in scale – more accurately, of a partial and thwarted change in scale. It was to a more important extent a result of the greedy exploitativeness and callousness of those who engineered that change in scale. It would have been equally possible to make available to the Aleuts the rewards which they thought would accompany the changes which overtook them. If this had been done, the recent history, present condition, and future prospects of the Aleuts would have been very different, as the case of their fellows under Russian and Soviet administration demonstrates (cf. Antropova 1964).

5. Variations in scale in India

In India I have conducted research in a small and isolated mountain village and its region (Berreman 1972a), and have contrasted it with larger, less isolated plains villages (Berreman 1960a). I have also worked in a good-sized city, contrasting social relations there with those of villages (Berreman 1972b). Inferences drawn from these experiences about the influence of scale on social organization comprise the remainder of this paper.

5.1 *Small versus smaller: villages of plains and mountains*

In contrasting mountain (*Pahari*) with plains (*Desi*) villages of north central India, I have elsewhere pointed out that mountain villages are small, scattered, and mutually isolated (Berreman 1960a). The topography largely dictates these characteristics. As a result, intense and frequent interaction occurs primarily within the village. Inter-caste interaction is relatively frequent within the village (some castes have very few representatives in a given village, so if these people are to interact at all it must be, perforce, inter-caste interaction). A single water-source, a single shop, the need for cooperation on heavy and urgent tasks, facilitate or require such interaction. Inter-village interaction is relatively infrequent because of the barriers of distance and terrain.

On the plains, by comparison, villages are close to one another, and the flat terrain and presence of roads make even distant ones accessible. Population density is much greater, caste composition within a village or locality is more diverse, caste boundaries are more closely guarded, and social separation is more rigorously enforced than in the mountains. Intense and frequent interaction on the plains occurs predominantly within the caste, and it easily crosses village lines to incorporate caste-fellows of other villages, including those at considerable distance.

Communication, homogeneity, and diversity

Intensive interaction leads to common culture and, in turn, is facilitated by it. Accordingly, in the isolated, small-scale mountain society, common culture is localized and to a lesser degree stratified; in the larger-scale plains society, common culture is stratified and to a lesser degree localized.

. . . In the hills there is little opportunity for cultural differences to arise or to be maintained among castes simply because there is little intercaste isolation in any one locality. On the plains the situation is reversed; caste isolation is the rule and intercaste cultural differences, especially across the pollution barrier, result. Common culture, like common language depends upon the interaction of those who share it. (cf. Gumperz 1958) As Bloomfield (1933: 46) has noted, 'the most important differences of speech within a community are due to differences in *density of communication*'. (Berreman 1960a: 785.)

Obviously, then, the kind and intensity of interaction is important. It is in this respect, perhaps even more than in frequency, that Pahari intercaste relations differ from those on the plains. Characteristically, such contacts on the plains are formal, 'contractual', restricted in scope and content, and are accompanied by a good deal of inhibition on both sides. In contrast, in the Pahari area they are more often informal, intensive and extensive. Plains castes exclude one another from knowledge of, and participation in, their problems and ways of life; Paharis exclude outsiders but are little concerned with concealing their affairs from local members of other castes. Pahari castes are thus not 'closed subgroups' to the extent that plains castes tend to be.

The accompanying diagram may help make clear the contrasts in plains and Pahari interaction patterns and hence cultural differentiation by caste and locality. In this diagram broken arrows indicate limited interaction, solid arrows indicate extensive and intensive, informal interaction. Interaction in plains culture tends to be horizontal (i.e. within the caste and across local boundaries), while Pahari interaction tends to be vertical (i.e. within the local area and across caste boundaries). (Ibid: 786.)

Thus, the degree of cultural difference found among the castes, areas, and perhaps even between the sexes, . . . varies directly with their degree of isolation from one another, defined in terms of rate and quality of interaction and determined by social and physical accessibility. (Ibid: 787.)

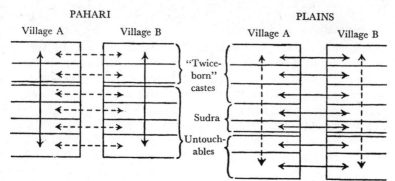

Figure 2. Contrasting interaction patterns

Scale, expressed as size of network, is central in the above discussion, as is intensity of interaction. The small scale of Pahari society – the isolation of its local units – throws people upon one another despite social differences, in a fashion not found in the plains. There, larger scale makes possible (but does not require) social separation – mutual social isolation – of the constituent groups within local communities, with resultant maintenance of social differentiation. Density of communication is both a product of and a means to cultural homogeneity. If everyone communicates uninhibitedly and effectively with everyone else on a full range of topics and in a full range of contexts, cultural homogeneity is assured. This is a characteristic of small-scale societies. It might also result from widespread and effective use of mass media and public education in large-scale ones, as governments have often hoped, but so far this has not occurred to any very conspicous extent. Social barriers, both self-imposed (e.g. as a manifestation of ethnic pride), and externally imposed (e.g. as a manifestation of ethnic discrimination), as well as cultural, linguistic, and physical barriers often prevent the communication which would facilitate communication conducive to cultural and social homogeneity.

Distribution of social knowledge

In small-scale societies, the social distribution of social knowledge is relatively homogeneous. *Pahari* villagers, for example, know a great deal about one another and about the internal affairs and internal organization of one another's castes. There are few secrets in the intimacy of small-scale life. This is less true in larger, more diverse, less culturally homogeneous plains villages, where service castes of low rank know those they serve, but where those served have a rather casual knowledge of their servants. The contrast is more evident and better documented in the contrast between villagers and urbanites. In urban society, people often know very little about most social groups to which they do not themselves belong. Those who do know are those who have to know: the poor, the vulnerable, the marginal, whose welfare, livelihood, and even survival is dependent upon others more powerful than themselves. They learn to know the habits and capabilities of the powerful in order to deal with them as effectively as possible. Those who are powerful need know only their own social group and their own power, its use and its effect, and this is generally all they do know. My urban research led me to the conclusion, 'people know well those who dominate them, but know little about those they dominate' (Berreman 1972b: 573).

5.2 Caste and scale

It has been suggested '. . . there is necessarily a close-set limit upon the size and complexity of a society organized through a caste (*jati*) system' (Bailey 1963: 113). Caste, in other words, cannot function or is impaired in a large-scale society in which there is no obvious racial basis for social distinctions because of mobility and diversity, and the consequent likelihood of misidentification and ease of dissimulation that would obtain in such a society. I have noted elsewhere,

It is probably true that in the anonymity and mobility of contemporary urban life, rigid ethnic (or caste) stratification is increasingly difficult to maintain when the indicators of identity are learned, for learned characteristics can be unlearned, suppressed, or learned by those to whom they are inappropriate. To manipulate these indicators is often difficult, as the persistence of the (physically indistinguishable) Burakumin of Japan makes clear, because the identifying characteristics may be learned very early (language, gesture), and may be enforced from without as well as from within (dress, deference, occupation), but it is possible, as instances of passing make clear (DeVos & Wagatsuma 1966: 245–248; Isaacs 1965: 143–149, *et passim*). The more personal relationships of traditional, small-scale societies, together with their formal and informal barriers and sanctions against casual or promiscuous interaction, militate against the learning or expression of inappropriate status characteristics. There individuals are well known, family ties are not concealable, dissimulation is a virtual impossibility, and physical mobility (to a new setting) is almost as unlikely as social mobility. Biological or other conspicuous indicators of status are thus largely unnecessary. Reliable, immutable, and conspicuous indicators of identity are thus more important to systems of birth-ascribed stratification in the anonymity and mobility of the city than in the village, but the internal pressures of ethnic pride combined with the external pressures of ethnic discrimination and the vested interests which sustain it make such systems possible in even the most unlikely-seeming circumstances (Berreman 1972c: 395–396).

I would here suggest that caste, as defined and organized in India, works most efficiently within a certain *range* of scale, limited at both ends. Evidently *Pahari* villages are too small and isolated for it to work easily. They are not only unable to support the full range of castes expectable in North Indian villages (and desired by many *Paharis* themselves), but they are unable to sustain or enforce the kind of rigid hierarchical social separation and differential socail behavior expected by people of the nearby plains. *Paharis* are therefore accused of being unorthodox in their caste organization; they are ridiculed for being uncivilized (*jungli*) and lax in their caste behavior. Accordingly they are regarded as being inferior in purity, and hence in rank and status, to plainsmen of corresponding castes. They explain their own deficiencies of this sort in very pragmatic terms: namely, that they have not the range of castes, the population, the wealth, the facilities and amenities, nor the leisure to observe the niceties of a complex, rigid, orthodox caste system.

On the other hand, contemporary cities seem to be too large and complex for India's caste system to work easily or well. City folk are unable to recognize and deal in an orthodox way with the wide range of strangers who cross their paths, or to attend correctly even to the many people whose castes they do know, recognize, or suspect. There are simply too many, their contacts are too brief or limited, the necessary information is too incomplete, the occasions are too public and uncontrollable, the opportunities for dis imulation too great, and the opportunity to protect oneself from polluting contact is too often missing. As a result, like *Paharis*, urbanites are often regarded and treated as compromised, polluted, leaders of a loose life, by their orthodox rural brethren, even when they are of corresponding castes.

Thus, in the one case the scale is too small to support the caste system in all of its complexity; in the other the scale is too large to permit the intricate and controlled interaction which the system ideally requires. It is in the intermediate scale of the densely populated rural regions of most of India, composed of many small, nearby, mutually accessible villages made up of many castes, that the system reaches its full oppressive flower.

5.3 Small versus large: villages and cities

Having looked rather closely at the small end of the continuum of scale in India, and having introduced the subject of cities in the two immediately preceding paragraphs, I turn now to a more general characterization of large-scale urban social relations in India based on my research in Dehra Dun, a city of nearly 200,000. I will utilize the rural villages of mountains and plains discussed above as contrastive cases of small-scale relations, and will again resort to the expedient of providing background data by quoting from a recent paper of my own. More sophisticated statements might be derived from the literature or constructed for this paper; but the following have the respective advantages of being first-hand and of having been prepared in another context where scale was not at issue, so that they are unlikely to be influenced by biases regarding scale that might be generated in the preparation of this paper.

5.3.1 Social relations

The village comprises people whose statuses are largely a function of their membership in corporate groups (families, sibs, castes). They tend to remain in their 'home territory' – the familiar setting of the village and its local region. . . . Villagers interact in terms of their total identities on a personal basis with others who know them well. Status summation is the rule: well-to-do people are powerful people of high ritual and social status; poor people are relatively powerless and of low status (with the exception of some religious roles where poverty is defined as consistent with or even necessary to high ritual status). As a consequence of these facts, there is relatively rarely a novel interactional situation to be figured out; rarely status incongruity to be coped with; rarely important interaction with strangers.

In the city, on the other hand, ethnic diversity is great. A large proportion of one's interaction is outside the 'home territory' of one's neighborhood, and is with strangers or casual acquaintances. Even those who are not strangers often know little about one another and see one another in limited, stereotyped situations. Therefore, a large proportion of interaction occurs in contexts where only specific statuses – parts of the social identity – are relevant or even known, and the elements of individual status (ethnic, ritual, economic, occupational, political statuses) are not as highly correlated as in the village. People therefore have to figure out how to interact on the basis of minimal information in highly specific, impersonal situations rather than responding on the basis of thorough knowledge, consistent statuses and generalized relevance.

City people usually know very little about the corporate groups to which their fellow city-dwellers belong and about the internal structure of those groups. This does not mean that the city is socially unstructured or even less structured than the village, but rather that its structure is less conspicuous. The structure lies largely in the regularity of behavioral responses to subtle cues about social identity and its situational relevance which come out of face-to-face interaction which is impersonal and often fleeting. This is reflected in the stereotypic differences between the social knowledge and skills of the country bumpkin and the cith slicker, each of whom is a laughing stock in the other's milieu where his hard-won social knowledge and skills are as inappropriate and irrelevant as they are effective and appropriate on his home ground. Both survive socially by reacting to the social identities of others, but the expression, definition and recognition of those identities and the appropriate responses are quite different.

The villager is well-versed on corporate groups, the individuals who comprise them, the history and characteristics of the groups and their members, and the traditional social, economic, political and ritual interrelations among them. He depends on ramified knowledge rather than superficial impressions. *The urbanite* is well-versed in the identification of a wide variety of strangers as representatives of both corporate and noncorporate social categories. He knows the superficial signs of their identity, their stereotypically defined attributes, the varieties of situations and the social information necessary for interaction with them, and methods of defining and delimiting interaction in the impersonal, instrumental world of urban interaction. He knows also when situations are not impersonal and instrumental, and how to act accordingly and appropriately. Urban residential neighborhoods are often relatively homogeneous ethnically, and stable over time, so that interaction approximates that in the village. Indian cities have for these reasons often been described as agglomerations of villages. What I have noted above about urban interaction applies, therefore, to the work-a-day world of the city – the bazar and other public places. It is less applicable to interaction within residential neighborhoods, and relatively 'private' settings.

In the urban situation, where status summation is less and is less relevant than in the village, and where livelihood is not dependent on high-caste landowners, power and privilege are not tied so closely or necessarily to traditional ritual status. People of low ritual status who have essential services to offer may be able to organize themselves, for they are in a position to exercise political and economic influence and to acquire or demand social amenities. Thus, the Sweepers of Dehra Dun, one of the most despised groups in the society, have been able to organize and surpass other low-status groups in security of employment, standard of living, and morale, because they are the exclusive practitioners of an essential service: providing the city's sewage and street cleaning systems. They are also a significant political bloc and a self-confident people. This is a distinct contrast to the situation of their caste-fellows in surrounding villages where their untouchability and dependence upon farming castes of high status insure deprivation, discrimination and all of their consequences (Berreman 1972b; 580–582, italics added).

. . .

Situational differences in the use of [social] terminology [*in the city*] are . . . complex. . . . A man of merchant caste who is fastidious about matters of ritual purity and pollution will discuss an impending wedding with detailed reference to the caste, sub-caste, sib and family affiliations of the participants, the caste and religion of those who will be hired to provide services, the region and social class of guests. A wide range of statuses will be important to him. In his drygoods shop, however, he will categorize customers only in ways relevant to the customer role, relying on stereotypes about the honesty, tight-fistedness, propensity to bargain, and buying preferences of various social categories he encounters. . . . A teashop proprietor, on the other hand, will look at potential customers in terms of religion and major caste categories because he has to attend to his customers' notions of ritual purity and the jeopardy in which inter-dining puts them. A barber will attend to certain categories of class, religion, and region in order to assure that he can please his customers in the hair styles they prefer and expect. Customers behave in complementary fashion. It is clear that these relations are not defined by the 'whole persons' involved – by the sum of the statuses of those interacting – but by those segments of the social selves which are relevant in the situation. The relations outside of one's own ethnic group are impersonal and fractionated; they are what sociologists have often termed 'secondary relationships'. They contrast with the personal, holistic, 'primary' relationships in the family, the village and other traditional settings where all of one's statuses are known, relevant and likely to be responded to (cf. Faris 1932) – relationships found in the city only within the ethnic group or neighborhood, if at all (Berreman 1972b: 573–574). Further on I note that in the city, where status summation or status consistency is far from perfect:

People expend considerable effort trying to assure that the statuses they regard as advantageous and appropriate for themselves are conveyed in particular contexts, and they expend considerable energy in trying to discern and respond to the relevant (if possible the most significant) and appropriate identities of others. This is where knowledge of the meaning attached to attributes and behaviors in various social and situational contexts is crucial to successful interaction, and where the manipulation of these meanings is crucial to identity maintenance. This is the crux of urban social organization.

. . .

The insight and understanding upon which successful social behavior depends, therefore, includes not only knowing the characteristics of groups and their members, but also on understanding the relationship of group membership to privileges, to the power which confers those privileges, and to the sanctions which enforce them. On the individual level this means knowing the social capabilities as well as the social identities of those one meets: what they expect and what they can be expected to do; what resources they have at their command; how they can be expected to act and react in particular circumstances and with what effect. To the extent that inter-group relations are characterized by stability, it is primarily a consequence of balance of power, not consensus on the desirability of, or the rationale for, the system. No stigmatized, oppressed or even relatively deprived ethnic group or social category that I encountered in Dehra Dun or in its rural hinterland accepted its status as legitimate. But many – perhaps most – individuals in such statuses accepted that status as fact and accommodated to it while cherishing a hope or nursing a plan or pursuing action to alter it (Ibid: 582–583).

. . .

Increased availability of education, mass media, and political participation, together with conspicuous consumption of luxury goods by the well-to-do, and callous disregard for the needs and desires of the poor by many of the well-to-do contribute to and accelerate the likelihood of change through enhancing awareness of alternatives, providing an understanding of the means to change and increasing the accessibility of those means. Urban India is the arena in which this is happening most rapidly. There the social structure is loose enough to allow experimentation with various alliances and social structures which have been elsehwere inhibited by the rigidity of traditional, rural social organization and the unitary relationship between the social organization and the distribution of power. Effective mechanisms for change may result, actuated by newly mobilized interest groups growing out of significant urban social categories (Ibid: 583–584).

These characterizations of urban social relations bring the discussion to the implications of scale which most interest me: those relating to ethnic stratification and its consequences in the lives of those who experience it.

5.3.2 Scale and stratification

Basically, the difference between a large-scale stratified society and a smaller-scale one, from the viewpoint of those within it is, I think, that the former is more permeable and flexible, offering room to maneuver in the ambiguity and anonymity its size and complexity provide. The effects of these qualities are not limited to stratification separation, and oppression – I emphasize these features because of my own interest in them.

Complexity, anonymity, escape, and passing : It is possible to disappear, to escape, to get lost intentionally or not, in a large-scale society in ways and to an extent difficult or impossible in small-scale ones. The anonymity, impersonality, fragmentation, diversity, complexity, and sheer magnitude of urban society make it possible for a person to go unrecognized and unidentified and thereby escape some of the consequences of his identity or status. Social mobility, identity manipulation and passing are possible even when ascription is the rule. One can attempt to dissimulate his identity permanently (by moving to a strange city or neighborhood and altering his speech, name, dress, occupation, lifestyle, etc.), or situationally (e.g. by similarly concealing from his colleagues at work his family background, ethnic identity, or place of residence), or temporarily (e.g. by putting on Western clothing in order to spend a night on the town incognito). The fleeting, fragmented interactions which

5

characterize large-scale, urban life facilitate such avoidance of the implications of ascribed status.

Bureaucratic responses : As societies get larger, those in power often intensify their efforts to counteract these phenomena in apparent awareness of, and anxiety about, their possible consequences: namely, a threat to the power and privilege which rigidity assures them, and an undermining of the controls which make possible that rigidity. Formal, bureaucratic means of keeping tabs on people (identification cards, computer banks of personal information, etc.) and clandestine surveillance techniques are often employed. Evidently the belief is that, unless closely supervised, people will take advantage of the opportunities offered by population size and density, complexity and anonymity, to seek the rewards normally reserved for a few, and to escape the onerous obligations an impersonal society imposes upon its members. Socialization and informal controls are regarded as inadequate to ensure or enforce the conformity those in power hope to maintain. In smaller-scale societies, less formal means of surveillance and social control accomplish the same ends.

Mobility, deviation, and accountability : The changes and manipulations of status which large scale facilitates are not necessarily illegitimate nor even deceptive. The large-scale milieu is likely to be one in which the very impersonality and fragmentation of relationships reduces the reliance upon ascribed characteristics and 'involute' statuses (those consisting of more or less rigidly defined clusters of compatible and mutually reinforcing elements, cf. Barth 1960: 142, 144), to define interaction. A person may find the city a place where he can enter milieux in which his ascribed statuses are irrelevant or secondary; where he can acquire identities and play roles to which he aspires that would be denied him in a small-scale environment. In short, mobility may there be legitimate – even expected. The individual may be able to acquire or emphasize statuses or aspects of status which he values or finds rewarding, and conceal or hold in abeyance others which bring painful consequences. In the city, achieved statuses may override traditional ascribed ones (in some situations and for some purposes, at least); claimed statuses may be difficult to challenge effectively.

In small-scale societies – in villages, tribes, and bands – strangers are few and are regarded warily. A person cannot legitimately escape his status. He is known in his totality to his fellows, is held accountable to them, and is responded to accordingly. His interactions with others are continuous and total; his statuses are well known, involute, inseparable from one another and inseparable from his personal biography. He may escape some of their implica-

66

tions by experiencing a drastic, public change in his social role, but this is quite different from the private, publicly unremarked and sometimes clandestine changes which occur in urban settings.

Thus, I knew a young untouchable in the *Pahari* village of my research who became a spectacular success as the vehicle for a powerful regional deity and thereby avoided many of the consequences of his untouchability (Berreman 1971; 1972a: 379–396). I knew another who was regarded as having gone crazy (ibid, 1971; 1972a: 396–397). Both were allowed freedom of action denied their caste-fellows. An observer might believe, as I do, that the individuals affected had a hand in the divine or fateful events which excused them from the full implications of their inborn statuses. But the ideology is (and must be in an ascriptively stratified society), that such escape is involuntary and is, in addition, rare. Therefore, the first individual was said to have been divinely 'chosen', the second to have been unfortunately 'stricken'.

One may also be expelled from a valued status in a small-scale society – outcasted to the social isolation of pariah status in village India; driven out of the village to become a lonely, feared, and despised 'outside man' in the Aleutians. These, too, are rare, imposed, and publicly recognized status changes, not voluntary or clandestine efforts at mobility or escape such as occur in the anonymity of the city.

In rural India, the only way in which an individual can rise in ascribed status is if his caste raises its status; and the only way in which a caste can rise in status is by receiving public acknowledgement that a mistake has been made theretofore in identification of the caste's true rank. This acknowledgement is accomplished through persistent status emulation (Sanskritization) by the caste's members to justify the status claim (cf. Srinivas 1966), combined with the acquisition and application of power to enforce that claim (cf. Berreman 1967b; 1972c; 1973). The caste does not 'rise'; instead it becomes redefined (*correctly* defined in the view of those concerned, both in and out of the caste). No individual social mobility occurs; no deception, misinformation, or ambiguity is involved. This is quite different from the urban phenomenon of individual mobility.

The crucial difference is that in a small society, the individual is under close and constant surveillance by others, including authority figures. In large ones, he may be unnoticed and unaccountable – or noticed and accountable in such disparate situations and roles that no one comprehends or cares about him as a person. In small societies, mistakes and deviations are quickly seen and reacted to.

In large ones they may go unseen, unnoticed, and unremarked, for the individual is less intimately tied to others, less conspicuous to them, and his actions are defined as less relevant to their lives and fortunes. In small societies the deviant individual's aspiration, success, or eccentricity may be regarded as a challenge to the moral order; in a large one it is more likely, if noticed at all, to be regarded as inconvenient, laughable, or perhaps enviable personal deviation. In a sea of variation, no one deviation is so conspicuous or seems so important as is the case in a pond of conformity.

6.1 Totality, status fragmentation, and role segregation

Small societies share with Goffman's 'total institutions' the fact that people live most of their lives in one another's presences, open to one another's scrutiny, subject to one another's evaluative responses (cf. Goffman 1961: 3–124). They interact in primary relationships – as total persons with known statuses, known personalities, known biographies, all of which are inseparable and all of which are relevant to the interaction. Thus, in the village, Ram Lal is Ram Lal the untouchable Blacksmith who, like most of his caste-fellows, is poor and regarded as lazy and dissolute, but he is also unusually intelligent and witty like his father, he is not addicted to hashish unlike his brother, and he is uniquely capable in divination. All of his relationships are conditioned by this knowledge which everyone shares. A man for whom he works is Shiv Singh, the arrogant, cantankerous and dishonest but high-status Rajput farmer who cheated his brother out of an inheritance and lost his first wife to a more considerate man. All of his interactions are approached by others in terms of this crucial fund of knowledge about him.

In the large-scale urban context, these two men would be responded to in very specific ways on the basis of the limited knowledge which comes from casual, role-specific contact with its limited relevance for those involved. In fact, whereas village interaction takes account of both person and status, urban interaction is often role-specific, taking into account neither person nor status. Statuses are fragmented; roles are segregated. Ram Lal is in the city likely to be perceived as Ram Lal the bumpkin cloth customer, Ram Lal the poor man asking a slightly-known shopkeeper for credit, Ram Lal the illiterate wishing to have a personal letter written on his behalf, Ram Lal the laborer looking for work, Ram Lal the untouchable seeking a place to eat or worship. Shiv Singh will be regarded as Shiv Singh the mountain villager seeking a ration of cement, Shiv Singh the asthma sufferer as Hakim's patient, Shiv Singh the niggardly taxi customer, Shiv Singh the landowning tax-payer (or tax-evader), Shiv Singh the Rajput temple-goer. Ram Lal and Shiv Singh as temporary or permanent urban-ites are likely to be unknown to those around them except in such specific roles, in such situations, pursuing such particular tasks. Nor surprisingly, in large-scale societies, institutions dependent upon detailed personal knowledge and face-to-face interaction are less prevalent, or at least less pervasive relative to the total social network, than in small ones. Sufficient mutual information is simply not available for it to be otherwise.

6.2 *Indexical and objective behavior*

In the small-scale society, therefore, people relate to one another on the basis of extensive and intensive mutual knowledge. In the large-scale society, many of their relationships are based upon superficial mutual assessments. As Wirth noted (1938: 12), 'the contacts of the city may indeed be face-to-face, but they are never-theless impersonal, superficial, transitory, and segmented'. The first of these kinds of interactional behavior is describable as 'indexical', whereas the latter kind can be termed 'objective'. These terms are derived from Husserl (cf. Farber 1943: 237–238), and Garfinkel, one of Husserl's contemporary sociological advocates (cf. Garfinkel 1967: 4–11).

> Husserl spoke of [indexical expressions as] expressions whose sense cannot be decided by an auditor without his necessarily knowing or assuming something about the biography and the purposes of the user of the expression, the circumstances of the utterance, the previous course of the conversation, or the particular relationship of actual or potential interaction that exists between the expressor and the auditor (Garfinkel 1967: 4).

I am asserting that such thorough, contextual knowledge is characteristically utilized in small-scale social interaction. In large scale social interaction the available data are fewer and less necessary – the behavior is more stereotyped, impersonal and is conditioned by obvious and significant characteristics of person and circumstance. Quoting Wirth, again:

> typically our [urban] physical contacts are close but our social contacts are distant. The urban world puts a premium on visual recognition. We see the uniform which denotes the role of the functionaries and are oblivious to the personal eccentricities that are hidden behind that uniform (Wirth 1938: 14).

This is a difference of degree, rather than kind, between urban and rural interaction.

6.3 *Communities, personal and impersonal*

Jules Henry has noted: 'in many primitive cultures and in the great cultures of A sia,a person is born into a personal community, a group of intimates to which he is linked for life by tradition; but in America everyone must create his own personal community' (Henry 1963: 147). I would add that the situation in America is essentially that of any large-scale, impersonal, complex post-industrial society as contrasted to small-scale societies. Just as 'every [American] child must be a social engineer' (ibid.), so must every post-industrial urbanite, for 'no traditional arrangements guarantee an individual personal community' (ibid.). Elsewhere it is unusual for a child to be surrounded by friends one day and deserted the next, yet this is a constant possibility in America (ibid.: 148), and so it is in the large-scale industrial society.

6.4 *The construction of community*

This, Henry insists, is stress-producing for Americans. I think that it is universally so. As a consequence, people seem to construct personal communities even in the unlikeliest of circumstances. The city is a distinctively impersonal community, yet it teems with personal communities, fragments of personal communities, and people seeking to construct personal communities (cf. Rowe 1964).

Here an important distinction must be made between small-scale and large-scale environments within the city; for while the tribal settlement and rural village are uniformly small in scale, the city has elements of both small and large scale. One of the shortcomings of the characterization of urban life set forth by Wirth and others is the failure to make this distinction and instead to treat the city as entirely large-scale. The characteristically urban, large-scale interaction in the city (fleeting, fragmented, anonymous) takes place in the marketplace, in bureaucracies, in many occupational settings – in short, in the impersonal milieux of 'public places', as Goffman (1963) calls them. At the same time there exist in cities personal milieux – 'private places' (Goffman 1963: 9) – families, homes, neighborhoods, social clubs. The former are the large-scale, impersonal, exclusively urban environments of which I have written above, and in which my urban research was carried out. Those environments are the source of Wirth's characterization of urban society. Private places were excluded from my urban research precisely because I wanted to discover how ethnic relations occur in the impersonal setting of urban public places in India (Berreman 1972b: 568). But private places are important to city people, as they are to people everywhere.

In Dehra Dun, every occupational group, small business interest, regional and linguistic category had its formal association; every neighborhood its small-scale relationships. Even gigantic Bombay has been described as a city of villages; or, perhaps more accurately, as a city of villagers. City people spend much of their time in the impersonality of secondary relationships, status fragmentation, role segregation, casual or stereotyped interaction, and part-person-hood. Yet they return at night or mealtime, at times of illness, trouble, crisis, or celebration, to more intimate environments reproducing the small societies from which they came and to which they often look back with more nostalgia than realism, overlooking the pressures and attractions which took them away in the first place. Similar circumstances frequently bring urban migrants back to the peasant villages from which they came, and for similar reasons. In family, neighborhood, club, ethnic association, union, teashop, pub, and street-corner gang, small-scale society and its concomitants are sought, generated, and preserved. The very terminology which epitomizes small-scale relationships – the terminology of kinship – is often adapted to such groups, furthering the illusion and the effect. (See Vatuk 1969, for an excellent analysis of fictive kinship in an urban neighborhood of an Indian city, and Vatuk 1972, for the analysis in its full context. Wirth has commented: 'In view of the ineffectiveness of actual kinship ties we create fictional kinship groups. In the face of the disappearance of the territorial unit as a basis of social solidarity we create interest units' [Wirth, 1938: 23].)

In small societies, the personal community is congruent with the total community. In large societies, the personal community is a small and often fragile part of the social world of those within it; its functions are circumscribed; it may be fractionated in that individuals may participate in several role-specific personal communities. Its existence is therefore precarious. But it is invariably important to those who comprise it. This is another manifestation of the fact that in small-scale relationships, virtually all constituents of social organization coalesce: roles, statuses, and personalities; formal and informal relations; expressive and instrumental activities; collective- and self-orientation; ascription and achievement; economics, politics, social relations, religion, etc. In large-scale societies, these all tend to diverge from one another as social relations become situationally and temporally fragmented.

71

In a small-scale society, people know too much about one another to separate the person from his status; in a large-scale society, they know too little of one another to attend consistently to either, much less to both. Either of these situations can be physically costly: total visibility and accountability can be experienced as total vulnerability, just as total anonymity can be experienced as loneliness or even nothingness.

6.5 *The quest for community*

There is a rather poignant motto engraved in letters of heroic size across the facade of the University of California's venerable Hilgard Hall at Berkeley: 'TO RESCUE FOO HUMAN SOCIETY THE NATIVE VALUES OF RURAL LIFE'. It reflects accurately the nostalgia for small-scale life in large-scale societies and the yearning for the presumed stability, security and 'authenticity' of small-scale social organization which underlies the recurrence of such organizations within large-scale environments (cf. Slater 1970). The same yearning is expressed in Western utopian communities of many sorts, and in the proliferation of rural and urban 'communes' which is part of the contemporary US youth culture (cf. Davis 1971) – a counter-culture (Yinger 1960) whose advocates are alienated from, and who reject, many of the manifestations of large-scale society.

Fred Davis has suggested, in his discussion of 'youth subcultures':

> The proliferation in the modern world of mass bureaucratic organizations, of closely calculated schemes of production and control with their minutely specified procedures and regulations, has greatly contributed to the felt divorcement of activity from product and of role from being, namely, the classic Marxian definition of alienation. As Mannheim [1940] argued, whereas these organizational schemes possess considerable 'functional rationality', i.e. they manage to get the work done efficiently, they nevertheless lack too frequently 'substantial rationality', i.e. they fail to address themselves to the body of human sentiments and meanings with which particular acts are invested' (Davis 1971: 11).

The consequences of large-scale social relations seem to be humanly costly:

> Whereas it is possible to exaggerate, as many social scientists have, the anonymity of life in the metropolis, the fragility of the modern kin-isolated nuclear family, the psychic dislocation resulting from

geographic and social mobility, and so forth, it nonetheless cannot be gainsaid that big cities, massive organizations, and an intense circulation of persons and ideas do make for more marginal differences in how people relate to each other, in how they conceive of themselves and their fellows. Compared to what anthropologists have noted for village and trival societies, modern urban existence does give rise to impersonality, expediential relationships, social distance, opportunism, and personal isolation. Despite the greater intellectual and artistic creativity fostered in cities, despite the enhanced personal freedom and opportunities for social advancement that urban-based modern technology has made possible [Simmel 1950], it is also true – or so the weight of sociological evidence seems to indicate – that modern man does feel more lonely, more anomic, more unsure of who he 'really' is and what he should aspire to than did his preindustrial forebears' (Davis 1971: 12).

The very ambiguity, flexibility, permeability, anonymity, and tolerance which characterize large-scale society and which attract many people to it in an attempt to escape the total accountability of small-scale life, are in the end anxiety-provoking for many people, who seem often to yearn again for what they or their ancestors once sought to escape.

. . . Hippies wish somehow to declare – or perhaps merely to believe – that life can be whole again, that identities can be made secure and relationships meaningful through a return to the little community, through direct engagement with the land and its products, through communal collective enterprise that abjures conventional status distinctions, and through allegiance to some more altruistic (if humbler) scheme wherein, true to the great Christian and communist philosophers, the quintessential rule of life is to be – from each according to his abilities, to each according to his needs (Davis 1971: 20).

To suggest, however . . . that these 'new forms' [the communes of various kinds] are but a simple recreation of the small peasant community of preindustrial times, a naive rediscovery, as it were, of the 'underlying' organic bases of social life, is to misread the true character of hippie communalism as much as if one were to deny it all significance whatsoever. Questions of sheer economic viability aside, much of the charismatic millenial spirit that animates the hippie commune is positively anathema to village life with its provincial mentality, mundane routines, and taciturn forms of social relations (Davis 1971: 21).

And Davis quotes an observation written in 1922 by the sociologist Schmalenbach (1961: 338), that community and communion are not the same thing; that 'much of the present-day yearning for communal coherence . . . is directed less toward a specific community than toward coherence as such'.

7. Inconclusion.

The discussion above demonstrates my feeling that size alone is difficult to apply as an analytical concept, both because it is a relative matter, and because it occurs in so many cultural, ecological, and historical contexts. On the whole and in general, size is no doubt an important variable in limiting and permitting some varieties and characteristics of social organization – but in specific instances its influence is difficult to gauge because a wide variety of other variables are simultaneously operative, masking its effect. Size is at best a broadly limiting factor of relatively little use in comparative studies. It seems to me more useful to make 'controlled' comparisons (cf. Eggan 1954), taking into account a variety of factors – depending upon the comparison being made – such as size, complexity, sources and modes of communication, agencies of socialization, types of interdependence, forms of social organization, value systems, cultural traditions, history, etc. – something I have attempted to do cross-culturally or cross-temporally in several papers (Berreman 1955, 1960a, 1960b, 1962a, 1962b, 1964, 1966, 1967b, 1969, 1971, 1972c, 1973).

Accepting for the time being, however, the general notion of scale as something which *can* be roughly operationalized and which *does* have social consequences, I would say that in general large-scale societies differ from small-scale ones in ways identifiable with complexity, diversity; and the resultant differentials in individual visibility and accountability, in social flexibility and permeability – in short, in ways suggested by the central tendency of those contrasts listed between Type I Societies and Type II Societies in Fig. 1. I believe that scale has a tendency to vary directly with the impersonality of social interaction, the impersonality of social control, with the complexity of social and cultural differentiation, with the possibility of social mobility and individual redefinition of identity, and with the anonymity of personal life – little more than that.

In closing, I will simply list in summary form some of the specific ways in which I have suggested above that scale influences social relations:

(1) 'Scale' as a concept to be used in the analysis of social organiza-

tion is most easily definable as the size of the maximal network(s) in which people in the social entity under study are significantly involved. This definition is so broad as to be of questionable analytical utility. Complexity of social organization is closely associated with size and, like intensity of interaction, is generally implied in the term 'scale'. If 'scale' is to be used in social analysis, its referent must be clearly spelled out, and the manner in which its constituent dimensions are to be operationalized and weighted must be specified.

(2) There have been many generalizations made by social commentators which relate more or less to scale as a variable in social organization. Some of these have been cited here and grouped around two polar types designated 'Type I Societies' and 'Type II Societies', corresponding roughly to Redfield's Folk and Urban types respectively. Further consideration of the legitimacy and accuracy of these descriptive typologies is recommended.

(3) For present purposes, I regard Type I Societies as small-scale, Type II Societies as large-scale.

(4) Increase in scale makes people vulnerable to forces beyond their control, experience, and even comprehension, and often makes them dependent upon similarly remote institutions and resources. (Aleut example.)

(5) Increase in scale often leads people to value and seek rewards not attainable within their society (i.e. to acquire reference groups in which they are barred from membership). At the same time people are likely to abandon, irrevocably, pre-existing rewards which may still be attainable. The barriers to attainment of the new rewards are often imposed by others, rather than being inherent. (Aleut example.)

(6) The results of (4) and (5) include both the feeling and the actuality of deprivation which, when unresolved, leads to personal and social disorganization. (Aleut example.)

(7) Change is likely to be more pervasive, more rapid and more readily tolerated in large-scale than in small-scale societies.

(8) Large-scale societies are occupationally more diverse; they contain more statuses, roles, and situations; they contain more belief systems, a wider range and greater number of social interactions, more barriers to communication between groups; consequently they are socially more heterogeneous than small-scale ones. Therefore, they exhibit social strata, ethnic pluralism, cultural diversity, etc. (India example: mountain-plains contrast, urban situation.)

(9) The social distribution of social knowledge is likely to be more uniform in small-scale than in large-scale societies. (India example: rural-urban contrast.)

(10) Large-scale societies are likely to be ideologically more diverse, with less value consensus than small-scale ones and more dependence upon power and bureaucratic enforcement to maintain them. Perhaps as a result, counter-cultures are more characteristic of the former than of the latter.

(11) Birth-ascribed social stratification – especially in the absence of physical distinguishability among the strata – functions most efficiently in a society that is intermediate in scale (where social relations are neither overwhelmingly personal nor anonymous. (India examples.)

(12) Statuses in small-scale societies tend to be involute; those in large-scale societies tend to be disparate, fragmented, internally inconsistent, and situationally variable. (India example: rural-urban contrast.)

(13) The quality of small-scale and large-scale social interaction, and the kinds of social knowledge and skills each requires, differ significantly. The first is involute, total, and takes into account both the individuals (their biographies and personalities) and their statuses; the second is impersonal, fragmented, and takes into account specific part-statuses in specific situations. (India example: rural-urban contrast.)

(14) As a consequence of (13), interpersonal behavior in small-scale societies is conditioned by deep knowledge of the individuals involved and broad knowledge of the context. That in the city is conditioned by stereotypic responses to superficial cues about categories of persons and types of interaction situations. (India: rural-urban contrast.)

(15) Large-scale societies offer their members more anonymity and mobility than do small-scale ones, and they are more permeable, flexible, and manipulable. Hence, people can change, escape, or dissemble their identities in ways and to extents impossible in small societies. People can disappear in large-scale societies, they cannot in small-scale ones. (India: rural-urban contrast.)

(16) Small-scale societies offer their members more predictability and solidarity than large-scale ones: however, at the cost of total visibility and total accountability, with resultant social inflexibility (India: rural-urban contrast.)

(17) As a consequence of (16), the mechanisms by which people may escape the consequences of stigmatized identity differ in large- and small-scale societies. The former include voluntary and often clandestine efforts at mobility or passing; the latter may be restricted to publicly visible and putatively involuntary status changes. (Indian examples.)

(18) More personal diversity and eccentricity is found and tolerated in large-scale societies than in small-scale ones.

(19) In large-scale societies, formal procedures for keeping tabs on people and for ensuring conformity replace the informal ones of small-scale societies, and counter the tendencies described in (15) and (18).

(20) The personal community in the small-scale society is more or less congruent with the society; that in the large-scale society is a small segment of the total society and is often relevant only to limited spheres of activity. Hence, in large-scale society there may be multiple but shallow or fragmentary personal communities. However, people show remarkable tenacity in creating satisfying personal communities even in unlikely circumstances.

(21) People in small-scale societies are likely to envy those in large-scale societies their personal flexibility, anonymity, freedom from informal controls, diversity of experience, and diversity of opportunity.

(22) People in large-scale societies tend to envy those in small-scale ones their presumed intimacy, security, and freedom from formal controls.

(23) People in small-scale societies tend to idealize, and to emigrate to, large-scale milieux.

(24) People in large-scale societies tend to idealize, and to construct, small-scale milieux.

(25) Other things being equal, the above statements about the relationship between scale and social organization are true.

(26) Other things are never equal.

REIDAR GRÖNHAUG

Scale as a Variable in Analysis: Fields in Social Organization in Herat, Northwest Afghanistan

1. Introduction: The scale of what?

1.1 *What kinds of sub-systems have scale?*

Characterizations of whole societies as being 'large-scale' or 'small-scale' are in many cases loose and vague. It is hopeless to try to decide whether scale really is an important characteristic of social organization, unless we can first establish a sufficiently precise method for determining empirically the scale of the phenomena in question. Such a method is a prerequisite for any discussion of the structural corollaries of the scale of a society.

What kinds of units should we use for validly characterizing a 'society' in terms of scale? It is difficult to start with the whole of a 'society' as the initial unit, because there is so much we must learn before we can empirically describe it. A case like Luxembourg can be described in emic terms as a state unit emcompassing a variety of smaller units. For many purposes – political, cultural, economic – Luxembourg's inhabitants are also part of larger surrounding systems that affect everyday life in Luxembourg. Some of these contexts are recognized in emic rules, such as the formal organization of the EEC; others are not so clearly codified, such as the wider international market, power, and ecologic flow patterns affecting life within Luxembourg. How should we then circumscribe the Luxembourgians' 'society'?

In any case we cannot immediately apply an emic view of society, e.g. a state or tribal unit, as a basis for defining in etic terms the relevant societal whole. The nature of that whole and its size cannot easily be known at the beginning of investigation. We can only hope to understand it through a process of discovery. It is impossible to know beforehand which level of scale is certain to display the most relevant determinants of overall social life in an ovserved population.

We can start observation at 'any convenient locality' (Radcliffe-Brown 1968: 193). But, we should be prepared to expand or contract the scale of the area and population under study if we can thereby more clearly understand the initially observed regularities.

We can imagine various ways of analytically dividing a larger societal whole and circumscribing the sub-units. The question is how, theoretically and methodologically, to derive units both valid and structurally critical. Taking up this problem, I will start by clarifying the term 'scale'.

1.2 *Defining scale*

I will use 'scale' to designate size, the 'scale' of an organizational unit being the number of people involved and the unit's extension in social space. An empirical system can be described in terms of scale, granted we can delineate its boundaries in social space and time, and can identify the social interlinking of involved personnel. I will attribute scale to social units which in any case encompass a set of individuals interlinked by organization and communication.

Scale, in this sense of size, includes two dissimilar dimensions: the number of personnel and extension in social space. A corollary of these is the density of people in space. Sometimes we must distinguish among these dimensions; we can further avoid obscurities in our discussion by referring, when necessary, to 'numbers', 'space', or 'density'.

'Structural complexity', though related to these dimensions, is distinct from them. By 'complexity' I am referring to the numbers of roles and the combinations and permutations of roles. Societies differ in the ways roles are distinguished and combined; they differ regarding numbers of role-codes and codes' productivity in generating varieties of social person-types.

A small societal unit may be structurally highly complex (modern Luxembourg), and one of large scale structurally simpler (the Mongol Empire). The Mongol Empire displayed a considerable number of kinship, ethnic, military rank, economic, and other roles; but at the same time it produced only a limited range of social person types, each type tending to display a standard combination of a certain number of roles. In contrast, Luxembourg society is more complex in the sense that it rapidly produces new role forms to be combined in rather non-repetitive types of social persons. A greater variation of role permutations thus characterizes the constitution of social persons in Luxembourg.

We can use the number of roles and ways of combining roles into social persons as variables in comparative exercises (cf. Barth 1972), and I make this point the basis for my notion of 'structural complexity'. Complexity then refers to the number of roles and the number and variety of social person-types. Further, complexity is an aspect of social and cultural structures in general, such as dis-

79

tinction of levels in social hierarchies and the degree of differentiation in communicative codes – but much of this relates to role patterns which I will focus upon in my discussion.

It is a matter of terminological convenience whether or not we include complexity as another specific dimension under one broad label 'scale'. However, since we want to compare the logical and empirical relations between size and complexity in social systems, we must question ideas about levels of complexity as corollaries of levels of scale. Our problem is the relations between size and complexity.[2]

Here it is convenient to distinguish size from complexity, reserving the term 'scale' for the former. In the following, 'scale' will mean extension in social space and number of personnel in a social system, and 'complexity' will pertain to the degree of role differentiation and the varieties of role permutations in the system. Scale and complexity are two separable aspects of society, and I want to study empirically the way they relate to each other.

2. The multiple levels of scale in one society.

My point of departure is Redfield's questions:

> . . . Considering a peasant community as a system of social relations, as social structure, how shall we describe its relations with the world outside that community? . . .

and

> . . . Because no one village is really independent, but is a part of a much larger and more complicated system, our interest is drawn towards the description of the more complicated system. . . . And how shall one study so large and complex an entity? . . . (Redfield 1967a: 128, 1967b: 24).

In this paper I present a method for the observation and analytic description of social life within its macro-context, a procedure developed during studies in the regions of Antalya, Southern Turkey, and Herat, Northwest Afghanistan.[3] In this analysis of social life in Herat I gradually clarify my methodological steps while moving from one empirical aspect to another, from a single to a more composite picture of the society.

Initially the description focusses on the little community, since this corresponds to the course of my fieldwork observations. This however, does not imply viewing the local rural community in Herat as especially significant in comparison with other types of organizational units there. In fact, the typical rural locality in Herat is an extraordinary weak form of organization with a limited potential for mobilization.

Local communities do not appear to have the same structural importance in all societies, or at all times during the history of one society. In the discussion below I contrast the structural importance of the local community with that of other organizational entities at different levels of scale within the larger societal whole.

In Redfield's remark it is implied that his peasants live within units of small scale, 'the little community', and at the same time within more inclusive 'systems' of much larger scale. But what kind of units and systems, and how large?

In addition to the units of village-district-province and the like, villagers in Herat recognize and live within a series of other organizational entities. Many of these are of much larger scale than the little community, and they differ in scale among themselves so that they do not all belong to the same equally 'macro' level. They also differ in organizational form and content, and the extensions and directions of the social relation patterns vary.

I will describe empirically some specific sub-populations that are dispersed in social space and interlinked in social organization. In each case I identify a social 'proper dynamics' that generate the organizational and statistical pattern in question. The idea is to look for the social dynamics that create direct and indirect links and repercussions within a population so that it emerges as an aggregate entity with attributes of scale and complexity. I will be interested in an organizational entity to the extent that it displays some specific structural implications which are irreducible to the pattern of other entities. 'Structural implications' means here effects upon the individual social person, as well as upon the societal system as a whole.

The empirical systems will be shown to contain emic codes, rules, and categories which Herati people know and apply, but it is in etic terms that I will define and select the entities. I treat them as super-individual systems conditioning the lives of individuals, whatever the subjective hopes and strategies of these individuals may be.[4]

These empirical systems vary, from well-defined corporate groups, to mere aggregates of interrelated actors who themselves may be unaware of any social interlinking among themselves. The units differ in form and scale, but they display in common certain basic features allowing for an uniform terminology. I will call these units or systems of social interconnexions 'social fields'.[5]

In the study of large-scale entities, anthropologists face special problems in data collection. Both in Antalya and in Herat I first initially spent a few weeks surveying the overall region, and then a considerable part of the total fieldwork period in one selected locality. From there I followed the villagers out into the region as they engaged themselves in specific tasks vis-à-vis different role- and network-partners dispersed over the area. At the conclusion of my stay I attempted a short re-survey of the region. Previous to the fieldwork I had read some anthropology, history, geography, statistics, and other writings on Afghanistan. When mapping large-scale fields, anthropologists can use secondary statistical and other material; but most importantly we have to adapt participant observation, and specific techniques for primary data collection, to fit the study of large-scale entities. We return to this question in the various following sections, particularly when discussing regional organization (3.5).

In the remainder of this paper I describe a series of social fields in Herat and discuss the procedural rules pertaining to their discovery. The aim is to find their organizational patterns, levels of scale, and interrelations with each other. Specifically, I will try to describe and evaluate the order among social fields, in the sense of their relative weight or dominance within the processes of maintenance and change of general social life in Herat.

I take 'society' to be a whole that contains the total set of social prerequisites and determinants for individual lives, the social production and destruction of human beings. Initially, the anthropologist cannot know how to circumscribe the relevant 'society', to measure it, or to count its members. In order to describe society in Herat I must first define relevant kinds of analytic units and discover how to study their interrelations.

Let us begin with a discussion of the local field, and then relate it to other more inclusive systems in Herat.

3. Fields at various levels of scale in Herat.

3.1 *Locality*

3.1.1 A short description

A striking feature of the average village in the Herat valley is the high and rapid turn-over in locality membership. The little community in Herat is only to a very limited extent 'a cradle-to-the-grave arrangement', as Redfield put it. In a neighbourhood of about twenty households, one third may have lived there two generations or more, another third a decade or two, and the rest only a few years or less. The typical village is like a wayside station: households come there, stay for a period, then leave. Villagers live in tight complexes or blocks of houses built of dried mud, but next-door neighbours have in many cases never met before moving into the same village.

Population density is high in the irrigated areas of Herat. A village of about twenty households may use an acreage of not more than 400–500 decares, which amounts to a population density of 200–300 per square kilometer. Average density in the canal areas is much higher, some places approaching 1000 individuals per square kilometer. A small neighbourhood within this compactly populated canal area will be my empirical focal point throughout the following discussion.

Most villagers are sharecroppers, tilling the land of a resident or absentee landowner. The latter typically resides in the town of Herat. Some sharecroppers also own a little land, and a few villagers are freeholders working exclusively their own land. Within the normal pattern of household development, members of freeholder families will themselves become sharecroppers and some share-croppers will rise to become freeholders. In general, the statuses of worker, sharecropper, and freeholder constitute stages, over a generation or two, in the cyclical development of agriculturalist families.

Agricultural workers and sharecroppers without land or oxen are the people who most often shift residence. Sharecroppers possessing one or two oxen tend to reside more permanently at one place; and if they also own a little local land, they may be among the old-timers of the village.

The lack of residential permanence relates directly to landowner-sharecropper relations. The landowner may choose not to renew the annual contract if dissatisfied with the work performance of the sharecropper household. The latter must then leave the agricultural land and the dwelling included in the contract; since sharecroppers may have no other tie to the locality in question, they will be forced to move away. The pattern has many brutal effects; during the process, many sharecroppers and workers become beggars, some collecting alms in their old neighbourhood, others roaming widely and never returning to the neighbourhood.

The households of a village display economic situations ranging from relative security to veritable despair. Freeholders and share-croppers with a little land and other productive means may enjoy a fairly good standard of living and an adequate diet. At the other extreme are unpropertied poor people, many of whom display a terrible syndrome of debt, hunger, and tuberculosis.

Even very small neighbourhoods are ethnically heterogeneous. Most people speak Dari, the Afghan version of Persian, but one, two or more other languages are also found. Many persons are bilingual. People reckon themselves as belonging to one of a number of 'tribal' or ethnic categories without any implications of corporate organization or territorial belonging. A small village may represent the categories of 'Tadjik', 'Afghan', 'Timuri', 'Taimenni', 'Moghol', 'Turkmen', 'Jat', and others, plus a multitude of sub-categories. It is common to find five or six different main categories within a neighbourhood of say twenty households.

The overwhelming majority of villagers belong to the Hanefi religious rite. Different Sufi sects are also present, and the introduction of one of them into a village may lead to some division, since many mullahs dislike such sects. Most villagers go to the mosque for prayers at least in the morning and at sunset. The mullahs are also geographically mobile; they stay only for a short period with a specific local congregation before moving to another place.

The political scene in the villages of the Herat Valley displays a relative absence of large factions and alliances to be mobilized in contests for community leadership and in conflicts over land, women, and other matters of honour. This is not surprising if we consider the Herati villagers' general situation. In land conflicts, sharecroppers have no reason to fight for their landlords' soil. The sharecropper is mobile, shifting his attachment to different villages and different plots, and the bond between him and his landlord rarely develops much beyond specific contractual rights and obligations.

Among Herati villagers, conflicts of honour are rare, and when they do occur, they seldom lead to violent feuds. A villager will have difficulties mobilizing local support for such issues. Due to the near-universal mobility, his relatives are not present as a solid block in one community but are scattered around as a dispersed network in the region. In conflicts of this kind, it is more common for one of the parties, typically the insulted one, to move away from the trouble, seeking a sharecropping job and residence in a sufficiently distant village.

If a big landlord lives in the village or has appointed an overseer to manage affairs for him, a kind of leadership is present in the village; but this pertains only to a limited set of economic issues. Left to themselves, village residents do not display any strong community initiative on the basis of their own neighbourhood organization. It is even difficult for them to mobilize for simple technical tasks with obvious collective benefits, such as repairing irrigation canals. In matters of this kind, state authorities at the district level frequently intervene, ordering people to act (see 3.2.1.).[6]

In the light of the geographical mobility and the ethnic heterogeneity of Herati villagers, it is striking how well people within the individual village do manage to coordinate their agricultural work. Irrigation procedures, canal maintenance, harvesting, and crop distribution require repetitive agreements, meetings, and intricate forms of cooperation among households. In the hectic work routine there is no place for differences of 'tribe' or religious interests, or for insulting other men's honour. The sharecropper is a veritable slave of his work; he labours for his family's bread and landlord's rent, and submits to the demands for work cooperation.

Summing up: (1) The average village in Herat is characterized by a strikingly high *turn-over*; and the overall agriculturalist population has a low degree of residential permanence. (2) Within the individual locality very few parts of community arrangements are based upon kinship. Any villager will find only a few of his relatives in his village of residence; the rest are scattered around the region.

(3) Individuals and households are *recruited* to a village by establishing contractual relations with local landlords, by purchasing land of their own, or, in a very few cases, by establishing themselves as rural craftsmen or shopkeepers.

(4) Villagers families *tend to stay* at one place as long as they are able to maintain economic viability and fulfil sharecropper obligations. Maintaining a household presumes an equilibrium among domestic consumption needs, labour force, resource control, and income. The effects of domestic development on personnel composition will determine in individual cases the ratio of consumers to workers in a household. The unit's access to land and employment depends upon local ecologic conditions and competition in the market for sharecroppers' labour. Greater competition means allotment of smaller plots to individual households, increasing rent and decreasing renumeration in kind to sharecroppers. Thereby the viability of individual households is precariously endangered.

(5) Very many households experience budgetary imbalance. The worker(s) of the family fall ill, or crops are insufficient, and this leads to borrowing and falling into debt – oxen are sold to cover immediate consumption needs, and so on. If the household's economic capacity is thereby reduced, the landlord may be unwilling to renew his contract with the sharecropper. The latter must then *leave* the locality.

On the other hand, households can also increase their assets: at certain stages in the domestic development pattern there is a favourable ratio of workers to consumers, whereby the unit may be able to accumulate a small surplus to buy oxen and land. The household will try to use its assets optimally; and if this cannot be achieved in its place of residence, the household may move to a village with more favourable conditions.

Combining the above points, we observe that the locality is (6) normally not arranged as a set of solid corporate groups or factions, and has (7) an extremely *weak potential* for staging corporate action and for defining and promoting common community goals.

(8) Some important *determinants* behind the above features of locality forms are found in landowner-sharecropper relations, irrigation technology, and Hanefi Islam which organizes the neighbourhood as a congregation; in many cases the mosque is the only really collective forum in the locality. It is characteristic, however, that religious life has extremely limited organizational consequences for the local population as a community. Moreover, all three determinants – property, irrigation and religion – are parts of social fields of larger scale than the locality itself.

3.1.2. Analytic procedures

Although locality can be seen as a social field in itself, we should not include everything observed from local scenes in the analytic entity treated as 'locality'. In the total picture, locality is just one field among others, and we need a multi-field picture to evaluate how significant locality is in comparison with other fields, i.e. how strongly it determines the formation of the societal whole and the social person. (cf. Grønhaug 1971, 1971b, and: in press).

Locality must be analyzed so as to facilitate discovery of units at scale levels larger and smaller than itself. On one hand, events in large-scale fields affect local level processes: regional personnel circulation, macro-ecological and economic flow-patterns, and so forth. On the other hand, there are units smaller than locality, such as the domestic field, and ultimately the levels of person and sub-person: role-repertoires and specific roles.

We can identify locality as a social field in Herat by looking at (1) the *relative durability* of interaction among (2) a *limited number* of persons living (3) close to each other within *limited space*. Locality can in this sense be seen as (4) a specific forum, or a *set of fora*, within which the members act in the presence of each other as social persons and in specifically intense ways.

Members of a locality handle (5) a *series of tasks* and issues vis-à-vis each other: co-residents are also co-workers, and in addition they relate to one another in other tasks and role-sets. Integration processes thereby create multiplexity in local relations.

The actual degree of (6) *emerging multiplexity* is the cumulative effect of specific integration processes, which in turn depend upon the tasks and issues in local interaction. Thus localities within one society, and also cross-culturally, can be shown to differ with respect to multiplexity. As a main empirical feature from the above, social relations within Herati villages display a comparatively low level of multiplexity. For this reason I have preferred to label the units 'localities', rather than 'local communities'.

Herati villagers stay only for limited periods in one locality. But whether they stay in the same small place for ten or five years, or only for one, (7) much *information* about their previous behaviour is nonetheless carried over from situation to situation. The locality thereby emerges as a social milieu where multiplexity develops in social relations and information is created and stored. This contrasts with many other fields in Herat – e.g. regional organization, where inter-personal relations are much more single-stranded, as will be shown later.

In any minimally stable milieu there are (8) events which participants regard as critical for their own interrelations. Such events encompass issues of work, power, kinship, ritual, and so forth, but members of the locality experience them as one continuous whole which they associate and label with their village or neighbourhood name. These events contain the potentialities of (9) *tension* and *fission*; there is a continuous need for negotiation and the establishment of *agreement*.

(10) The points above show the *small scale* of effective locality in Herat – one to a few hundred people; as well as its *proper dynamics* of emerging multiplexity, fusion, and fission in relations among locally residing actors. Thereby, we have isolated locality as a *field* of social interconnexions with characteristic organizational dynamics and a specific scale – size, extension, and density, and also a typical pattern of development over time. Locality corresponds *to only one* of the many aspects of the lives of locally residing actors.

Localities in Herat vary in scale, multiplexity of internal relations, cohesion, and in the potential for communal initiative and mobilization. Within limits, they differ as determinants in the formation of the social person. The above picture characterizes the typical mode of local organization found among agriculturalist villagers in Herat.

Locality studies are then especially concerned with what happens in intra-local relations when a set of individuals, within the context of larger and smaller fields affecting local processes, reside together for some time in a limited area.

3.1.3. What is not locality in Herat

Should we not specifically discuss the ecology or economy of the village, the little community as a system of kinship or stratification, the religious aspect of village life, and so forth? Village life obviously displays features which can be understood only with reference to such categories. Indeed, I have already considered these as elements within the locality system. But in this way we do not obtain a proper understanding of these categories.

In the case of Middle Eastern and Central Asian societies, as in so many others, it is more fruitful to treat systems such as economy, stratification, kinship, religion as social fields of their own, whose organization and scale are normally not concomitant with locality. When we pursue in Herat the empirical relations that correspond to these various fields, we find networks and patterns of organization that extend far beyond the single locality.

It would be perfectly valid to treat the little locality as an ecosystem, as an ecologic field, but the relevance of this for the present task is questionable. The nature and impact of ecologic forces will be seen much more clearly if, beginning in one locality, we pursue the social relations that are in fact activated in the use of locally relevant energy resources. We will then find network and ecologic arrangements that encompass great numbers of localities.

We can similarly speak of villagers' religious life. Following the above procedure we can point to religious events in the neighbourhood that are connected with events of work, kinship, and local politics – all of which make up community life at large. The same actors' relations in the larger set of religious fora situated outside their own village, however, are a different thing. Although applied locally, Hanefi codes are not produced there; they emanate from within a far more extensive field of communication. Like ordinary people, religious specialists in Herat are mobile. Participation in Muslim ritual does not depend upon being member of the locality. The organization of religion, like that of kinship and ecology in Herat, displays its own network forms with their own levels of scale which cannot be understood solely as aspects of the little community.

These brief remarks on kinship indicate that the villages are not kinship-based groups, and that Herati kinship cannot be seen as a primary aspect of locality life. The individual family-based household utilizes its relations with kinsmen as sources of help and support, but on the interaction level, the kinship system can be more clearly depicted as fields of network organization extended in the region.

Redfield presented his 'concentric series of circles' and 'eccentric series of squares' as diagrammatic devices to clarify relations between the local community and the more complex society around it (cf. Redfield 1967a on 'A community within communities'). He also asserts that local people view outsiders in terms of the two ideas, distance and difference (1967a: 113). There is however, also a third one, that of issue, task, and meaning. With reference to specific issues, individuals take part in organizational entities that cut across locality as well as other organizations based upon other tasks.

From the viewpoint of the single household, local, ecologic, religious, and kinship systems represent four different social fields, demarcated by distinct patterns of organization, values and symbols, tasks, issues, fora, situations, networks, groupings, and rules for including and excluding personnel. Let us now see how the same personnel are involved in a whole series of fields which display different forms and levels of scale.

3.2. *An ecosystem as a social field*

3.2.1. Its scale and aggregate form

Within the area under study, ecosystems can be delineated by differing levels of scale. Three ecological sectors – dry-farming, nomadic, urban – can be described and then tied together into a picture of the region as one big ecosystem. Within the region, several ecological subsystems can be distinguished, each including numerous villages. Valid units for description as ecosystems are also one or a few villages which take their water from underground or open irrigation canals or isolated wells.

I have chosen for description an ecological subsystem which can be conveniently circumscribed and which represents a resource adaption – canal irrigated agriculture, practised by several hundred thousand of Herat's inhabitants. Water diverted via man-made canals from the Hari-Rud River is here the limiting factor. The stream itself descends from high central Afghanistan, passes westwards through the province of Herat, and then bends to the North, disappearing into the desert sands in Soviet territory.

In the river valley to the east and west of the town of Herat there are several long irrigation canals, one of which I shall describe. Like the others, this canal is simply a big ditch about 40 kilometers long with a width of 10 meters at its source and less than one meter towards its termination point. The essential features of irrigation technology as found today have apparently remained the same for centuries.

Approximately one hundred thousand individuals live in villages drawing water from this canal. In addition, many people from the drier areas come as labourers during the harvest season. Absentee landlords, in the town and elsewhere, receive their parts of the yearly crops; nomads trek through, pasturing their animals on village lands, taking water from the canal, and exchanging products with villagers; and beggars and others also receive some of the produce. Population density in the canal area thus runs to several hundred per square kilometer – a dramatically different picture from the thinly-populated tracts of scattered villages in the vast deserts and mountains to the north and south of the river.

The social organization of the canals contains several levels of coordination and control. As outlets from the main canal, smaller irrigation ducts lead to the villages. The source of such a 'village canal' is an opening in the bank of the main canal which has specific dimensions stipulated and controlled by state authorities. A few years before my fieldwork, all such outlets were framed in concrete according to specific dimensions. In itself, this work implies neither modernization of irrigation nor more productive use of water; according to informants, it was simply one of many measures taken within the traditional system of water distribution in Herat.

All land connected to the main canal is denoted and stipulated in an old 'Register of watergiving', kept in the district government's office. Although the district government administers an area larger than that of this particular canal, it has the traditional task of effecting an equal and just distribution of water among local land-units within the canal area. The register pertains to land and water only; it is not a cadastral survey.

The dimensions of the village outlet opening are proportional to the size of the area it irrigates. These are the only legally accepted outlets from the main canal to the villages and through them each village is formally allocated a fraction of the main canal's total water flow. The use of water wheels and motor pumps along the canal is forbidden, since this would disturb the calculated distribution of water via the fixed outlets.

When one outlet serves two or more villages, water is allocated in periods of hours and according to respective field sizes by opening and closing the gates to individual neighbourhood ducts leading off the 'village canal'. Irrigation management within the neighbourhood is left to the farmers themselves. For example, villagers appoint a local 'water giver' to irrigate their rice plots which are normally planted in a contiguous village tract and must be flooded daily during the dry season. Such an authority minimizes quarrels, but he is nonetheless carefully controlled by neighbours. Wheat, on the other hand, is individually irrigated at weekly intervals; this also requires considerable coordination among households.

It is surprising that the number of inter-household conflicts on the neighbourhood level is so limited. On the whole, irrigation rules and routines function to minimize disagreement among the individual agriculturalists using the water. Neighbours in irrigated villages do have their quarrels, but not so much over the allocation of water.

Coordination at higher levels of canal-organization is far more complicated. The whole canal area consists of a complex network of small and large channels, crisscrossing each other by tunnels and bridges still mostly built of stone and brick. These and other constructions frequently break down, whereby even small localized damages can threaten several villages with flooding or lack of water.

If single villages had the organization capacity to mobilize themselves and define their responsibilities vis-à-vis others, matters of canal maintenance might be more readily solved. But in fact canal-area villages facing these critical tasks display a characteristic lack of autonomy and ability to make decisions. Even technically trivial damages emerge as intricate and difficult inter-village, even bureaucratic, affairs. Repairs are rarely undertaken before many messages have been passed between village and district head quarters, district officials have inspected the damages, and soldiers have been sent back and forth with letters and instructions. Finally, the district government orders landowners and sharecroppers to pool labour and money and start working within an announced deadline.

The role of district and provincial authorities in controlling water-*distribution* is salient. This function is in fact ritualized every New Year during the annual cleaning of the main canal along its total course. The canal is closed at its source, and one and a half thousand villagers a day are set to work with their spades, under the parading control of the district governor, the military commander, soldiers, etc. – all to the music of village 'Jat' musicians.

The most important types of conflicts in the system arise between the lower third and the upper two sections of the main canal. For several decades now, water has been permanently scarce in the lower third. It seems that, with the presently increasing population density, the canal's irrigation capacity is virtually exhausted before water can reach the terminus. Since all the users of canal water need more than is formally allocated to them, illegal tapping frequently occurs. But people in the lower section have no place to steal from, while their fellows in the upper two sections will dig holes in secondary canals designed to serve the lower ground. Apparently a moral principle is involved which seems to say, 'stealing from a stranger is at least not so bad as stealing from a neighbour'.

Due to this dispartity in water supply, important dissimilarities appear between the lower and the upper two sections of the main canal area. In the upper two sections wheat, rice, and cotton are cultivated, while the lower third, lacking sufficient water for rice and cotton, has only wheat. In drought years, damages are worse in the lower section than further upstream. Land is also cheaper in the lower third of the canal area. It is people of the low section who most frequently address the district government with complaints about water thefts committed by upper section inhabitants and with petitions for improved methods of equitable water distribution.

The government has traditionally tried to equalize water distribution by closing for one day each week all the outlet gates along the upper two sections of the main canal, thus diverting all the water to the lower section. A few years ago an additional measure was introduced. Across the main canal, at calculated intervals along its course, concrete steps were built which keep the water level within each interval at a controlled height. Thereby, the interval levels in all three canal sections could be compared and controlled. The Kabul government ordered the implementation of this new arrangement after receiving a petition from the producers and landowners of the lower canal section.

However, the introduction of these concrete steps did not bring sufficient improvement. In 1970–71, drought struck the entire Herat area and damages remained greater in the lower section than upstream. People in the upper sections also suffered; in both drought and normal years they now receive less water than before the introduction of the 'interval steps'. Some of the higher land tracts in the upper sections no longer receive sufficient water for rice and other demanding crops. Productivity as well as land prices have fallen in these specific sub-areas.

Today's problem is not only one of equal distribution. It is also an overall shortage of water. Traditional irrigation technology in Herat simply cannot supply enogugh water, regardless of how it is allocated.

People in the low section exclaimed to me, 'Since water has come to our village by that canal for two thousand years, why doesn't it come now?' Their own answer was, 'too much theft further up', but the basic answer is that water supply does not increase, while the size of the dependent population does.

This process represents the Herat version of the 'ecology crisis'. Over recent decades the population of the canal area has grown, due to both natural increase and net influx of people from the region's drier parts. Along the water course, the irrigated area has been extended so that today (without any parallel improvement in irrigation technology) more land is drawing water from the canal than only a generation ago. The river and canal yield the same amounts of water as previously, while today more people need water for more land and more grain.

Additionally, we can observe that the effects of a bad harvest on the sharecropper's household income depend upon the ratio between his and the landlord's shares of the annual yield. In any case, water scarcity and a poor harvest will compound the sharecropper's economic losses by automatically reducing his share in absolute terms.

No matter how small the annual yield, the sharecropper must pay rent to his landlord. In Herat this is currently one-third or one-half of the harvest, depending upon whether the sharecropper possesses his own oxen. Although in itself a poor harvest might support the family that produces it, there may well not be enough after the landlord exacts his rent. Since a considerable number of families experience budgetary difficulties even in normal years, it is not surprising that heavy debts among villagers are an integral part of the whole picture (cf. Ferdinand 1962).

As extreme case, whole neighbourhoods in the lower section were deserted during the 1970–71 drought because of the absence of water. People there told me they had never before experienced such a disaster.

In conclusion, some broader organizational implications should be pointed out. By taking part in water allocation from the main-canal, the agriculturalist is involved in the event system of at least three different macro-fields of social organization. First, water is a resource which implicates the irrigation farmer in a large-scale ecosystem. Secondly, the use of water is tied to land as property, since water is fractioned out to land and not to producers as individuals. By receiving his portion of canal water, the agriculturalist thereby enters the macro-system of property and class. Thirdly, canal water is subject to state control within the field of public administration. What Wittfogel termed the 'law of changing administrative returns': (Wittfogel 1967: 109) seems to apply here in the following way:

Isolated desert and mountain wells and canals are free of external government interference, since it would be too expensive to administer these dispersed water sources effectively. However, despite the general scarcity of administrative resources, the compact and densely populated basis around Herat town lends itself to some degree of government control. Thereby, agriculturalists using the canal's water enter the macro-political field and become involved with representatives of the state.

In sum, social events occurring in canal irrigation are simultaneously also events in several other social fields.

3.2.2 Proper dynamics, and some analytic procedures

The general dynamics of ecology display a patterned flow of organic energy. More specifically, we can approach the proper dynamics of the canal irrigation system in the following way: It is an ecosystem where management units in the human population, coesting with each other and with animal and plant species, carry on agricultural production with water as the limiting factor.

Agriculturalists exploit the irrigated fields, and the crops they harvest extract minerals from the soil. It is highly characteristic of this type of agriculture that irrigated fields are neither exhausted nor impoverished. Critical minerals are circulated back to the soil in numerous ways – nutrients are carried by the canal water, strong winds move in sand from the surrounding steppes and desert, and Herati agricultural technology replenishes the soil with plant, animal, and industrial fertilizers. The fertility of canal-irrigated fields has been maintained over years of intense cultivation, involving to some extent double-cropping as well.

The amount of water available is, on the other hand, strictly limited. The Herati agriculturalist has considerably less irrigation water than, for example, farmers in monsoon-fed Southeast Asia. Rice cultivation in Herat cannot possibly achieve the immense productivity levels reported for tropical paddy cultivation (cf. Geertz 1970), and local technology excludes paddy nurseries, transplantation, and protracted flooding of plots. Although industrial fertilizer and Green Revolution plants can raise the level of productivity in Herat somewhat, the shortage of water ultimately prohibits any pronounced intensification of agriculture as a whole in the canal area.

Given the present social and technological circumstances, this fact constrains the marginal return of labour input on any landplot and the number of consumers that can be fed from it. If the human population dependent upon canal area crops, as defined by rules of property, exceeds the feeding capacity of these crops, the whole system functions to exclude the surplus number of people from the canal area or its distribution arrangements. Social mechanisms (cfr. 3.1.1.) simply push these people out – in many cases, to a beggar's life and premature death.

The canal system itself will persist with its highly productive fields as long as a sufficient, but not too large, number of agriculturalists stay to tend it. Ecosystems of Central Asian irrigation agriculture involve harnessing of sunlight, energy transformations, mineral circulation, biomass production and distribution, all in a highly permanent and resistant pattern. It is no reification to say that these are veritably living systems in space and time. Individuals of different ethnic backgrounds enter from outside and become parts of the irrigation ecosystem, but over their twenty centuries of existence, the Herat canals and their social organization seem to have more thoroughly shaped and moulded incoming people, than conversely.

This striking contrast between the permanence of Herati irrigation technology and the relative transience of the involved human population also reminds us of similar properties of irrigation arrangements elsewhere in Asia (cf. Leach 1961, Geertz 1970).

In order to understand ecological proper dynamics more clearly, we need an approach that takes into account not only men's relation to natural environment but also their place within systems of politics and property (cf. Barth 1964: 17).

Today's ecological situation of land pressure and resource scarcity can be fully understood only in the light of social distribution rules defining irrigated land as property, and produce as owner's rent versus worker's payment, thereby dividing the population itself into class categories. The *badar* ('he who has') and the *nadar* ('he who has not') relate to ecological resources in very different ways.

The 'ecology crisis' is simultaneously a distributional crisis, because some crucial pre-conditions for the former are of an economic and stratificational nature. An enormous portion of the annual produce is transferred from the producer households to owners and creditors residing largely outside the canal area. In total, much more than the half is exacted from producer households as rent, interest, and other payments to landowners, creditors, and others.

Recent monetarization has also effected the canal ecosystem by replacing some subsistence goods with market goods. The state has been unable to counter increasing poverty. Its modest administrative efforts, including a modicum of agricultural extension services, crop and fertilizer innovations, have proved insufficient.

Summing up: the field of canal organization is seen to be an ecosystem of a patterned energy flow between a set of natural elements comprising the selected niche, and a number of human action units functioning as producers, consumers, and controllers. The system is characterized by proper dynamics of ecological feedback that account for the maintenance of high-yield irrigation agriculture over time. Significant parts of the proper dynamics include the pattern of conflict within the human population, dominated by tensions between inhabitants of the lower and the upper two sections of the canal area; and the practice of centralized administrative decision-making and conflict resolution. The aggregate population interlinked by these dynamics can easily be delineated and circumscribed in terms of the three aspects of scale: numbers, spatial extension, and density. Likewise, there seem to be few analytic difficulties in accounting for the temporal aspect; the individual canal organization appears to be a social field with a durability of probably a millenium or two.

Considering this, I would like to remark on a specific point of analytic procedure. In general, ecologists manipulate scale as a variable in their ecosystem analysis. Ecosystem can conveniently be described in terms of size, extension, density, and durability:

> An ecosystem consists of a biotic community of interrelated organisms together with their common habitat and can range in size, scope and durability from a drop of water together with the micro-organisms which live within it to the entire earth with all its plants and animal inhabitants (Geertz 1970: 3).

As for the other fields discussed in this paper, empirical circumscription is validly achieved when a systemic interconnexion system, a proper dynamics, is found. The same proper dynamics however, can display themselves on different organizational levels, in a hierarchy of small and large fields organized by the same elementary dimension (cf. Odum 1963: 10).

At the level of the main canal's organization, we found an ecosystem that is large, diverse, stable and relatively independent of adjacent systems. At this level the ecological proper dynamics could be seen with adequate clarity. The isolated canal system is not at all an arbitrary entity; it is empirically a relatively closed system with an inner dynamics and a scale of its own.

We could also describe ecosystems in Herat at different levels of scale. A larger one – at the regional level – might be too diverse and complex for simple description over a few pages. On the other hand, a smaller sub-system would be less diverse than the main canal and represent a less autonomous entity.

The same elementary dynamics – e.g. of ecology – can manifest themselves at several levels of scale, although the dynamics themselves become more composite as we go from less to more inclusive

96

and diverse organizational levels. This point is clear enough in the case of ecological fields in Herat; below we will see that it pertains also to other, qualitatively different fields.

The significance of the ecological field within the overall social system in Herat has still not been evaluated. I have tried to describe ecology in a way that shows the proper dynamics of ecology which affect the individual person and the societal whole, and facilitate the discovery of other relevant fields. As an example, irrigation ecology in Herat seems to imply the institutions of property, class, and the state; and the question arises of how to treat these as social fields and evaluate their significance vis-à-vis ecological and the local fields. First, however, let us turn to a field apparently less directly dependent upon ecology and material matters.

3.3. Levels in religious organization

3.3.1. A religious field, its scale and proper dynamics

The vast majority of Herati people are Sunni Muslims of the Hanefi persuasion. Their focal ritual practice is the *namaz* prayer five times daily, and their central forum is the mosque which is found, either small or large, in every neighbourhood. The basic role-set is that of Muslim believers as brothers, and a critical role-solution that of common prayer at the mosque.

Anyone properly performing the purification and prayer ritual is eligible for participation, and beyond this no further conditions are required of people praying together. The praying congregation may consist of three persons, or several thousand individuals related by nothing more than their common Muslim identity communicated in the ritual. This role-set thus represents a tremendous potentiality for bringing throngs of people to prayer and establishing an instant congregation. The role-set is not so effective, when further organizational implications are considered. These depend upon conditions of the locality and other factors not springing from the religious role-set alone.

Every village neighbourhood has a mosque led by a *mullah* according to orthodox Sunni law (*Sheriat*). In marked contrast to this element of religious life are those people who choose the mystic way (*tariqa*) to God, in a Sufi sect or order, led by a *sheikh*.

Here the basic role-set is that of brothers within the 'circle', of disciples under the 'guidance' of the Sheikh. I will briefly sketch the form of role-set and network organization in the Sufi tariqat, its aspects of scale and time, and its proper dynamics of religious sign production and communication. My intention is to discuss

7

whether such a religious grouping can be seen as a social field of its own.

At one level Sufi tariqats are categories including quite large numbers of people. As an example, the Naqshibandi Sufi tradition is found in many Muslim countries. People I stayed with in Antalya were Naqshibandi as were the Sufis of my main fieldwork locality in Herat. There are probably millions of people who refer to themselves as Naqshibandi, but the meaning differs: indeed, it is an open question what kind of relations, if any, exist among Naqshibandi people in various countries. At this level we are talking of an aggregate of empirical codes and communication practices distributed within a population in space and time. The entity has scale aspects; theoretically, it could be represented on the kind of maps made in linguistic or religious geography. The empirical unit is something similar to a language 'community' – that is, all the people of various countries who to some extent practice the Naqshibandi codes. This is roughly analogous to a scattered population of individuals who speak the same language. But at the level of interaction, a tariqat in Herat has the form of a 'relatively bounded network-organization'. Membership is based on personal discipleship under the leadership and guidance of a sheikh. Disciples come from various localities in the area, since tariqat involvement does not spring from membership locality. Some sheikhs live permanently at one place, e.g. close to the shrine of a saint. Others set up quarters for limited periods in one locality, then move to another. The centre of the sect's life is the sheikh's residence, with a room for the mystic _zikr_ ritual performed by the circle of Sufi brothers.

A successful sheikh develops his reputation in the area, and disciples bring new recruits via relations of kinship, acquaintance, and so forth. In the field I saw villagers become members of a sect under a sheikh who had established himself in the neighbouring locality. I got the impression that the number of active members in such a sect organization tends to be limited. I would estimate there are between 200 and 300 more or less active disciples under one sheikh. Sheikhs rarely manage to build up a large number of adherents; the following processes brake the growth of tariqat organization.

A sheikh has competitors: not only other Sufi sheikhs, but primarily the mullahs of the mosques and Koran schools. The mullah versus the sheikh, 'Sheriat contra Tariqat', represents a classic conflict still played out in Herat.

The prozelytizing sheikh thus breeds opposition to himself, and this is part of the reason for his transiency. When he becomes involved in life at one place, it is difficult for him to maintain any exalted position. However, when he moves, followers find it costly to visit him.

Another point probably related to the small size of the tariqat group is the unimportance of literacy which I observed in Herat Sufi life at the village level. Villagers are generally illiterate, both secularly and religiously (Arabic), and much more so than in Antalya. The way to Sufi spiritual fulfillment passes through individual exercises and participation in the circle of brothers, where face-to-face contact is the mode of communication.

Problems in the routinization of a tariqat are salient in connexion with leadership and succession. Finding a worthy successor is difficult; if he is found, there is the danger that he may take over too early or move away with part of the following. When a sheikh dies, the tariqat milieu tends to fall apart as an ongoing concern. The group's life span is limited.

An area may have several years of hectic Sufi activity under a sheikh, and then pass into a period lacking any tariqat group activities. Eventually, a new sheikh arrives with a slightly different ritual repertoire, and some of the old sheikh's followers will 'go to' him, while others will not. There will be significant continuity in the use of ritual idioms, but not in the life of unified groups.

This may very well be the micro-level process underlying the distributional pattern of Muslim Sufism in Central and Southwest Asia: Sufi idioms and practices are widely dispersed, but the practicing groups organized around sheikhs tend to be small and fairly localized.

Any sheikh can thus draw upon the rich inventory of Sufi idioms found among people in an area with centuries of Sufi tradition. The Naqshibandiye 'way' is part of this idiomatic inventory from which any sheikh can select elements, which he then combines in his own way creating a specific style and presentation for his followers.

In sum, Sufism as an inventory of idioms and sign practices is a widely spread tradition, a symbol language known by millions. But at the level of active groups, tariqat units in Herat are small and short-lived.

The proper dynamics of this religious field can be shown in the following way. A tariqat network developes around a sheikh while his career as a Sufi leader develops and disciples are recruited. For participants, tariqat membership is a fairly well-defined thing, and being a Sufi brother under sheikh so-and-so, implies a clear social identity. Via the role-sets of the tariqat organization, rather exclusive information circulates; and by using the specific ritual idioms, members are marked off from non-members. While disciples aspire to Sufi fulfillment events are staged and discussed within this entity of interlinked personnel. By means of network links messages are communicated, rituals are staged, and gifts presented to the sheikh who redistributes them while entertaining members. Group boundaries appear emically in rules for the inclusion of disciple members and exclusion of the unworthy and sceptical. The organization works as long as the tariqat role-sets are activated, and as I have indicated, displays the phases of proselytizing, recruitment, and growth; difficulties in routinization decline, and dispersal – parallelling the career and death of the sheikh.

The core of the proper dynamics pertains however, to meaning and signification. Tariqat ritual ('*zikr*') is the staging and production of specific symbols defining the inclusion of participants in the circle of brothers. Being within the ritual circle is a symbolic medium for seeing oneself as part of God's greater reality. The disciple leaves the everyday world and moves into the circle of brothers submitting to a sheikh and a sphere of specific meaning. The acts are mystic exercises, sermons, silent prayer and meditation, rhythmic exclamations (e.g. 'Illallah' – 'Illallah' or 'Allahu' – 'Allahu') and extensive series of vehement bodily movements with hundred in a series.

The ritual passes through stages, from a quiet introduction to an ecstatic climax, after which the group falls back into silence; this cycle is normally repeated several times during one evening. Some individuals display ecstasy more intensely and for a longer time than others. A kind of part-whole meaning seems to be important. Actors move in and become parts in the ritual circle. Emically, the bow in *zikr* ritual is 'abandonment' ('Islam') of oneself to God, and the ritual whole is a medium for coming close and 'seeing' God and eternity. God is signified in the ritual, and for the actors that do the signifying, the signified entity becomes clear in the *zikr*. The group of actors produce a sign that denotes an entity (God). According to their code, the signifiers themselves approach that entity, which they envisage through their own signification. This signification is achieved by techniques which the novice must strive to master. But the trained and gifted Sufi transcends preoccupation with such rules and comes close to the signified divine entity in a display of ecstatic behaviour. This is a special case of establishing signs in social process (cf. LaBianca 1976).

A Sufi brother said to me after a *zikr* meeting, 'Our everyday life and misery do not count. God is important'. I understand this kind of religious despisal of the temporal world as a reflex of the ritual signification itself. When an individual's whole involvement in the group ritual signifies God and the relationship between God and man, he literally sees himself as part of eternity: everyday misery becomes a dull reflection of the meaning in ritual.

The characteristic element of these proper dynamics is then one of signification, of sign production and communication. This process underlies the specific form of the tariqat milleu and organization and makes it a relatively bounded system of interconnected personnel, a field with proper dynamics and a scale of its own.

3.3.2. Scale levels in religious organization

Within Afghanistan there are hierarchies of religious fora and leaders. One might depict central versus peripheral fora in religious communication and study the circulation of idioms, drawing on analogy with the model of universalization and parochalization, developed for India by Marriott (Marriott 1969).

In Herat, higher rank mullahs and sheikhs are found in and around the city. It would be wrong, however, to see religious hierarchy as homologous with the region's locality structure. Religious networks criss-cross the other fields. Many types of religious personnel are involved: mullahs, sheikhs, students, and dervishes.

The annual cycle of Sheriat mosque life takes place within at least three levels of organization. Everyday prayer takes place in the small neighbourhood mosque (*mesci*). The main Friday prayer and sermon in Sunni Islam can take place only in a larger mosque (*cami*) equipped for that purpose; such a mosque must be placed in a local community of more than 40 households. On Fridays, Herati villages therefore leave their immediate neighbourhood and go to the nearest 'Friday mosque'. For the celebration of the feast of Eid at the end of the month of Ramazan, the men of many villages come together in numbers of 1500–2000 to pray under one imam.

I leave open the question of how to treat these levels in terms of fields. Instead I will ask whether the international community of Muslim believers can be seen as a social field, and if so, what are the critical empirical criteria for answering this question.

Occasionally events occur which after some time, via chain reaction and repercussions, seem to affect Muslims in different parts of the world by activating international Muslim debate. Through their careers certain individuals have accomplished this: for example, Jamal-ud Din al-Afghani travelled in India, Egypt, Turkey and elsewhere, appealing for a pan-Muslim stand against imperialism. In the late 19th century, pan-Islamism was a theme of debate among elites in the Ottoman Empire and elsewhere.

During the 19th century, Muslim leaders started to argue for Islam's superiority over Western science and technology. I was surprised to find myself involved in that debate with Turkish villagers. I was amazed however, when illiterate Herati peasants invited me to the same discussion in practically identical terms. I also find astonishing the similarity in arguments for the purification of Islam which I heard in Antalya and Herat, and for example in Java as reported by Geertz (Geertz 1957).

Communication of ideas within the international Muslim community occurs via fora like Mecca and less important shrines, the printing press and other media, top-level Muslim meetings, and through the networks of imams, sheikhs, and others. Events occurring in one part which effect other large parts of the system, would indicate the existence of a community. As examples: What were the repercussion of the Caliphate's downfall in Muslim countries? Of Atatürk's struggle against the Great Powers? Of the Arab–Israeli conflict in its various stages? Such events are discussed among the elites of various countries, sometimes even in village mosques and other peripheral fora.

If relatively bounded systems of inter-communication exist, the notion of social fields applies. We can describe people's religious activities as being part of several levels of religious organization, i.e. hierarchy of small and large fields. Such an analysis would be in the tradition of Kroeber, Redfield, and others, who have been engaged in the anthropological study of civilizations as coherent wholes. Much of the empirical work belongs to other disciplines, but the overall picture and the analytic discussion of forms and processes are anthropological themes.

3.4. Small- and large-scale fields of citizen-state interrelationships

For relations between citizens and state agencies, the units can be delineated in the same way as done for locality, ecology, and religion. Again I start the description with a number of agricultural villagers as the selected personnel set.

Villagers relate as clients to landowners, traders, saints, and others taking roles of patronizing middlemen. The low class client offers electoral support, material payment, and the promise of prestige, in return for the middleman's addressing a state agency to elicit decisions and resources in favour of the client. In Herat, the patron-client relation is not always a multiplex and personal one. There is a kind of political market: middlemen are sought due to reputation, and they compete with each other for support and renumeration.

The middleman niche is made possible by the distance between bureaucracy and village people. The former lack resources to govern the population effectively, and the latter lack both the codes to deal with officials and a platform based on local or other organization.

The canal organization is a case in point. Great numbers of villages experience the same troubles, which they cannot handle themselves. A landowner can patronize them by persuading the administrating to take action. Grain distributed by the government as aid to the drought-stricken agriculturalists in 1971–72 was channelled largely by informal middlemen rather than through the channels of provincial bureaucracy.

As for scale, a reputed middleman may have a considerable number of actual and potential clients in need of his services vis-à-vis the state or in interpersonal conflicts. The villager-middleman-bureaucracy connexions are institutionalized, operating as cases of social organization with a degree of closure and permanence.

The proper dynamics in question pertain to the flow of demands and services between citizen and state; taxes, military service, expressions of loyalty from people to government; regulations, claims for loyalty, and aid from government to people. The process is one of feedback: i.e. a cybernetic order (cf. Deutch 1963). This process is an aggregate and composite one. At its core lie the more elementary distribution of power and autonomy in the patron-client relation, and the recruitment and mobilization process through which the patron builds up a power enterprise using strategies in local-level and central fora (cf. Bailey 1970; Eidheim 1971, chs. 2 and 5). A political field in Herat can be seen as a set of such enterprises and governmental agencies, in relations of competition and alliance. In everyday life, the effect is that the citizen role is drawn into such political relation and is moulded by them. The characteristic aggregate feature is that of an administration unable to govern villagers effectively by bureaucratic rules, and villagers unable to articulate their interests according to class or locality rules. With respect to this dimension involving the state and politics, the same personnel in Herat are part of a series of less and more inclusive fields of varying levels of scale.

3.5. *Regional organization as a social field*

3.5.1. Why study the regions, and how to find them

Above, I have argued for a multi-field analysis and stressed the point that specific fields should be studied in the context of their interrelations, not in isolation or for their own sake. Turning to the theme of regional organization, we must delineate the 'region' by demonstrating both its characteristic attributes and its inter-connexions with other fields of different scales.

The various specific fields do display a certain autonomy as systems, since the dynamics of qualitatively different fields cannot be reduced into each other. Nevertheless, the fields do effect each other, and some kind of economic dynamics seem to influence the functioning of all of the fields discussed so far. These dynamics are thus especially critical for understanding the whole set of fields. But we have not so far discussed the nature of the economic dynamics. To obtain their proper characterization, we need a new empirical picture displaying the concrete form and aggregate pattern of the production and circulation of economic values in Herat. From there we can search for the relevant field, delineate its scale, and try to identify its underlying dynamics. The first question is, in which empirical area should we start looking for the field of economy?

Since the same elementary dynamics can be manifest at several organizational levels of scale (cf. 3.2.2.) we could alternatively describe household, locality, or some other unit as economic systems. It is now wothwhile, however, to consider a really great number of people dispersed in the Herat landscape, and investigate the possible effects of the economic interconnexions within such an entity. A bird's-eye-view of a large entity with its elements can more conveniently show the characteristic features of the composite economic organization in Herat: its forms of labour division, pro-ductive regimes, modes of circulation, and economically based stratification. The single actor and household must be understood as part of such a larger system comprising the different but inter-related economic sectors of agriculture, pastoralism, trade and crafts, as well as a number of social classes and forms of status groups. We can further observe from the above description that the great differences in wealth and stratification in Herat do in fact presuppose a large population size. Finally the picture of a large field will conveniently display the nature of local-global relations, the interconnexions between life in Herat and the macro-levels of national and international economy and politics.

I will choose the level of 'region' in Herat to make clear these features and dimensions. A region can be defined in many ways. Cultural geography and 'regional science' provide many viewpoints, which cannot, however, be dealt with here (cf. Isard & Reiner). Initially, it is difficult to know to circumscribe a region, or by which principle to define its organization. Like 'society' and the other units discussed above, regions must be discovered before they can be defined. Where to draw its boundaries is something we know as the result of investigation and not prior to it.

For comparative purposes, the concept of 'region' cannot primarily or exclusively be defined in economic terms. In some societies, the dominant regional dynamics is apparently effected by processes in religious communication, although Islam in present-day Herat or Antalya does not work in that way. As another example, the effects of state decision upon people's everyday life in Scandinavia are many and formidable; to a large extent, state activities structure regional organization there (cf. Brox 1966). As an intermediate case, Turkish state activities more decisively affect regional patterns in Antalya than the Afghan administration influences Herati regional organization (cf. Grønhaug 1971; in press). But in both cases this is less pronounced than in Scandinavia where state bureaucracies mould and re-mould regions within their respective territories.

In anthropological literaure the concept of 'region', when defined, is normally used as a synthetic or syndrome concept. It is difficult to conceptualize 'region' for the purpose of comparative analysis. In any case, defining regions in terms of physical geography or administrative divisions is irrelevant, prior to an analysis of social organization in the area (cf. Barth 1966a). Forms of regional organization and attendant processes differ among societies. In each case, we have to find out which dimension is dominant in the pattern of regional organization. By now we can, however, take clues from the analyses of the smaller fields in Herat which indicate the importance of the economic dimension.

At the level of phenomena, a regional picture should show a hierarchy of large and small localities, and a patterned flow of personnel, produce, services, and messages comprising an organization which ties together people from the constituent localities. A hypothesis about regional organization deserves attention, if it points to some simple principles that organize the whole of a large population into distinct categories of people, displays some significant interdependencies between these categories, and accounts for the hierarchy of localities in the area.

3.5.2. Analytic procedures

I will consider the Herat region as a field of relations among the spatially distributed main categories of personnel within the area around the town of Herat which includes my focal village. The region will be described as an organizational field for the distribution and circulation of land rights, labour, animals, produce, and services in trade and crafts.

The personnel categories of 'farmers', 'nomads', and the like, are aggregates which I have constructed through observations of households and other micro-phenomena. The main procedural steps from the micro-level to aggregate categories and their regional interconnexion can be outlined as follows.

Initially, I map the main types of economically relevant *units* – households producing wheat-and-rice versus only-wheat, long distance versus locally ranging nomadic households, landowner families, business firms, public offices, shops, and so forth. They are described as decision-making and action units, each type possessing a specific personnel and resource inventory and a characteristic dynamics of organization. I summarize by *aggregating* my material into a larger universe of description, displaying the total variation of main forms of units, and making an over-all estimate of the respective numbers of different types of units found in the region. (Cf. Barth 1966a).

Following events and processes, I generalize from case stories to show the characteristic organizational dynamics within the different types of units. I study these units both in isolation and as elements in the larger whole which have been affected by over-all regional change during the last decades. The different unit- and sector-analysis are then combined into a dynamic picture of aggregated inter-unit relations. At this level we need additional data on the forms of encounters and confrontations among units of the different relevant categories. During fieldwork I was able to conceptualize these inter-unit relation pattern and tried to observe as many as possible of those types of encounters which manifested inter-category relations. Moving around in the area to map unit- and inter-unit behaviour, I was in fact beginning the analysis of regional organization. In the analysis proper, I try to *simulate* how initiatives from one unit result in counter-moves from other similar and dissimilar units, producing patterned series of chain-reactions and repercussions. By tying together several sub-systems via their feedback-interconnexions, there emerges a generalized picture of the region as a social field with specific proper dynamics displayed through the simulation exercise, and with a scale equivalent to the size of the population that appears to be organized by that dynamics.

At all levels, data on social events and *social event* analysis are critical. And finally, as part of simulating regional organization, I present analysis of a regional 'macro-event' that displays the characteristic features of regional organization as an entity.

3.5.3. A short description

The urban-rural relationship is a significant element in Central Asian regional organization. The urban centre in this case is Herat (cf. English 1973). Although accurate population statistics are lacking, it is reasonable to estimate about 100,000 inhabitants for Herat City. It relates to its hinterland by trade via the bazar and by contracts between urban landowners and village sharecroppers. With its present boundaries the province of Herat includes about 40,000 square kilometers, whereas the city's actual hinterland, which also includes parts of the adjacent provinces, totals roughly 60,000 to 70,000 square kilometers. And we can assume the corresponding population is approximately one million people, which represents an average density of about 15 individuals per square kilometer. In fact, density varies dramatically from a few individuals per square kilometer in the arid areas to several hundreds in places irrigated by the canals.

As for the hierarchy of localities in the Herat region, there is one big city and a multitude of small rural communities. The link of the 'town' between city and village is weak – following my impression, weaker than in Muslim parts of the Mediterranean area. In Herat, the towns of this intermediate size typically consist of some public office buildings, shops, and residences, while in their overall composition they appear as big villages. The essential regional picture is then that of Herat City as the core, with lines of transport, control, and communication passing directly into rural localities.

The estimated population of one million can be categorized as follows:

1. agricultural producers:
1.1. agricultural producers with water for wheat only,
1.2. agricultural producers with water for both rice and wheat;
2. pastoral nomads staying in or passing through the Herat area.
3. people with their main affiliation to the city:
3.1. landowners, big traders, administrators,
3.2. small traders, craftsmen,
3.3. daily paid labourers, urban 'Lumpenproletariat', and very few migrant labourers.

107

Roughly, these categories represent the following percentages of the total population: 1.1. – 50%, 1.2. – 30%, 2. – 10%, 3. – 10%. This distribution is persistent, although individuals may pass from one category to another.

The mobility of people in Herat nullifies any attempt to isolate definite regional boundaries. Recalling the problems of describing local community, religious and ecological organization, we find it similarly difficult, in terms of empirical phenomena, to circumscribe a 'region' as a concise unit. But, proper dynamics as an abstraction can be more clearly defined. I shall attempt to disclose these dynamics of the region by portraying what happened to people in Herat during the drought of 1971–1972, showing how relevant occurrences in different parts of the region were interrelated during the course of this pervasive event.

The 1971–72 drought meant that annual precipitation was reduced by a few inches. The following picture demonstrates the sensitivity of the whole of social organization in Herat to even small ecological fluctuations.

The drought affected differently the various categories of the population. For those agriculturalists who normally have enough water for *both wheat and rice*, the 1971 wheat harvest was essentially equal to that of normal years; water supply remained adequate for weekly irrigation of wheat. The cotton crop of these producers was also average. Contrary to fluctuations in wheat prices, cotton is purchased at stable prices by a state controlled monopoly: in 1971 many producers received for this crop a money income typical of normal years. But rice crops were meagre in almost all villages in the region. A good year's return is 15:1 (yield:seed), while 1971 yields only trebled, doubled, or gave no return at all on seed.

Therefore both producers and owners suffered a serious loss of income; this represented especially critical consequenses for sharecroppers. In 1971 many such households could not meet family needs with their shares of the harvest; they had to take up loans to cover the deficit. Villagers are normally in debt; the drought increased the debt of poor villagers and made it more difficult for them to repay loans, since another year's postponement leads to increased interest rates. Imbalance of household budgets due to loss of income and insufficient credit forced many to sell their oxen to obtain food. Only people possessing their own oxen can work as 'fifty-fifty' sharecroppers. The loss of one's oxen thus leads to a lower socio-economic position; sharecroppers without their own oxen receive one-quarter of the harvest or much less if they work on a daily basis.

The misfortunes of those normally producing *only wheat* were even greater. Many such fields were parched both years; at best, they showed trebled investments in seed. These people also lost an additional source of income. In normal years they work for rice producers as seasonal migrant labourers. When their own wheat harvest is over, they move to the irrigated areas and cut rice for a share of the crop. The drought and reduced rice crop eliminated demand for this labour force. In those very few wheat-and-rice villages where rice yields were close to normal, some labour was needed. But since the supply of labour vastly exceeded demand, wages for daily work were depressed to an extraordinarily low level throughout the region. People seeking work filled the paths and roads of Herat.

In order to survive the critical months, villagers sold their oxen, took up more loans, sold household furnishing and women's gold, and started petty trading with these and other items. Beyond that, begging was one of the remaining alternatives.

Pastures used by the *nomads* are generally public land owned by the state. No fees are paid for the use of summer pastures in the mountains, nor do specific tribes monopolize territories. Distantly ranging nomads winter in the western and northern lowlands, close to the Iranian and Soviet borders. Some nomads own land and water resources there, though most land is public. Passage through village districts and pasturing on agricultural fields are normally free of charge. But, the conditions vary for grazing in agricultural areas; fees are sometimes demanded. Many nomads follow itineraries, lasting up to 40 days, which pass from western or northern lowlands up to the mountains of Central Afghanistan, while others have short routes of a few days duration, which lead along the slopes north and south of the Hari-Rud River. Households and camps change the direction and length of their migration routes according to changes in flocks and qualities of pasture in the various areas.

An exclusively nomad household needs a minimum number of animals in order to keep a balanced budget. The necessary number of animals, and the general opportunity situation of the nomad household, must always be considered in relation to the continually fluctuating prices in non-nomadic sectors of the economy, especially the price of wheat.

Pastures were decimated during the drought. Sheep and goats became thin, producing a less than average amount of wool. Extraordinary amounts of animals and meat were offered for sale. Since wheat was scarce and expensive, the exchange rate of animals and animal produce for wheat fell drastically in the nomads' disfavour. Although this exchange rate fluctuated from month to month, the overall trend described here dominates the wheat-meat-relationship for one to two years.

Observing this crisis in nomadism, one might expect a gross migration of nomads to villages and the city. Significantly, this did not happen. Most nomads successfully survived the critical months without abandoning pastoralism. They managed in different ways.

Those nomads ranging closer to Herat City cut brush in the desert, transported it to the city on camels, and sold it as fuel at prices inflated by a drought-caused scarcity of fuel. Similar to villagers, nomads engaged in petty trading in animals, carpets, and household furnishing. But pastoralists did not switch to agriculture – villages were already swelled by ranks of unemployed agricultural workers – nor did they settle as proletarians in the city. Rather, they reduced consumption, lived from their own animals, and took up loans – for example, from wealthy relatives settled as landowners and traders. Although their flocks were reduced, they lived through the crisis as nomads. Finally, the winter of 1971–1972 brought enough rain to assure better pastures. The rain meant a new possibility to re-build herds to an adequate or better level of wealth than before the crisis. Throughout the crisis, this prospect remained more promising to the nomads than turning with empty hands to some other sector of the region's economy.

In the *city*, economic activities were depressed. The city of Herat is extremely sensitive to economic fluctuations in the countryside, since its activities are largely financed by the transfer of produce from villages. Many traders and administrators are also landowners, and one general effect of the drought was a gross reduction in the income of property-owners residing in the city. This had the further effect of a reduction in house construction, which is a main source of wage work in the city. Since crops had been reduced, wheat and rice straw became scarce on the market. This left brickmakers without their normal fuel supply. This important building material thus became scarce and exceptionally expensive; the city's brick-works decreased their output. With rising construction costs and dwindling personal incomes, the upper class people of Herat built less during the drought. As a result, there were fewer jobs and less income available to wage workers.

In normal years, wage workers are also employed in the city to pack pistachio nuts, raisins, wool, and other produce. All of these activities are tied to the agricultural sector; and in all of them the demand for wage labour decreased. As a further repercussion, most traders dealing in agricultural goods had their business reduced, so that the need for porters in the bazaar was diminished.

In general, total regional productivity, including services and wholesale and retail trade, decreased during the drought.

We have seen how the drought had specific implications for the various categories of personnel: how landowners, workers, peasants, nomads, and others suffered to different degrees and by different mechanisms. One overall effect should be underlined: the systems production of poor people. Many households are economically marginal, and the drought had the effect of pushing them further down the socio-economic ladder. A clear manifestation of this was increase in the number of beggars – male and female, old and young, ill and healthy.

On the other hand, some people benefited from drought. They were the people who control a big enough surplus to influence grain market prices, to grant interest loans, and to buy land. During the crisis they sold grain on a seller's market and bought land on a buyer's market. Other property-holders without such savings suffered from the crisis and emerged less wealthy, selling land to cover expenses.

Summing up, the regional interconnexions display themselves as a on-going field system. The empirical pattern is seen in the network relations and the channels for economic resource flow in production, trade, and on the labour market. I have described the dynamics of the agricultural, nomadic, and urban economics, and the dynamics of the regional economy as a higher level system interconnecting the three. This is the proper dynamics of the regional organization in Herat, tying together the population of one million people as an organized entity.

Looking outwards, the regional picture enables us to relate life in Herat to larger fields, e.g. fields in international political and economic relations. Two important things have happened in Herat during the last fifteen years.

Firstly, the USA and the USSR have built an extensive road system by which Herat has become connected with most of Afghanistan's other cities and also the surrounding foreign countries. Secondly, economic life has become more monetarized. Especially in connexion with development aid from abroad, money, mainly from the two biggest powers plus Western Germany, has been pumped into Herat via Afghan state channels (cf. Ministry of Planning 1970, sections on 'Money and Banking', and 'Prices'). The region, and its multitude of households and ecological and other sub-systems are thereby more directly connected to international price fluctuations, in a way completely beyond the control of Herati people. This is one specific tie between Herat and the national and international systems by which factors

111

from the outside are channeled in as determinants within the region itself.

Up to the time of my fieldwork, no concomitant industry had been started in Herat, and the level of improvement in agriculture was low. Herat still has no hydro-electric or other power plants designed for supplying industry.

Trade on all levels, however, has been increasing, and more business goes on in Herat than in earlier decades. When it comes to distribution of wealth and the creation of new jobs for the increasing population, it is an open question whether this means real development. Monetarization means that the villager substitutes household products for goods largely imported from abroad (e.g. clothes). Surplus from trade cannot yet be invested in industrial enterprises in Herat; wealthy people transfer their profit from Herat trade and agriculture to Kabul and elsewhere where money can be more profitably invested. An improvement in the power and transportation situation should change this pattern.

With prospects of financial support from Iran, a railway is being planned. Like roads and money, a railway may transform regional activities, as well as organizational patterns in agriculture, locality, and other fields.

3.6. *An economic field*

From the description of the region we can now identify those economic dynamics that tie together the regional population. The Herat economy comprises the activities of people dispersed within and around the city. Moving within this large geographical area, people pursue their economic alternatives. Many landowners residing in the city use profits made in one village for investing in additional land located in other parts of the region. Producer households similarly circulate within the area, following changes in their opportunity situations.

At the level of phenomena we have been describing regional organization. But in the course of analysis, regional form has itself appeared largely as an epiphenomenon of economic processes. If we now disregard specifically regional features, the hierarchy of localities and spatial communication network, and focus instead upon the processes of economic production and circulation, we can envisage the above picture as an economic field. The regional entity is large enough to display a sufficiently permanent and autonomous economic system which adequately represents characteristic productive regimes and social strata. This economic field includes different productive regimes and modes of distribution. The former include pastoral nomadism, agriculture and crafts, and a number of sub-types such as irrigated and non-irrigated agriculture, and pastoralism combined with the collection of fuel. As a main point, the relation between labour input and productive results differs in these various regimes. For example, we saw the contrasting ways in which nomadic and agricultural households coped with the drought.

The impoverished nomad can realistically hope that his reduced herd will regenerate to a level sufficient for maintaining an independent household and a satisfactory standard of living. The dispossessed agriculturalist has no analogous opportunity for again attaining wealth. His income will be restricted by the rate of remuneration for his labour and the ratio of workers to consumers in his household. One aggregate result of this difference is a contrast between the elements of stratification generated in the nomad and the agriculturalist sectors, respectively. Common macro-factors imposing themselves from national and international fields will bring forth dissimilar effects in the two sectors.

One important mode of property distribution is that of the independent freeholder who as producer and owner controls his household's means of production. This mode prevails in the nomadic regime (though modified by an element of debt among nomads), and among urban and rural craftsmen as well as traders (family shops). In the agricultural regime, peasants of this type are nowadays found mainly in the peripheral and less productive parts of the area. Most of the cultivated land in Herat is in the hands of non-producers. Some sharecroppers own a little of the land which they work, while the rest is controlled by landlords. The domination of landowner/worker relationships in agricultural production and distribution has implications for the overall economic field in Herat. Surveying the economic field for the dominant mode of distribution and circulation, we are impressed by the overall prevalence of market relationships. People are related to land via the market as buyers, sellers, and renters. Villages often resemble a kind of agricultural factory where dwellings serve merely as workers' quarters. Local agriculturalists seldom elaborate symbols which identify their families with the land – a trait so typical of 'proper peasants'.

Most significantly, the landowner/sharecropper relationship is itself market-oriented and part of the overall market. Sharecropping contracts are annually renegotiated, and labourers are continually competing for sharecropping rights and wage work. As a feature of the regional market, the ratio of landed property requiring labour to landless labour seeking employment determines the level of landowners' rents and sharecroppers' remuneration. In recent decades labour supply in Herat has increased faster than the area of cultivated land. Since labourers underbid each other, their pay shows a relative decline in terms of produce per unit of labour.

The market relationship between landowner and sharecropper-wage worker dominates both this sector and the overall field of economic production and circulation in Herat.

Three important features for characterizing this type of economy should be noted: First, a great number of the production-consumption units in the Herat economy are family households, and many aggregate features of the overall economy are generated by these domestic units. This is obvious if we consider the nomads and various types of family firms engaged in trade and crafts. This point is less clear in agriculture, due to the dominance of non-producing landowners. But since a large number of work decisions are left to the producer households, even this sector has many characteristic features brought about by the domestic units. Without pursuing details, I would say that as part of the overall economic field in Herat, there is an organizational element we may call 'domestic' or 'peasant'.

Secondly, the market-oriented landowner/labourer relationship as the dominant feature of property distribution and control in Herat is vital because it determines the intensity of producers' work, the division of production, the expenditure of income, and the levels and patterns of investment. Landowners use a substantial portion of their income to maintain themselves as a kind of leisure class; that is, to maintain and raise family status, notably through conspicuous consumption and education. Herati landowners do not substantially invest their income in the improvement of agricultural productivity.

Finally, we can observe a capitalist element. The allocation strategy of 'money-commodities-money' is the core of trade in Herat. Many landowners channel agricultural surplus into trade, money profits and further investments following the same pattern. Success stories are told about nomads who have turned profits from pastoralism into land and trade, thereby becoming big landowners and traders in the city and, in some cases, founding family firms operating on national and international levels. But these stories usually follow a course which takes the entrepreneur to Kabul and other places outside Herat.

The reason for the stagnant capitalization of economic life in Herat cannot be demonstrated within this paper. I will only point to the constraining effects of the landowner/sharecropper relationship itself. While the landowner consumes a portion of his income, the remainder can more easily be turned into profits via trade and entreprises outside Herat, than through investment in local land worked by sharecroppers and oxen.

In sum, economic life in Herat is market-dominated. In this specific sense, relations of production and distribution contain a critical capitalist element which should not, however, be associated with 'mature capitalism'. I have accounted for market dominance in Herat by referring mainly to the specific traditional and domestic conditions of that region and Afghanistan. It would be false to attribute this market dominance to effects of the international capitalist system. Although I have pointed out some recent changes implying recent stronger local influence of the international capitalist system, external economic inputs have until now had comparatively little effect upon economic life in Herat. Nor have I implied any necessity for capitalism to become increasingly dominant in the future development of socio-economic life in Herat. We can imagine other paths of change.

3.7. *The question of one field dominating others*

We may now raise the question of the relative dominance of one or more of several interrelated fields. Here we shall empirically discuss the hypothesis that the economic field is especially determinative within the set of fields presented above. We have gained a general impression that the dynamids of the market in circulation of land, labour, and produce are strikingly unhampered by non-market elements of the economy and by the proper-dynamics of other fields.

The same personnel take part in all of the fields described. When a person participates in the Herat economy he acquires social roles that determine or steer further allocation of roles to him as he takes part in other fields. His economic role and the opportunities implied by it determine the level of resources in his domestic unit, his platform for taking part in locality organization, his access to and control over land and water, his manner of relating to state agencies, and in many ways also his involvement in religious organization. Hence, in the construction of the social person in Herat, the labels of sharecropper, freeholder, landlord, trader, craftsman, nomad, and so forth, do not refer merely to occupational roles. They imply entire clusters of roles, opportunities, and attributes. The social allocation of other roles is steered by the operation of economic roles and role-sets.

Thus, the overall organizational potential of Herati (1) local communities and (2) kinship organization does not fully materialize. This is due to people's residential instability, which in turn is caused by determinants in the sharecropping economy. The effects of (3) the ecological crisis in Herat can only be understood when we consider economic organization; it was the mode of property distribution that worked so as to let the drought – an ecologic phenomenon – create food-scarcity to a major part of the population. (4) The Afghan state's administrative poverty is partly explained by the organization of the economy – e.g. the hopeless task of collecting taxes from traditional Afghan agriculturalists and pastoralists. It is more pertinent, however, that the actor's role in political patron-client relations is conditioned by his economic situation. Residential instability also markedly restricts any effective contacts between state agencies and villager households, and negates efforts of individual households and civil servants to build up mutual working relations. The state interferes in canal irrigation, but merely as a kind of arbitrator in intra-canal conflicts generated in an economic-ecological system that operates rather independent from the state. As for (5) regional organization, its gross features appear as veritable epiphenomena of underlying economic dynamics within which the landowner-producer relationship is a highly dominant element. The regional account shows even more clearly than the description of locality, the vehemence of economic forces in Herat and their massive and composite effects. Finally (6), economic determinants allocate to actors in Herat differentials of power and resource control, placing them in highly different life situations, thereby effecting people's involvement in religious milieu and the mode of religious communication itself. The symbols of Sheriat and Tariqat Islam were not originally made in Herat; other people use them elsewhere under highly different circumstances. But the emic meaning of these symbols is produced from the context of Herati people's economically dominated life.

At the level of status and role, the question of inter-field dominance can be seen as a matter of determinative or 'imperative' roles: one role-type, when allocated to an actor, then steers him to the further allocation of roles (cf. Barth 1969). The processes and intensities of steering in role-allocation comprise a theme that must be studied empirically: we can do so by following the respective fields' relative effects over time upon role-allocation in the social construction of the social person (cf. Grønhaug in press; part III).

We can empirically follow the processes of inter-field dominance by studying the role transformations which occur as the actor moves from arena to arena, from field to field. In the case of Herat, we can see how the actor's economic roles imperatively effect the social allocation of other roles to him.

When analyzing this theme, we must distinguish among three

levels: the person, the field, and the societal formation as a whole of all interrelated fields. The social construction of the person can be described in terms of role-allocation, while the fields themselves can be seen as aggregates of related role-sets. We can thereby study the specific effects of an assumedly dominant field by examining formative processes at the levels of both the social person, and societal formations.

This conclusion should be connected to the issue of 'complexity' as stated in the introduction. We are now analytically able, not only to compare societies as being more and less 'complex', but also to compare the processes relating dominant and dominated elements in complex wholes. We can cross-culturally account for dynamic directions over time in social person and societal formations.

It thus seems fruitful to distinguish between 'scale' and 'complexity', and manipulate the scale variable to identify modes of empirical complexity. We can further operationalize the notion of complexity by studying the number of distinct fields and the way they interrelate in societies.

In this way, the question of structural dominance in 'societies' and smaller entities may be formulated in operational terms and be empirically analyzed. As my main point, we can do so by applying some elementary notions from our common anthropological language of social organization and culture.

The above conclusion can be submitted to tests of demonstration and falsification. For example, we can clarify the statements about inter-field dominance by partly or wholly repeating the study focussing our observation upon alternative personnel-sets in Herat such as nomads or urban upper-class people. We can obtain further precision through historical material shedding light upon social (dis-)continuities over time in Herat and comparative exercises in terms of relevant analytical dimensions. Concerning the latter, it would be particularly interesting to include societies in Central Asia and elsewhere in which irrigated agriculture, stratification, and state organization are important components. A point made by Barth during the final phase of the symposium sketches such a comparison:

> I was also struck by the similarity and difference between *Herat* ... and my *Swat* valley in the other end of the *Afghan* area, which is ecologically similar you know: A nice big valley that is too dry for cultivating unless you have irrigation channels, and you do have them. Why then is political life so staggeringly different in those two places? You can surely approach it by looking at any kinds of integrations that are created by how people in fact

aggregate their activity in domains: That the feudal kind of patron-client ties that are fundamental to social life in Swat are a major premise for all the other features that distinguish that valley from the *Herat* valley. Because of this construction of social persons as patrons and chiefs and landowners versus clients and peasants, they will make the kind of society that you have in *Swat*, or when they do not have it or have alternative concepts of how you construct a person like *Herat*, they will make a *Herat* society (Barth, in Blom 1972, session 10, p. 5).

4. Final remarks: social fields as analytic units

I have applied to the organization of this material a notion of *social fields* as the critical analytic units. A field is a relatively bounded interconnexion system stretched out in socio-space. The size of a field is attributed to the magnitude of personnel which it organizes. It is essentially with this meaning of size that I have defined *scale*, and in the analysis I have varied the levels of scale in order to discover fields and distinguish among them.

The quantitative aspect of numbers, size, and density are relevant, as well as the temporal aspect of durability. Organizational *proper dynamics* are a further definitional attribute of a social field; by manipulating scale as a variable, I could identify different social dynamics characterizing the various respective circumscribed entities.

One field contains a distinct set of the social prerequisites for individual lives in society, i.e. for the social construction of social *persons*. And a set of fields can be combined into an account of the *society* as a whole. I see society as an overall system of the total set of social prerequisites operative in the social formation of the persons studied.

A social field is an aggregate of social relationships which are sets of complementary roles. Social relationships are interconnected in the social person in the sense that a number of roles are combined in the person that is part of the totality of fields making up his society.[8]

In the study of social fields, the *discovery process* includes the observation of empirical *events* in which *task* and issue-oriented relations become activated. The action units themselves must be identified and characterized in terms of their organizational composition and inventory, then mapped and summarized as aggregate pictures. The critical data concern the generation of organizational patterns through inter-unit relations, the social occasions for their activization, the moves, and repercussions of moves of actors vis-à-vis each other. Through the simulation of social processes we discover fields as bounded entities of organizational interconnexions. We start by describing patterns in *emically* codified events, and move toward *etic* accounts of fields as super-individual systems.[9]

The next step concerns the question of *dominance* in inter-field relations – the problem of 'order of orders' to paraphrase Levi-Strauss (1967). Each field is in itself a system of dominating and dominated elements, but the more complex question concerns the relative dominance of one (or more) of the several fields comprising society.

The order of orders has two aspects: the causative functions of specific fields in the formation of social person and in the societal formation as a whole. Pursuing this question we can study generatively both the processes of the social construction of social persons and the social construction of society itself (cf. Barth 1966, 1972).

Considering dominance, I assume that all fields are interrelated and causative of each other, but also that some fields and relationships are more determinative and causative than others, a point demonstrated above. A specific field becomes dominant because the roles it implies affect role allocation in general for most people, and because its social relationships integrate the population in an especially effective way. Thereby that field's proper dynamics can work with greater force both upon the actor and the society as a whole. I imply no notions of structural harmony or equilibrium. Rather, I have shown a case where some fields have destructive effects upon others, and where there are social processes of destruction of social persons.[10]

The procedure does not arbitrarily presume that large fields are necessarily more important than small ones, or that specific fields are more important than others. Rather, I have tried to design the analysis so as to facilitate operational investigation of such questions.

At the *phenotype* level, a social field as an empirical pattern of social events, cultural codes, and organizational circumstances pertains to one society. At this level, a given field may be conceptualized in terms of an empirical syndrome which has little or no comparative value. But the empirical patterns designating fields must be analyzed in terms of more elementary determinants or processes, and at this *geneotype* level we can make use of analytic concepts and statements. Above, I described the proper dynamics of locality, irrigation, region, and economy in Herat as composite or aggregate processes, and thereby trying to identify their empirical nature. As a further step I then resolved these proper dynamics into logically more simple notions easier to use in comparative discussion.

On one hand, then, the idea of fields as aggregates of events

119

extended in social space and time is designed to account for the *unique* and substantive properties of a society as it exists at a given point in history. On the other hand, the integration of formal analytic concepts and statements into the procedure adds to the potential of the field concept as a tool for *comparative* analysis (cf. Grønhaug, in press).

The social field concept is a version of the general *system* idea. Events within one part of a field system affect its other parts more directly than sectors outside that field. The field is an interrelated whole with a degree of boundedness distinguishing it from other fields. The notion of field as a relatively bounded entity in relationships of 'export' and 'import' with other fields is an *'open systems'* variant of general systems theory (cf. von Bertalanffy 1973).

'Society' must then be thought of as system of systems. Social reality is by its nature *multi-dimensional*, and we must account for as many qualitatively and quantitatively different aspects of societies as possible, while maintaining a consistent language about the commonly 'social'. For this task the multiple field approach may be of some use.

The relevant dimension for describing societies can be conceptualized in terms of *proper dynamics*. We have noted how a single dimension of proper dynamics manifests itself at several, more and less inclusive *organizational levels* of scale (cf. section 3.2.2.). However, Herati society cannot validly be imagined as a single hierarchy of organizational levels in only one dimension. We must envisage society as a composite of *many hierarchies* (of economy, religion, power, etc.), each hierarchy representing specific proper dynamics and displaying specific organizational scale levels.

When considering the scale of society, dichotomies like 'micro: macro', 'small-scale:large-scale', 'community:society', etc. can be misleading. We must understand society as a composite of several hierarchies, each containing multiple levels of scale, and not merely as a two-level entity (cf. Sinha 1972; Schwartz 1972; Grønhaug 1971a, 1972, in press).[11]

Finding the scale of a specific society thus appears to be a frustrating problem. Since Herati society is multi-dimensional, and each dimension manifests itself at many different levels of scale, how can we then talk of Herati society as being of this or that numerical size? It seems that any answer to this begs for further specification.

I think of society in relation to a focal set of actors, and I see their society as that overall system which comprises the total set of social prerequisites for their construction as social persons. The overall society of my Herati sharecroppers consists of several fields at

120

different levels of scale. It would be erroneous to select one of the fields with its specific scale and label it 'Herati society', since all fields in Herat are operative in the formation of the sharecroppers and their social partners.

The best we can do is to talk of the size of fields as specified organizational dimensions. Later we can try to identify the most dominant of the fields and point to the effects and functions of that field in the construction of persons and society. From this point of reference we can then consider the scale of the dominant field as a critical organizational level in a society. But this dimension is not identical with the scale of that overall society, something which cannot be expressed in simple numerical terms. The following remark clarifies this:

> Demographic scale is what we mostly talk about when we are thinking of scale, sheer numbers of people within any countable segregate, and the only question is what can be counted? We find we can count almost anything better than we can (count) societies (Schwartz in Blom 1972, session 10, p. 11).

In Herat I have pointed to the regional economy as the critical level of organization; it includes a population of about one million. Integration within the regional economy has its own dynamics with determinative effects upon smaller sub-systems operative in social person formation in Herat. People there are also part of larger fields: the Afghan state, Islam, the world-wide economic-political system. The analytic task is then to locate and evaluate the significance of the impacts of such larger fields, and study the processes of change whereby specific macro-fields become more or less determinative in the lives of people in Herat.

Thus, the significant question for understanding a society as a whole concerns the processes whereby a set of actors is, or is becoming, part of a social field that has, or is acquiring, decisive determinative effects upon all the fields that include those actors. We can tackle this problem by analytically resolving the notion of 'society' into elementary components of fields. We can identify the scale of fields. But without demonstrating a specific field's determinative significance for the overall society, it is meaningless – or at best bewildering – to regard the scale of a *field* as the scale of the *society* in question.

Scale as simply numerical size is an interesting variable, since we can use it to identify different significant fields, especially to find the extension and functional mode of the determinative field(s) in a society. Thereby, we can more clearly understand the dynamics of the social construction of society itself.

SURAJIT SINHA

Co-existence of Multiple Scales and Networks of a Civilization: India

1. Introduction

I have been accustomed to examine the multiple levels of complexities in Indian society in terms of evolutionary levels (Sinha 1955, 1958, 1962), or as continua between tribal and caste/peasant roles (Sinha 1965). In these formulations, scale of society – as strictly defined in terms of maximal size of the population involved in significant networks of social relationship – has not been rigorously considered as the decisive variable. I must also admit to an initial skepticism, that while distinguishing the small-scale societies from the large-scale ones we may perhaps end up very close to repeating the classical polar dichotomies following Maine, Tönnies, Durkheim, and Redfield, or some variants of Parsonian pattern variables.

By combining the criteria of techno-economic levels with that of 'scales' in the sense of the Wilsons (Wilson & Wilson 1945), we find in the Indian sub-continent the co-existence and inter-penetration of diverse levels of productive technology and associated scales – symbiotic hunters, swidden cultivators, plough-cultivating 'tribes', agriculturist caste-peasants in rural centres, traditional urban communities, and modern urban/industrial centres (Sinha 1968, Bose 1968). To this list could be added the isolated and primitive tribes of the Andaman Islands. All these scales operate under the super-arching networks (scale) of a pre-industrial traditional 'civilization', undergoing a process of reorganization as an emerging modern 'nation'. India thus provides a great natural experimental ground for examining the problem of diverse 'scales'. The smaller 'scales' are under the pressures of the larger ones, and the super-arching network of civilization/nation in its turn bears the mark of adaptation to the pressures of numerous 'small-scale' social constituents. The Indian case particularly interests us on account of its unique preservation of particularism (parochial/narrow/small scales) in the midst of many strands of universalistic norms and structures.

2. Basic structural attributes of the different scales

As we move from the level of primitive hunters to settled agriculturist caste/peasant villages there is a progressive increase in the
size of the local community and a movement in the pattern of
organizational complexity from segmentary to organic solidarity
(Bailey 1960, 1961, Sinha 1965). But we should note that segmentary
particularism is deeply embedded and preserved at the caste/
peasant scale of complexity. Let us examine the situation more
closely:

2.1. *Primitive hunters*

If we take the Onge of Little Andaman as the archetype, the total
population of the tribe is about 140, and density is about 1 person in
2 sq. miles. They are divided into a few wandering bands of about
15 people belonging to 4 or 5 nuclear families with their demarcated
territories. The organizing structures are: nuclear family, band
(around a permanent communal hut), and a notion of ethnic group
or tribe whom they label as 'men'. There is no development of
lineage, clan, formal leadership, or elaborate role specialization and
stratification. The local groups or bands used to be divided into two
nearly endogamous clusters – the forest dwellers and the coast
dwellers.

2.2. *Symbiotic hunters*

Unlike the Onge who are, or until very recently were, completely
self-sufficient as hunters and gatherers, there are a number of
nomadic and semi-nomadic hunting and gathering groups in the
Indian mainland who live in or close to the forest and maintain
their livelihood partly by exchanging forest products with the
agricultural products of neighbouring peasants in the plains.
Sometimes these symbiotic hunters oscillate in their livelihood
pattern between the level of hunting and gathering and swidden
cultivation.

In the case of the Birhor of Bihar and Orissa we find that their
total population was only 2,755 in 1941. According to S. C. Roy
(1925) they are divided into two sub-groups: the Uthlu, hunters
and gatherers, and the Jaghi, the settled group. We are concerned
here with the Uthlu section. Their basic unit of community
organization are wandering local groups, *tanda's*, which are uni-
ethnic and consist of about 15–20 households and about 50–60
people. In the winter the 'tanda' members roam about in smaller

123

units of about 10–15 persons belonging to 3–5 nuclear families. It is difficult to estimate the effective scale of their society in terms of circles of inter-tanda relationship, but it is not likely to exceed 200 persons. Their organizing social structures are nuclear family, shallow patrilineage, and clan. There are some specialization in terms of secular and religious leadership of the tanda but there is no social stratification. A few tandas may get together in a hunting expedition. The Birchor also have ceremonial friendship with the low-caste Hindus in the adjacent plains. They sell their forest products to the Hindu peasants and settled tribals in exchange for agricultural products and money. Although they have imbibed some elements of the magico-religious traditions of the regional Hindu peasantry, they still remain virtually isolated from the framework of the caste system. They are, however, aware that they are looked down upon by the Hindu peasants as an 'untouchable' group and they, in return, do not accept cooked food from the lowest Hindu castes.

2.3. *Swidden cultivators*

Although the bulk of the Scheduled Tribes in modern India are settled plough cultivators, there are a number of groups in North East India and a few groups in Central India who live in swidden cultivation. Population size and patterns of social organization vary considerably at this level of technology, depending on the terrain and degree of pressure from the encroaching peasant society. There are groups like the Juang with a population of 15,024; Hill Maria with a population of 11,500; Lushai (Mizo), 54,007; and Khasi, 356,155.

A recent study on the carrying capacity of land under shifting cultivation among the Juang of Keonjhar, the Mizo of Lushai Hills, and the Maria of Abujhmarh Hills indicates that population density per square mile among these communities varies widely: Juang – 63.2, Mizo – 13.2, and Maria 6.1 (Bose 1967: 191).

In spite of variation in population size and density, these groups share the following characteristics: permanent uni-ethnic villages with about 140–150 persons; some development of lineage and clan; usually development of voluntary associations like bachelors' dormitories and institution of secular and sacred leadership at the village level. The effective scale of these societies would perhaps not exceed 1500 people spread over 10–12 villages. In some groups like the Khasi there is a tendency toewards formation of clan-based chieftaincy with jurisdiction over a number of villages; but the social structure is essentially unstratified and segmentary.

2.4. Settled agriculturist 'tribes'

Some ethnic groups, in spite of sharing the basic productive technology of plough cultivation of the Hindu peasantry, are administratively regarded as 'tribes' on the basis of their relative social isolation and 'backwardsness'. Difficulties of drawing a sharp division line between 'caste' and 'tribe' have been widely discussed by Ghurye (1942), Bailey (1960, 1961), and Sinha (1965), and need not be repeated here. If for heuristic consideration we accept the label of 'tribe' for these groups and examine their case, we find that usually they are larger in population as ethnic groups than the swidden cultivating groups; also, they live in larger local communities in relatively more densely populated regions. A tribe like the Santal, for example, had a population of over 3 million in 1961. Although these 3 million Santal are spread over 3 States of India, they maintain a remarkable standardization of cultural pattern throughout this extensive terrain. Meaningful systematic social contacts, however, do not stretch beyond a circle of about 12 villages containing about 2–3,000 Santal, although a series of such contiguous circles ultimately cover a major population of the tribe. Their distribution, however, is interspersed with caste/peasant villages, and even in the districts of their major concentration they do not exceed 20% of the total population of the districts.

In essence, the organizing principles of Santal society are similar to those of the swidden cultivator groups. The Santal tend to reside in partially isolated hamlets almost exclusively inhabited by them. But these hamlets may be parts of larger multi-ethnic revenue villages. In their hamlets they live their social life more or less limited to their own ethnic group – at the revenue village level they have to take note of the presence of several Hindu castes with whom their contacts are largely limited to the economic sphere. Family, lineage, sub-clans, and clans are the basic structural units of the Santal; their lineages are usually deeper than those of the swidden cultivator tribes. Santal villages have a number of traditional officials, with about 12 villages organized under a Chief, Parganaits. People from a number of villages combine together during the annual communal hunt. On this occasion, social offences which had remained unresolved at the village or *pargana* level are decided.

The Santal provide an interesting case where a large population, exceeding 3 million at the level of ethnicity and ultimate limit of endogamy, can be sustained by a segmentary unstratified social organization linked symbiotically with multi-ethnic Hindu peasantry in the regional agrarian economy.

125

2.5. Settled agriculturist 'tribes' near the threshold of caste/peasant scale

While the Santal maintain their social and residential isolation from the Hindu castes despite symbiotic economic linkages, and manage their social life on segmentary principle, a cognate ethnic group, the Bhumij, have been deeply enmeshed in the caste-peasant network. I have described in several papers how the Bhumij in South Manbhum not only live on the average with 5 other ethnic groups, but are also very much a part of the hierarchic former feudal state of Barahabhum, covering a population of 2,44,733 living in 595 villages spread over 635 sq. miles and belonging to 65 ethnic groups (Sinha 1962, 1966). The Bhumij of Barabhum live in two worlds in two contexts – segmentary and egalitarian in intra-ethnic sphere and essentially hierarchic (both caste and feudal) at the inter-ethnic level and pargana level. With their segmentary organization the Bhumij maintain a smaller scale of society than the segmentary Santal. However, with their hierarchic linkage they are not only a part of a multi-ethnic chieftaincy, but their upper strata are linked with wider networks of royal Rajput lineages (Sinha 1962).

2.6. Caste/peasant rural society

2.6.1. The village community

In 1961, 82% of India's population lived in some 567,000 villages. The decisive bulk of this population operates under the social framework of the caste system. Villages vary widely in size, from a few isolated homesteads to nearly 5,000 persons. But in 1941 nearly 2/3 of the villages of unpartitioned India had less than 500 people.

Villages in India vary widely not only in size, but also in ethnic complexity. On the basis of 1911 census tables, Marriott has estimated the following figures for effective village communities and the number of ethnic groups in the villages in five regions of India and Pakistan (Marriott 1960).

Region	Estimated mean population per effective village community	Number of local ethnic groups
Kerala	1,058	17 or more
Coromandal	813	14
Upper Ganges	414	9
Middle Indus	20–250	3 or 4
Bengal Delta	189	2 to 5

Marriott has demonstrated how elaborateness in caste-ranking is correlated with the number of ethnic groups living in a village. Marriott's study is a pointer to the fact that there is considerable scope for research on the varying organizational principles for maintaining villages of different range of size and ethnic complexity. One of the major implications of his work is a notion of the limiting factor of size and related degree of ethnic heterogeneity for the operation of the caste system. Whereas a small village with a few ethnic groups is not conducive to the operation of the caste system, if ethnic heterogeneity is carried beyond a limit of close mutual observation of ritually defined rules of interaction, the system will fail to operate in a consistent and elaborate manner. Cohn highlights this point as follows:

> The absolute growth in population will have consequences for the social structure as well . . . the day-to-day functioning of the caste system depends on knowledge that can only be gained in a face-to-face group. Caste, as an interaction system, and the maintenance of local caste hierarchies depends on knowing to what groups individuals belong and what behaviours are expected from them . . . As the population of India increases, the size of the villages increases and the percentage of people living in large villages increases . . . as much as 40% of India's rural population may be living in large villages today. Can the face-to-face aspects of the caste system be as effectively maintained in villages where, more and more, not everyone knows who everyone else is nor does he know about everyone else? In the large villages, inter-caste relations may become increasingly economic relations and contractual rather than intertwined with social and ritual relations. (Cohn 1971: 158–159).

We already have a sizeable number of village studies on multi-ethnic, fairly large-size villages from different parts of India. These studies indicate that, unlike uni-ethnic tribal villages, multi-caste peasant village societies are highly stratified, as well as being segmented along ethnic and lineages lines. Lineages and castes in the villages have considerable autonomy in social relationships, while there are also multiple linkages which bring the segments and strata together in the village in various combinations. All these studies again highlight the multiple routes of extension of social networks beyond the village. It has been emphasized that these extensions do not move in a linear series of centralized, progressively higher and higher circles and levels of social integration. Different segments of the village population – sects, castes, lineages – have their own distinct patterns of extension. So the scales will vary not only in terms of size and ethnic complexity of the village, but also in terms of varied patterns of extra-village linkages for the different segments and strata of the village society.

2.6.2. Caste and sub-caste

At this point I should like to discuss briefly the 'caste' dimension of social scale. Caste does not operate merely at the village level but has also a sphere of horizontal solidarity spreading over many villages.

In the 1901 census 2,378 castes were enumerated – with average number per caste estimated as 120,000. Such an average, however, does not give us a grasp of the real situation, for the size of individual castes varies considerably. It is well-known that the self-regulating corporate social groups or circles which set the effective limit of endogamy as extended in groups are often the sub-castes: and the number of such sub-castes in India is anybody's guess. An idea of the extent of segmentation of castes into sub-castes may be formed on the basis of the fact that in the 1891 census it was reported that the Jat and Ahir were each responsible for 1,700 entries (as sub-castes); the Kurmi for nearly 1500.

> In 1931 Tehri-Garhwal, a tiny state in United Provinces with an area of 4,180 square miles and a population of only 350,000 had no less than 387 sub-castes of Brahmans and 1,025 sub-castes of Rajputs. Between sub-castes . . . the social barriers are nearly as strong as between castes; little inter-dining and intermarriage being permitted. (Davis 1951: 166.)

Formerly, the territorial range of a sub-caste Panchayat was usually co-terminous with the territorial extent of a local prince/chieftain. The local chieftain was the final arbitrator for disputes which could not be solved by the caste councils.

In general, the marriage and social networks of the upper castes/ sub-castes are more far-flung than those of the lower castes. This brings a distinct dimension in the problem of scale while comparing castes/sub-castes.

Iravati Karve has succintly summarized the flexible agglomerative mechanism of caste society as follows:

> To sum up, (1) the caste is an extended kin-group spread over a definite region. (2) It is never self-sufficient like a tribe because it is specialized generally in one type of occupation. (3) This deficiency is made good by many castes coming together in a village and being bound up in a pattern of mutual duties,

obligations and rights. (4) Castes are arranged in a hierarchical order which however, leaves some freedom for particular castes to strive for higher position. (5) The caste society allows new units to come into its web at a time and in a position which is largely indeterminate. (6) Castes remain in peripheral contact with each other, with very large freedom for each caste to follow what it considers to be its traditional pattern. (7) It illustrates the agglomerative character of the whole Hindu society. The society is not a product of continuous splitting of something which was a unit but has arisen out of a loose coming together of many separate cultural entities. (8) Historically this pattern might have existed even before the Aryans came, who merely took it up and perpetuated it. (9) This type of society of juxtaposed groups seems to have arisen at a time when different people came together without any single people being strong enough to impose its political or cultural domination. Most of these societies might have been tribal in nature and each retained its separate character in the new set up. (10) This society continued to exist in its old pattern as it had (a) the elasticity to accommodate ever new elements and (b) offered security through a long period of political insecurity and foreign domination. (11) The philosophical systems developed very early in the history of this society, while truly objective were also at the same time such as to offer a complete justification of the most important aspects of this society. (12) Besides, the ideal structure erected by this society its mode of internal articulation made it possible to survive outside attacks and internal schisms. (Karve 1961.)

2.7. *The civilizational network*

While describing the village we have already mentioned the multiple routes of extension of relationship. One interesting and important way of looking at the village is to see it as the basic unit of spatial nucleation of the social and cultural structure not only of a region but also of a whole civilization. Taking the clue from Kroeber's notion of 'part-society', Redfield conceptualized traditional peasant society as being based on interaction between little traditions of the unlearned masses of the little communities and the Great Tradition of the literate at the centres of civilization (Redfield 1956, Redfield & Singer 1954). Redfield hinted at the importance of locating the 'hinge groups', the 'cultural brokers' that mediate between the little traditions of the village and the Great Tradition of the urban centers (Redfield ibid). While the notion of Little and Great Tradition has gone through several phases of critical re-examination, the importance of mapping out the social organization and network of various types and levels of civilizational centres has been generally accepted.

In the case of Indian civilization perhaps the most significant contributions in this line are those of Marriott, Cohn, Singer, and Saraswati. In an interesting article, 'Networks and Centers in the Integration of Indian Civilization', Cohn and Marriott observe:

> The integration of Indian civilization depends on at least two kinds of supralocal social patterns: networks of relationship and relationships with centres. India's characteristically loose and partial integrating of great social and cultural diversity may be attributed to the fact that her networks are varied, widespread, and complex, while her civilizational centres are multiple, overlapping in jurisdiction, and internally heterogeneous. India's networks and centres thus serve respectively as channels and models at once of diversity and integration. (Cohn & Marriott 1958: 7; see also Marriott 1955.)

The above pictures make the application of the notion of scale in the Indian scene complicated indeed. A notion of local, subregional, and regional scales of social interaction may not convey much sense because the particularized social worlds do not operate in such neat territorial chunks.

Perhaps the most intriguing aspect of pre-industrial traditional Indian civilization was a model of almost infinite capacity for expansion, based on intense localization and near self-sufficiency of the local communities' self-regulating castes, and loose, diversity-conscious expansion of relationship along many routes in which the process of universalization at the centres of civilization also accommodated the particularism of ethnicity and lineages. This model partially accommodated the demands of the local chieftains or of the superior monarchs in regulation of social norms. But many crosscutting networks were built beyond the political sphere. This loose expanding network also had the advantage of convenient withdrawal into the smaller sphere of local community in case of adverse political situation. This was appropriately realized by Marx in his conceptualization of the Indian version of the 'Asiatic Mode of Production':

> Those small and extremely ancient Indian communities, some of which have continued to this day, are based on possession in common of the land, on the blending of agriculture and handicrafts, on an unalterable division of labour, which serves when-

ever a new community is started as a plan and scheme ready cut and dried. . . . The simplicity of the organization for production in these self-sufficing communities that constantly reproduce themselves in the same form . . . supplies the key to the secret of unchangeableness of Asiatic societies. The structure of economic elements of society remains untouched by the storm-clouds of the political sky (Marx 1955: 34–35).

What Marx did not properly assess was how the pursuit of excellence in the religious/moral, aesthetic and intellectual field, broadly under the control of Sanskrit-learned Brahmans, propelled the diverse routes of the network of the civilization, cutting across the spheres of influence of the 'despotic' kinds.

2.8. *Re-organization of traditional networks and channels of communication in nation-building*

I have indicated so far how traditional pre-industrial Indian civilization thrived on intense localization of social life in caste/ lineage segmented and stratified villages, on comprehensive role of little kingdoms, self-regulating particularism of castes, diversified and loose network of regional communication around centres ultimately building up the all-India networks and centres of civilization.

The modern Indian nation demands a much more centralized and standardized behavioural pattern for quick mobilization of resources. Iravati Karve writes:

'The greatest challenge to this society has come in the modern times (a) when Britain welded it into one political entity for the first time in its long history, (b) when it gained freedom from the foreign power as one nation and adopted a democratic constitution, and finally (c) when it is hoping to adopt the modern technology' (1961: 1).

Under the pressures of technological development and operation of modern democratic processes, the contents of cultural communication are becoming simplified, standardized, and democratized; the channels of cultural communication are also getting standardized. Marriott has discussed the general contour of this process in two interesting papers (1959, 1963). Milton Singer has discussed the problem of democratization and modernization of cultural performances in Madras city (1959, 1968). Saraswati and Sinha have discribed the process of modern adaptations of the ascetics of Kasi (1970) and of the temple-complex of Kalighat (Sinha 1972).

The Indian mode of infusing particularism within universalism, however, continues to exhibit its adaptive resilience in the modernization of political and techno-economic life. Thus caste-combines as pressure groups are mediating between traditional parochial segments and modern political democracy (Rudolph & Rudolph 1967). The adaptive roles of caste and joint family in modern industry have been indicated by Singer (1967). I have pointed out the creative role of traditional Guru-Shishya idiom of communication in scientific research institutions. (Sinha 1970.)

3. Summing up

The above speculative discourse first of all reveals the glaring paucity of systematic data for adequate mapping of the social worlds of persons living at different levels of productive technology and scales of society in India. I have only indicated the conventional approximate structural principles organizing social life at various levels and scales. What we obviously need is intensive knowledge of the details of quantities and qualities of social encounters, and of contents of cultural communication at various levels.

Concretely, I would expect that this symposium will provide some guide-lines for enlarging our understanding of the Onge, Birhor, Hill Maria, Santal, Bhumij, multi-caste village scales of society, and also of the super-arching scale of the civilization.

We already have some broad notions of things possible at the various tribal scales and also of the scale (of localization) necessary for the optimum operation of ranked caste systems at the village and urban levels. We now need to discuss whether some answers to the problem of creatively and adaptively preserving ethnic/local/regional particularism in an emerging modern nation may be conceived in terms of re-arranging the interlocking of hierarchies of scales at the village, ethnic, supra-local regional networks and of the over-arching nation.

ERNEST GELLNER

Scale and Nation

1. Nationalism

One of the obvious features of the modern world is the increase in the scale of social political units. In the past, large – sometimes enormous – empires existed, but these were relatively eccentric. Above all, they were sociologically contigent. Their existence was not necessary. On the whole, the units which composed them could survive as well, or nearly as well, or indeed better, if the totality remained fragmented. (*If* the Wittfogel thesis is correct, then some of the major river valleys, dependent on irrigation systems, may be an exception to this). By and large, it is the empires which require explanation, whilst their break-up, or the persistence of fragmentation, do not. Self-sufficiency, local autonomy, and fragmentation appear more natural and inherent in the available social equipment than their contrary.

The situation is now changed. It is the large and effective units which seem natural, and it is their breakdown and fragmentation which is eccentric and requires special explanation. Small units do indeed survive, but one may well suspect that they are parasitic on the larger ones in various ways.

All social units that manage to survive rely on a variety of mechanisms for their self-perpetuation. A sense of loyalty and identification on part of the population is one of the factors which contribute to such cohesion as happens to be achieved. It is a factor which, quite plainly, is not always present in the same measure or proportion. It appears to be stronger in the modern world, in the attachment to the large units which are so characteristic of it, than it was in the past. What is even more noteworthy, this strength of the sentiment seems to be quite independent of deliberate manipulation or stimulation by those political units which are the happy objects of this feeling of loyalty. Of course they do often foment and encourage it, but it can be and often is powerful, quite independent of such encouragement. The striking demonstration of this is the force of such sentiments on behalf of large units which do not yet exist at all – in other words, of irredentist feelings on behalf of units

133

which as yet exist in the aspirations of their adherents only, and which consequently do not yet possess the resources or means for encouraging the sentiment. It is the sentiment which brings them into being, rather than vice versa.

All this is of course an oblique way of referring to the force and importance of modern 'nationalism'. In this name, we possess a term for designating the quite distinctive type of sentiment of feeling of loyalty and identification elicited by modern political units. Two traits which make up this distinctiveness have already been singled out: that the objects of these sentiments are generally larger than the traditional objects of social and political loyalty and identification; and that the sentiment can precede, and thus be manifestly independent of, the objective existence of the political unit which it singles out for its favour. In other words, nationalism is not an *ex post facto* ratifier of actual political might, but possesses a kind of independent criterion of legitimacy of its own.

There is a further distinctive characteristic of these modern and large political units. It is intimately connected, I believe, with the other two: this is the nature of the division of labour within them.

2. The division of labour

There are two well-known theories concerning the direction of the general and overall development of human societies. One asserts that the general direction of development is towards greater complexity, greater differentation, and hence also greater interdependence and functional comlementarity. The other theory, which tends to be slightly less global and all-embracing, and more specifically concerned with a trend especially conspicuous in the modern world, asserts that on the contrary our world is tending towards greater standardization, conformity, uniformity: in brief, towards a mass society. It is not difficult to think of great names in sociological theory as supporters of either of the two theories. Each of these theories is plausible, suggestive, and illuminating; at the same time, when articulated in their stark simplicity, they would seem to be in headlong collision with each other. How can two theories which assert such dimetrically opposed propositions both appear so plausible, so illuminating?

In my view they are indeed both valuable and largely true, notwithstanding the fact that when articulated without qualification in their most basic and simple terms, they are indeed in conflict with each other. What follows is not the need to abandon one or the other, but to refine them both in such a manner that their compatibility, indeed their complementarity, may become evident.

134

Take first of all the famous thesis of increasing differentiation and complementarity, the doctrine of the replacement of mechanical by organic solidarity. Initially, in the 19th century, the appeal of this theory was enhanced for many of its adherents by the fact that it fed the hope of some kind of fusion of biological and social theory: the increase in the differentiation of social organisms seemed somehow to continue the story of the increased differentiation of living beings in general. Thus nature could be envoked to ratify a social trend, and social developments would confirm the wisdom of nature. This consideration is no longer so influential. But the pervasive theme of increasing differentiation has been rediscovered and revived; in a new terminology, it plays as great a part in contemporary theories of 'social development' (in the new sense of a specific theory of industrial transformation), as it did in the more far-reaching, history-embracing sociological theory of the past century.

Apart from the encouragement it offers for the hope of a unified general philosophy, the plausibility of the idea is also sustained by other considerations. It receives support above all from a very visible and manifest contrast between the past and the present, between the poor and the rich, between the small and the large society (and here the argument is visibly connected with our general theme). Small societies are also poor societies and mostly unspecialized ones. (Leave aside for the moment the fact that some poor ones are also large.) Rich societies tend to be large and to practice a high degree of division of labour: in other words, to display great internal differentiation. Durkheim 'stole' this idea from the economists and showed that it had effects other than wealth: it pervaded the very texture of society, and profoundly modified the manner in which it had a hold over its members, its style of cohesion. There is indeed a great contrast between a clan society which is segmentary in Durkheim's sense, and a society such as ours. One of the striking and I think profound features of many clan societies is the distrust, contempt, fear, and ambivalence felt for the *specialist*. The moral norm is the unspecialized clan citizen: the specialist, whether technical, ritual, political or any other, stands above or below, but not within society. If he is below, he is openly despised, but if he stands above, he still inspires feelings of hostile ambivalence, even when his power does not threaten the ordinary clansmen. The extent to which specialization is indeed held to be *dishonourable* might well sadden any follower of Adam Smith: never mind whether it helps us to produce more, better and cheaper pins, the tribesmen seems to feel – specialization is nevertheless ignoble.

By contrast, more complex societies lose this revulsion against the specialist, and come to think of themselves as an assembly of

135

specialists. The resulting functionalist theory of social cohesion antedates Durkheim and can be found popping up in many places and times. For instance:

> There was a time, when all the body's members
> Rebelled against the belly; thus accused it: –
> that only like a gulf it did remain
> I' the midst o' the body, idle and inactive,
> Still cupboarding the viand, never bearing
> Like labour with the rest; where the other instruments
> Did see and hear, devise, instruct, walk, feel
> And, mutually participate, did minister
> Unto the appetite and affection common
> Of the whole body. The belly answered, –
> ... it tauntingly replied
> To the discontented members, the mutinous parts
> That envied his receipt; ...
> 'True it is, my incorporate friends,' quoth he,
> 'That I receive the general food at first,
> Which you do live upon; and fit it is,
> Because I am the store-house and the shop
> Of the whole body: but, if you do remember,
> I send it through the rivers of your blood,
> Even to the court, the heart, to the seat o' the brain;
> And, through the cranks and offices of man,
> The strongest nerves, and small inferior veins,
> From me receive that natural competency
> Whereby they live; ...
> ... 'Though all at once cannot
> See what I do deliver out to each,
> Yet I can make my audits up, that all
> From me do back receive the flour of all,
> and leave me but the bran.' What say you to 't?

(Shakespeare, Coriolanus)

The enormous increase in the division of labour and the pervasiveness of its social, political, and economic consequences is scarcely in doubt. If the attainment of coherence in sociological theory required us to abandon this doctrine – which, while it does not exactly have the status of the Second Law of Thermodynamics, comes as coherence would clearly have to be abandoned.

3. Standardization

And yet, the law or statement of trend which appears to stand in diametrical position to the first one seems virtually as well documented. In part, the plausibility of either generalization hinges on the selection of the kind of society we invoke by way of contrast to our own. In the former case, the obvious contrast is the segmentary tribe, with its clans all resembling each other and being differentiated numerically rather than qualitatively, (this being Durkheim's contribution to the notion of segmentation). The clans also resemble the larger tribe as a whole, of which they are a part, *and* also their sub-clans, in organization, so that similarity is preserved vertically as well as horizontally (this being, in essence, Evans-Pritchard's contribution to the notion of segmentation). If such a society is selected and juxtaposed with ours, there can be no doubt concerning what stands out as the salient difference: similarity amongst units and individuals in the one case, and differentiation in the other.

But we are not obliged to contrast modern society with the clans of segmentary tribes. We can also contrast it with something like traditional Hindu India, or the traditional Ottoman Empire and its millet organization. These two, more even than traditional Europe with its proliferation of guilds, corporations, estates and so forth, bring out quite a different contrast. When placed alongside social forms such as these, modern society seems and indisputably is atomized, drearily homogenous. Regional and group differentiations are ruthlessly eroded by a standardized style of life and of production. The theme is familiar not merely from the work of sociologists but equally from the countless and not unjustified cries of anguish of those who cannot bear to watch character, individuality, uniqueness disappearing from our world.

Here once again we possess a generalization which surely cannot be in serious doubt, and which nevertheless, as indicated, is in manifest conflict with the other equally convincing, observation. A simple but superficial solution would be to say that the actual curve of development is more complex than we had supposed: that the path from simpler tribal societies to complex civilizations, such as the Hindu or the Muslim ones, is one from smaller to greater differentiation, but that subsequently the direction of this particular tendency is reversed. This would fit in with, for instance, a similar thesis put forward concerning the general trend of human inequality. (Cf. Lenski 1966.) But it would be a superficial solution. What is involved is more complex than a mere reversal of the direction of the trend at a certain historic point.

The economic complexity, diversity, the richness of the division of labour in modern industrial society is greater than that of a caste or millet society, great though it is within those types. It would be sufficient to enumerate the number of separately produced components, each produced by persons who possess a distinct specialism, which go into some complex modern product such as, say, an aeroplane. Of course, against this evidence it could be argued that the *distance* separating the various kinds of technicians or their skills is not as great of that separating a different kind of craftsman in a traditional society. Here we are getting closer to the heart of the matter.

It is not merely the case that diversification has increased further (as by some criteria it has indisputably), but also that it is different in *kind*. This qualitative difference is crucial, yet it would be missed by an explanation which contented itself simply with noting a reversal in direction.

The central feature of a modern industrial society is that, in addition to a very elaborate division of labour, it is also one which changes rapidly and is hence doomed to occupational mobility. This distinguishes it from any traditional society, however complex its division of labour. It is diversified not only over space but over time: it is not merely that people do different things, but that the same people do different things at different times, or at least successive generations of the same family do different things. It is not merely that there are many diverse kinds of mobs, but that the same people or members of the same family do different jobs in succession. The jobs available themselves change.

Change characterizes not merely the process of industrialization, but remains a permanent feature of industrial society. Change subsequent to the industrialization may be less profound and fundamental, but it nevertheless remains fairly radical. In the future, *perhaps*, the time may come when an industrial society is also a stable one, and relinquishes further change. So far, there is little evidence of this happening. For a variety of reasons – ranging from the alleged economic mechanics of a market society, to the psychological expectation of continuous improvement and the raising of standards, or the political requirement of ever-increasing Danegeld in various directions, or international rivalry – industrial society has not been able or inclined to rest on what, for any other society, would have been indescribably comfortable and relaxing laurels. For this kind of society it has always been a bed of thorns. It must continue to change.

The consequences of the pervasiveness of this kind of division of labour over time as well as over space are enormous. Division of labour *plus* mobility, or division of labour over time as well as space, is quite different in its social implications from mere division of labour over space, accompanied by a good measure of stability· It requires that the personnel involved in this process be willing and able, in terms of skills, mental equipment, and general readiness, to change jobs and to change their productive social milieu.

This readiness has two aspects: it requires a readiness of individuals to change their job or craft specification in their own lifetime; it also requires the same to be feasible, and to constitute the reasonably normal expectation, over generations. This in turn implies that the main agency of professional training should be not the family but a specialized educational institution. This is of course one of the most conspicuous features of modern societies: they either possess universal elementary education, or they aspire to achieve this, with a seriousness far more convincing than that which characterizes their efforts in pursuit of other officially proclaimed aims.

The requirements of mobility over time are of course reinforced by another feature in any case connected with them, namely the high level of minimal educational and technical competence presupposed by modern productive efforts. Not only is it not feasible to hand over professional training to the family in view of the professional rigidity this would engender – it also is not feasible in as far as the level of technical competence required is higher than can effectively be inculcated by the family unit. The educational process itself grows, becomes complex, is diversified, and cannot be incorporated in the skills and competences of a father or a family group.

The basic shift of the process of education from the family to a specialized educational institution is one aspect of the situation: but it is not the whole of it. The educational system itself, though it possesses incomparably greater resources than the family ever possessed, has had to cope with the fact that the future professional allocation of the pupils passing through it is unpredictable and unstable, and cannot even be assumed to remain stable for any one individual. It must train them, but it cannot train them specifically. It can only give them a kind of generic training, leaving the specific job training to a much later stage.

We can now see the way contemporary society differs both from the undifferentiated 'segmentary' tribes and from the very highly differentiated complex societies such as those based on the institution of the caste or the millet. Modern societies possess a very homogenous educational system which provides a basically common generic training for the whole population, or for as much of it as possible, and on the basis of which a far more specialized and extraordinary diversified system of occupations is erected as a kind of second stage. It is an essential attribute of modern diversification, of this extraordinary division of labour, that it is a 'second storey', erected on that base of a shared basic education. This above all differentiates it from any past division of labour, however ramified, and it is this which enables it to cope with the division of labour over time as well as over space. A modern society in some measure resembles a modern army with its shared 'basic training' and its specialized jobs superimposed on it, and its hope that the basic training is sufficient to enable any one of the specialists to be re-schooled for another specialism without much loss of time.

Something further should be said about this universal generic training. One should not be too misled by its nominal content, or by the manifest rationale or question-begging self-characterizations of that content. Educational systems claim to prepare those who pass through them for the full life, to make them into good citizens, to develop their human potentialities, ad inf. These are pious phrases. In no field is there a greater gap between real and manifest function than in education – if only because educationists naturally have the gift of the gab. In terms of actual content specifications, the types of skills of literacy, general information and orientation, and numeracy, which are at the heart of the basic educational system, are indeed continuous with traditional educational institutions, or with some of them. Nevertheless, this continuity of content, and of accompanying justificatory verbiage, should not be allowed to establish the idea that there is any important continuity between the educational institutions of traditional and of modern society. This view is of course part of a favoured self-image of the educational system. There are many who like to present the modern system as an extension, to all men, of privileges and values previously reserved for some only.

Sociologically, this is largely an irrelevancy. The continuity is largely illusory. Even in traditional societies, at any rate in complex ones, the family did not monopolize the process of education. More complex skills and types of information had to be inculcated by schools, guilds, apprenticeships, and what-not. Good clerks, literate men to whose keeping the holy and secular writings of society could be entrusted, and who could perform such services as judges, administrators, or tutors, could seldom be produced by an unaided family tradition, and could generally only be produced by specialized educational centres. Nevertheless, these only produced one kind of specialist amongst others. This is where the important difference lies. Modern elementary education, which has no doubt inherited much of its curriculum and ideology from those specialized centres, fulfils a totally different role. Even if content overlaps, its use and significance is quite other: there is a world of difference between the use of certain skills to define a *special* social role, one among others, and on the other hand their use as an universal condition of citizenship. Elementary schooling now provides a kind of universal minimum, the necessary precondition for almost *any* job in the society, though perhaps not a sufficient one. It does not produce a privileged elite, but merely satisfies the minimal conditions for full citizenship. (The fact that it no longer produces a privileged elite or guild, while retaining many ideas, slogans, rationalizations, and trappings dating from the days when it did, may be the main factor explaining why it has such trouble maintaining discipline, and why it cannot control its students. They enter institutions which have the promise of privilege quite visibly inscribed over their portals; but once inside, they discover that this is merely a survival from the past. No wonder that some of them are furious and, having been deceived with a false promise of privilege, take it out on the institution in the name of egalitarian principle.)

Thus, in brief, the complex nature of modern technology and the high-powered training it presupposes, in conjunction with rapid mobility and the requirement of job-switches within one lifetime and between generations, ensure that modern society is *both* more homogeneous *and* more diversified than those which preceded it. It is more homogeneous in that it presupposes a shared universal basic training of a very serious nature; at the same time, on the basis of this shared foundation, a rapidly-changing superstructure is erected, which contains far more and more profoundly diversified elements than were found even in the more complex traditional societies. It is of course difficult to see how 'distance' between kinds of jobs or performances would be measured. In terms of a kind of manifest physical similarity, or even the type of principle involved, the distances between jobs in a modern industrial society are probably greater than those which exist in a traditional setting. At the same time, a kind of felt social and psychological distance is much less, simply in virtue of the importance, of the deep internalization of that basic training which *is* shared and presupposed by all the jobs.

Thus both the generalizations with which we started are in a sense true. Their harmonization is not a matter of some mechanical splitting of the difference, or of saying that a trend went in one direction up to a certain point, and was then reversed. It is a matter of a more subtle analysis, which highlights the way in which *each* of them is true, yet compatible with the other.

4. Loyalty to large units

It is possible, on the basis of these very simple but pregnant premises, to construct a theory of nationalism. Nationalism is notoriously one of the most powerful forces of the modern world, but oddly enough one which has received relatively little systematic treatment by sociologists. I have expounded this theory elsewhere (Gellner 1965), but shall restate it here with some comments on criticisms that have been levelled at it. (E.g. Kedourie 1970, Minogue 1967; see also Smith 1971.)

It is widely agreed that the extraordinary force of nationalism in the 19th century and since has contradicted many widespread expectations concerning human comportment – both high-minded ones, and others not so high-minded. It has contradicted high-minded expectations of universal brotherhood and love. It has equally contradicted much less high-minded expectations of universal rational self-interest and materialist self-seeking. Men have violated humanitarian ideals and rational self-interest alike in the cause of various nationalisms. The most popular theory which purports to explain it all runs as follows: the old Adam will out. The call of blood or group loyalty or territoriality, awakened who knows by what – modern disruption or perhaps the loss of a faith in God – overcome the flimsy barriers set up by fragile rationality or universal affection. Once these slender barriers are down, the powerful current of atavistic feeling carries all before it.

This picture is dramatic rather than illuminating. That men are vicious, violent, and irrational is not in doubt. They are also lazy, lethargic, slaves of custom, frightened, and fond of their pleasures. It is by no means clear why the first group of characteristics should suddenly begin to win so handsomely over the second set. Furthermore, the theory does not explain why those deep and turbulent passions should suddenly begin to exercise themselves on behalf of rather abstract and distant allegiances, encompassing large populations, and refrain from differentiating significantly within them. Men have in the past found it possible to assuage their need for loyalty, and their need for hate, by struggles between small and intimate communities: for very obvious reasons, such local and concrete allegiances and animosities can be much more satisfying emotionally than distant and abstract ones. What remains puzzling, on the theory which bases itself on the resurgence of atavistic feelings, is why curiously abstract loyalties should emerge just at the very time when they did, rather than at any other time, and why they should prevail over other, more customary forms of group feeling and antagonism. To explain this we must look at the social structures within which men act, rather than attempting to argue directly from some alleged inherent tendencies of the human heart.

The central features of a modern division of labour which we have selected are the following: maximum diversity over time as well as space, in other words *mobile* diversification. All this on the base of a *shared* common minimal culture, including reasonable measure of literacy and numeracy, which alone make possible the switches from occupation to occupation over the span of a single life or 'career'. The level of this shared minimum is such that it cannot be inculcated by a family unit, but only by an elaborate educational system.

Thus every man is a clerk. Max Weber stressed the significance of the way in which Protestiantism made every man his own priest; but the extension of clericly literate status to every man, inherent in the economic transformation under discussion, is perhaps even more significant.

What follows? Mobility tends to destroy – in as far as they are not already destroyed – the various intermediate kin and social units. They do not disappear altogether, but their importance in either production, or in the maintenance of social order – in other words, in the economy and in politics – becomes very small. Life becomes a matter of specialized, partial contacts and contrasts. Contract replaces status, partly because status is hard to maintain in very fluid contexts. An unspecialized, diffuse, multi-purpose relationship is then largely restricted to the nuclear family, which thereby acquires extraordinary importance and emotional significance. All this, of course, is only a simplified schema of the situation.

But with every man a mobile clerk, who gains his entrance to full social, economic, and political citizenship only through that minimal shared training, the really important boundary becomes the one which delimits the range within which this mobility is practicable. That range is the range of the language and/or the culture which happen to be the media of the educational system which formed the man in question. In the medium in which the educational system operates, the man can also function, and its limits are then in general the limits of his effectiveness and acceptability. His investment in the language, not of his mother as the mythology would have it, but of his *école maternelle* as the French put it, is enormous.

It is these culturally imposed limits of mobility which are decisive, and which thereby generate the limits of loyalty and the concepts in terms of which effective loyalty can be felt. Other kinds of units have no comparable hold over people. Even in societies such as

Japan, where men stay with the same industrial enterprise for a lifetime, they do not necessarily stay with it over generations. But a culture is, in principle, for keeps.

Nationalism is basically a movement which conceives the natural object of human loyalty to be a fairly large anonymous unit defined by shared language or culture. It is 'anonymous' in the sense that its members do not generally have positive links with each other, and that the sub-divisions within the nation are not of importance comparable with the larger unit. (This is quite different from many tribal social forms, where the clan may be just as important as a tribe, the sub-clan just as important as a clan, and so forth.)

Traditional societies, however diversified in the social roles they possess, when stable over time, tend to be tolerant of deep, permanent human and moral chasms between their members, or rather class of members. Above all, the sheer number, multiplicity of such chasms, prevents any one of them from standing out and polarizing the whole society. In a complex stratified society, the sheer number of status distinctions weakens the moral impact of any one of them. Colour, for instance, matters less when people use many other grades and ascriptions. But if it remains as the only one visible, shameless, ascriptive sign of rank. . . .

To us, nurtured on egalitarianism and in a social milieu which makes it plausible, the moral gap between two castes, or between master and slave, may seem deeply repugnant, humanly unintelligible. Perhaps there is indeed a slight *inherent* human revulsion for such social forms, insofar as at least those who are the losers in such relationships tend to rebel against them once constraints are removed. Be that as it may, the inherent revulsion does not appear to be strong enough to prevent very effective widespread acceptance of such moral chasms, in milieux in which they are sanctioned and hallowed by custom. People seem willing to accept and internalize any degree of inequality, however extreme, provided it is *stable*, complex, and habitual. The lack of symmetry and universalizability seems to be compensated by symmetry over time: however unequal we may be, if it was the same yesterday and the day before that, and will be the same tomorrow, it is acceptable. You may be discriminating against *me*, but you are not discriminating against me *at this moment*. Thus equality over time appears to make up for inequality over space. This is odd, but it is so.

It is here that the modern world destroys the balance and makes acceptance impossible. It destroys equality, symmetry, universalizability over time – in other words, stability. As if in compensation, homogeneity over space, and over the range of social roles, comes to be required. Anything which obstructs it – caste, estate,

144

and such – tends to be eroded. Fluid, loose classes, or classes that at least seem to be such, are tolerated instead.

The various past classifications, the moral chasms between classes of people, were accompanied by cultural differences, by differences in style of life and comportment. When the chasms themselves become unacceptable through widespread mobility, the accompanying cultural differences themselves tend to become blurred. Society once was like a box of children's plasticine: at first, each colour is neatly separate, but as children play with the different colours and tend to make them up, in the end it becomes an indistinct grey mass. There are still cultural differences, of course, within national communities, but they are gradual and nonextreme, and it is generally possible to 'pass'. It may of course take a generation or, as folklore has it, three. But that is not an intolerably long time to wait.

The trouble arises, however, where one of the old chasms is accompanied by differences which cannot easily be blurred: not all bits of plasticine will really mix with others. One example of this is of course cultural differences associated with differences in pigmentation. You can change the cultural differences but not pigmentation, and this prevents 'passing' and in turn pushes the cultural differences back into place and reinforces them. But genetic traits like these are not the only ones which can have this affect. Very deep and profound cultural differences, notably religious ones, can be virtually as irrevocable as physical ones.

It is at these boundaries that new nationalisms are born. A chasm accompanied by differences which, for one reason or another, cannot become blurred becomes a septic sore in a modern society. Mobility across it is not possible and the blurring cannot be achieved. People on either side of it come to have an investment in maintaining the boundary – and not only those who are located on the favourable side of it, whether it be favourable economically, politically, or in any other way. Of course, in any society the rich tend to fear and dislike the poor; what a horrid life-style they have! They smell, they do not wash, their children are nasty, and so forth. This is no disaster when the nature of the differences is such that there is no way of stopping individuals, even or especially large numbers of individuals, from crossing the boundary. You may not like them but you cannot do much about it. It is a mild source of embarrassment, that is all. But if you can stop them – or rather, if those who cross the boundary continue to be conspicuous as ex-members of the despised group – trouble is inevitable. Of course, in the traditional set-up, a few might also have crossed the chasms but, owing to occupational rigidity, there was no need for them to do so.

Under modern conditions, it is precisely the economically imposed mobility which makes rigidly ascribed status, frozen by deeply-ingrained cultural traits, unacceptable.

Thus the natural limit of the political unit, if not bedevilled by the chasms, is the limit of the validity of its educational certificates. But where their limits do no correspond to the deep chasms, the old inequalities that cannot be obscured, there is the basis for an irredentism, a nationalist movement on behalf of either a unit which does not exist yet, or at least on behalf of radical redrawing of existing boundaries.

This, in substance, is the theory linking the new style of division of labour with a new pattern of political units, units – large and co-extensive with cultural homogeneity, where the relevant shared culture is that of the modern-type primary school, not of the old folk culture. I believe this to be the key to the central phenomenon of modern times, nationalism.

5. Some objections

The previous argument merely attempted to state, in the simplest and schematic terms, the nature of the basic connection. This general schema took little notice of local variations in the way in which the pattern comes to impose itself. Though tied inherently – if the argument is correct – to the new type of division of labour, which is often referred to as 'industrialization', nationalism can either precede or follow industrialization in its more specific and narrow sense. Industrialization, in the sense of large-scale factory production, can be in full swing before the tension between culturally differential groups really asserts itself; or, especially in our century, the disruption caused by the tidal wave of industrialization *elsewhere* can by itself activate these processes. The details vary: the principle remains the same.

For instance, Kedourie argues (1970, p. 19) against the view 'that nationalism is a movement which develops in the poorer part of the empire in reaction to the wealth of the imperial rulers'. But the contention that this does sometimes happen, and is indeed highly characteristic, is not the essence of my theory, nor is it co-extensive with it. It is only what it implies for *some* kinds of circumstance, which are indeed common ones. It is true that whilst poverty in certain circumstances does breed discontent, just as in other no less important and numerous instances it breeds a passive and fatalist resignation. But the argument never claimed that poverty alone breeds discontent. Notoriously, it does not, as Kedourie rightly stresses. It is mobility which disrupts the acceptance of an inequality, and mobility *in conjunction* with even relative poverty does breed discontent, where much greater poverty in stable conditions does not. Kedourie goes on to point out, correctly, 'many well-known nationalist movement rose among populations which were not manifestly poorer than their rulers, whilst other nationalists movements appeared among preparations which were clearly more well to do than their rulers'. As he says, Poles, Italians and Czechs were not manifestly poorer than their Russian, Prussian, or Austrian masters. Greeks and Armenians were richer than their Ottoman Muslim overlords. This is indeed so. But poverty is not the only chasm which exists between people, and which in conjunction with cultural differences becomes intolerable under modern economic conditions. An economically privileged stratum may be politically under-privileged. This conjunction is indeed a very common pattern in many traditional states, which can tolerate economic enrichment only amongst segments of the population which are at the same time made politically powerless. Enrichment amongst those not debarred by religion or otherwise from political office would be dangerous and indeed disastrous for the powerholders. In stable conditions, communities of this kind continue to exist, relatively well off – the rulers tax the traders but cannot impoverish them in most cases – while at the same time politically under-privileged, and, with the resignation so characteristic of stable societies, these communities accept their lot. But under modern conditions, both their economic privilege and their political disfranchisement become intolerable, in one way or another, to occupants of both sides of the chasm. If the frontier is not marked by anything insuperable, mobility in both directions results, and the erstwhile deep difference is obscured. If, on the other hand, the old frontier is marked by irremovable markers, then *two* new nationalisms are born.

Kedourie invokes German and Japanese nationalism during the period between the two wars. Admittedly, neither of these countries had suffered from foreign occupation or colonization. This objection has a certain force, insofar as the theory probably cannot explain, on its own, why a relatively satisfied nationalism – that is to say, one already possessing a national state more or less corresponding to its aspirations – should become particularly violent and explosive in certain conditions. The theory merely explains why these units should become natural at a certain stage of social development, and why it is difficult to go against the principle by which they are delimited. Once a system of nation-states is established, and the states co-exist in hostile rivalry and with military sovereignty, fluctuations in the degree of accompanying violence and passion will no doubt occur, and the theory itself cannot explain these fluctuations. Having said this, one can point to the fact that the factors which led to the acuteness of these two nationalisms are not far to seek. In the case of the Germans, they included economic rivalry with a minority group which was economically and culturally prominent, and which had difficulty in obscuring the old chasm; and it also included recent loss of territory which by the normal nationalist criteria could plausibly be claimed. And in the case of both German and Japanese nationalism, there were the disadvantages of late-comers in an international competition in which – illogically, as it later turned out – prestige was still measured in terms of territorial empire. In the post-war world, the lack of correlation, or inverse relation, between size of territory on the one hand and wealth, power, influence and contentment on the other, became very manifest. Before the war, however, few people had the capacity to see this. This particular trait was indeed an atavism, dating back not perhaps to the sense of territory in the Stone Age, but at least to the prestige rankings in international politics established in the 19th century.

Kendourie also disputes the view that 'the need for economic growth . . . generates nationalism'. Here one could above all object to his conception of economic growth: 'If people have wants which they are eager to satisfy – and this surely is the mainspring of economic growth – it is only by applying their ingenuity, inventiveness, and capacity for labour to precise and specific tasks that they may hope, with luck, to satisfy these wants'. But in fact, economic growth in developing societies has nothing to do with 'wants which (people) are eager to satisfy'. This may seem paradoxical, but it is true. The need for economic growth in a developing country has few if any economic springs. It arises from a desire to assume full human status by taking part in an industrial civilization, participation in which alone enables a nation or an individual to compel others to treat it as an equal. Inability to take part in it makes a nation militarily powerless against its neighbours, administratively unable to control its own citizens, and culturally incapable of speaking the international language. Pre-industrial man is human, in the modern world, only in a latent sense, by courtesy. There is no point in beating about the bush: this is how things are.

Individual motives are neither here or there. The rulers generally want to be powerful and above all, to *remain* rulers, and some of their subjects no doubt would like to be rich. There is nothing unusual about all this. But the reason why 'development' has become a valid international ideal and yardstick of political performance is that it is conceived, rightly, as the gateway to the kind of life-style and organization which alone confers equality and full recognition in our world. This at least is almost universally agreed.

What then is the style of organization which is a pre-condition of full international citizenship? In essence, it contains precisely those traits which we singled out as a precondition of the style of loyalty known as nationalism. But it is not only the case that the development drive in the Third World aims at producing the very circumstances which will make nationalism easy (though indeed, rulers and educators in those countries constantly preach to their tribesmen about the need 'to become a nation'); it is also that the disruption which it had already produced causes a movement towards the crystallization of new cultural units, which will be acceptable by the new nationalist criteria. So nationalism and development, properly understood, are intimately linked after all.

Further on in his interesting work (page 132) Kedourie cites further instances against the theory. 'Large industrial enterprises have taken root and flourished in multi-lingual societies: in Bohemia and the United States in the 19th centuries; in Hong Kong, Israel, French Algeria, India, Ceylon, and Malaya in the 20th'. But Bohemia was in fact, notoriously, one of the fountains of nationalism, both for Germans as well as Czechs. The United States is notorious for the way in which its educational system has acted as an agency of transforming ethnic groups into a culturally homogeneous mass, until it failed in our time to do the same for the coloured groups, thereby once again producing a nationalism.

The same is true for Israel. The educational system was successful in moulding a relatively heterogenous immigrant into a homogenous nation, until the oriental Jews arrived en masse. Since then, it has not been entirely clear whether, with a greater effort, the educational system would repeat its initial success, or whether on the contrary a new nationalism would be born. Needless to say, the international situation has complicated matters by providing strong inducements for this new emergent Sephardi nationalism to remain moderate. To invoke Malaya, Ceylon, and above all French Algeria as instances against the emergence of nationalism is odd. India is indeed an interesting case. One can only suggest that the shared Hindu culture is more important than the diversity of languages, and that in certain cases 'language' (culture) is more important than language in the literal sense.

E. COLSON

A Redundancy of Actors

1. General discussion

Wilson (1971, pp. 7–8) defines a change in scale as 'a change in the number of people interacting and the closeness of their interaction'. She comments that it is arguable that the total amount of interaction increases, despite Durkheim's belief that this was so and that the increase led to a greater interdependence of those involved, but she is interested in a different question. Wilson is intent on tracing the way in which intense involvement with a few people is replaced by a more diffuse interaction with the many, rather than with whether or not the total amount of interaction increases. She appears to see the process as a continuous evolution towards a more complex society with a universal ethic and an acceptance of general responsibility.

Barth (1972) is also not concerned with whether or not the total amount of interaction increases, since he is concerned rather with changes in social organization associated with increase in scale and indeed argues that the changes are of a quantum nature. His identification of three empirical types of social order – associated with small, medium, and large-scale societies and differentiated by the number of statuses available in the individual *repertoires* and the community *inventory* as well as by the way the actors in different situations come by their *definition of the situation* which involves them – may or may not stand. His overall thesis that societies must either undergo a radical reordering or suffer major stress when they attempt to cope with larger aggregates of people appears to be in order. But it would be difficult to demonstrate how the reordering takes place from an examination of the coping mechanisms of any existent small-scale society faced with an increase in the numbers of its members attemping to carry on interaction with each other. Those available to us are in the process of being engulfed within complex organizations which seek to change both the local order and the local people by fiat and persuasion. The latter are exposed to an education which is meant to provide them with new ideas about society and a loyalty of larger units while at the same time it provides them with skills to serve that larger community. The wireless

150

and television also help to create the semblance of a larger society by providing a national set of characters, known to all, whom all can talk about and so have a common body of gossip when they meet.

Nevertheless, I am persuaded that Barth is right and am prepared to argue that the underlying process on which the re-ordering is based is one of exclusion which holds constant the intensity of inter-action with others who are seen as rounded characters capable of engaging sympathies and making demands which must be met. Although I recognize that the ability to tolerate contact with others is variable as between individuals and for the same individual over the course of a lifetime, the ability still appears to be limited. Few of us are able to sustain long-continued interaction, more or less within the same time-span, with more than a limited cast of characters. The development of the social order is a process whereby the majority of those we encounter are relegated to bit-parts or to membership in the crowd, while principal characters are so distri-buted about the stage that we need face only a portion of them at any one time.

Wilson and Barth assume a process of reaching out towards others which results in incorporation of the many now available within one's social world. I am arguing rather that people seek to maintain a fundamental status quo of involvement in the face of increasing demands upon their attention which threaten to extinguish their ability to interact in any fashion with sheer exhaustion. Initiators and principal movers in the process are those whom I shall call 'stars', for I assume that individuals vary in their ability to attract others even under conditions of social and economic equality, and that it is these favored individuals who are most threatened by an increase in scale. Moreno and Lundberg long since demonstrated the existence of 'stars' who attracted others in even most informal settings. They also demonstrated that those most often chosen by others as preferred for interaction were themselves likely to name only a very few with whom indeed they would associate. John Barnes made the same point when he argued that, even in 'tribal society', 'originators of action must be selective: they cannot mobilize the whole society every time anything needs to be done'. (Barnes 1968: 127).

The prime conditions which permit an increase in scale are those associated with an increase in population and/or an increase in the ease of communication. Either condition threatens some members of a social unit who thereby become vulnerable to increasing demands upon their interest, time, emotions, and ability to respond, as well as upon the material resources they control. So far anthropologists have concentrated on examining how people use their opportunities

151

to choose associates to maximize their access to goods, services, and followers. Much less attention has been given to choices which in effect limit interaction and contract the social sphere to a limited number of persons who have access to the favorite.

Yet we all know that the contraction occurs and something of the costs to us if it does not. Witness the jokes about social climbers who shed their old associates as they concentrate on building relationships which offer them greater advantages – in social comedy, at least, we also have a fair description of the devices used against the climbers to limit their access to the social circles to which they aspire. Witness also the way in which academics come to minimize their contacts with colleagues in their own universities as they become active in the world of national and international conferences and committees. The same inelasticity in the supply of 'social interest' lies behind the formation of cliques within academic departments as these increase in size, and so behind the resulting redefinition of disciplines which permits members to appeal to intellectual differences to legitimize their separation. It also explains something of the weariness of faculty faced with many students competing for attention and support.

This inelasticity has nothing to do with the number of roles available or with any conflict in roles. Most of the actors may be playing the same role, as students against faculty, but each enactor of the role has his own demand for attention, and it is this which makes the situation untenable. Faced with a redundancy of actors the tendency is to withdraw from the scene. Even small-scale societies with minimal organizations may show signs that their members regard most of their fellows as redundant, save as members of the crowd, with a concomitant limitation of interaction to only a small proportion of those theoretically available.

For the past sixteen years, Thayer Scudder and I have been involved in a long-term study of the Gwembe Tonga of Zambia. In repeated visits we have kept track of the same villages and the same people who were part of our original sample established in 1956–57 (Colson 1960 and 1971; Scudder 1962). This particular study began in 1956, but I had first visited Gwembe in 1949 before a road was built to connect the middle portion of the Gwembe Valley with the rest of the country. At that time Gwembe District was extremely isolated; on their home ground, its people carried on a social life of marked self-sufficiency. Although by 1956 they were being brought very rapidly into contact with the rest of Zambia and had become subject to a great deal of governmental interference, people still thought of themselves as largely independent in managing their own local affairs. Each newcomer, whether by birth or immigration, was placed within the social system by being assigned a clan. This in turn defined which roles he or she might play in relation to specific other members of the society. Along the Zambezi River, people lived in large neighborhoods which ranged in size from about 150 persons to just over a thousand. They were proud of the size of their neighborhoods and enjoyed the stir of activity and bustle of humanity, which they compared to the life of the Central African towns.

In one neighborhood of approximately 800 people, a division had taken place into two separate localities by 1956. The larger one had a concentrated population of about 600 people. Adults and even adolescents knew each adult member of the locality by name and could probably sort such members by clan, as parents and children, as spouses, and by sibling groups. On one occasion I checked with two informants and found they either knew or could give an informed guess as to the whereabouts on that day and at that hour of every other member of the locality. All this, plus the movement of people across the village area from homestead to homestead, gave the impression that the whole 600 were bound together by a high rate of interaction in which all were involved.

Closer inspection of the evidence suggests that in fact they restricted intensive interaction to a small fraction of those available to them, and handled contacts with the rest as though they were members of the crowd or by a superficial courtesy which permitted them to meet and pass on without further involvement. Such courtesy required recognition of an encounter rather than assignment of persons to roles or their treatment as complete persons.

Although the locality looked to be a continuous stream of buildings, these were organized into homesteads whose boundaries were clear to residents even though they might be invisible to the outsider. Homestead populations varied from one to fifteen adults, including young men and women just ready for marriage, and the very old who were completely dependent on others. One homestead shown in our records as having 26 adults had either already divided or was just at the point of division. In the daily round, people depended on other members of the homestead. For additional labor, they recruited work parties, whose membership rarely extended beyond fifteen workers although it might be much smaller. The corporate kinship groups, which pressed the claims of their members, were matrilineal lineages. Their effective membership again was very limited. It was unusual to see more than ten to twelve lineage mates assembled for any occasion. With respect to the lineage, people were aware of their inability to incorporate a large number of kinsmen into a close-knit group prepared to act together, for they said explicitly that if they became many they separated into different lineages, while if numbers shrank those who had acted as different lineages came to act together and saw themselves as one. Even with respect to the dead whose shades might intervene in human affairs, the same policy of limitation of numbers was in effect. From eight to fifteen shades seemed sufficient for the purposes of any living individual, and the rest were relegated to the forgotten dead who could be summoned only as a crowd behind those invoked by name.

The limitation on the number of people who interacted with each other also affected the pool of potential spouses. Most marriages were endogamous to the neighborhood and indeed to the locality. By 1956, they were also arranged by the couple imvolved. Young people of the locality frequently met in the large dances which sometimes absorbed all members of the locality. Gwembe Tonga of the Zambezi Plain, unlike Plateau Tonga, have no system of preferential marriages. Choice of partner ought therefore to have shown something like a random distribution, and at first inspection this seemed to be the case. Only an intensive knowledge of the community has enabled us to discover that men very rarely choose a wife unless some earlier link has brought them together on frequent occasions within the same homesteads. The actual marriage pool for each individual therefore again shows a restriction on free choice which dismisses most of those physically present but defined as outside the range of action. Even 600 people, though they can be known by name, compose too large a world for all to be given principal roles or even to be considered as potential enactors of these roles by all their fellows.

The situation within this particular locality is much the same as that in each of the other neighborhoods in our sample. For that matter, it is not unlike the situation in Welsh villages of the 1930s, as described by Rees and re-analyzed by Peters (1972: 127–132).

The success of Gwembe people in limiting their interactions is pointed up by our own difficulties as field workers returning again and again to the same villages. Because we are seen as people with wealth and influence, we are 'stars'. People choose to remember any claim once established against us. Each visit adds to our fields of interaction as strangers move into the villages we follow and more children grow up to replace the few old who die. We cannot afford to antagonize anyone and must cope with being a focus for many claims upon our attention-span, time, and resources. Satiation quickly sets in and we lose our ability to attend to the expectation of response. After a few days of intense interaction, we find outselves becoming less and less tolerant in encounters with others. In fact,

154

we suffer from 'people shock', although this fact was masked by our belief that as city people we were accustomed to encountering many more people in our daily lives than we do in Gwembe. We ignored the fact that customarily we react to people in crowds or on the basis of short-term impersonal contacts which require a minimum of effort and involve no storage of the details of the encounter in our memories for future recall. Such contacts are therefore less exhausting and more tolerable than our contacts in Gwembe which carry with them past and future as well as the present moment. We have had little experience of prolonged involvement with more than a few people in a non-field situation and have learned to respond to most of those we meet as objects rather than as individuals. 'People shock' is probably more exhausting than 'culture shock', about which anthropologists have written so much, and may be a major component in that phenomenon. Even when anthropologists do not return to old friends, as we do in our long-term study, they are faced with the necessity to try to imagine complete persons when they encounter people with a different culture. They are not provided with a set of minimal roles or statuses with which to consign the majority of those they encounter to oblivion as part of the crowd – indeed, they have no rules which allow them legitimately to prefer one over another of those who present themselves.

Our earlier explanation of the weariness associated with the return to Gwembe was in terms of the effort required to re-learn those we had forgotten. We assumed local people easily tolerated the same high rate of interaction they forced upon us. A better explanation seems to lie in the implications of social scale and the realization that we suffer from an overload of interaction because we behave in a fashion which the Gwembe people themselves cannot tolerate and avoid.

They must encounter one another frequently as they cross and recross the same space, but they minimize the thought and effort that must be invested in the majority of their encounters. Although everyone has the potential to fill the majority of the limited number of roles defined by Gwembe society, only a few are likely to be chosen as actors by those casting the various occasions which bring people together. Organizers recruit only the necessary number for carrying out the various tasks they set themselves. People are most likely to encounter a large number of others in the crowd phenomenon of the dance or on the occasion of a funeral. But on these occasions, most of those present can be defined as mutually together in space rather than as mutually interacting. In so far as interaction does take place, it is through the medium of the formal greetings which do not require those greeted to be assigned to any role or force upon the initiator some choice which involves him as a person.

Perhaps the most effective analogy for understanding the situation comes from the computer, and its memory banks. Gwembe Tonga store a large amount of information about the roles available to them in an immediate memory bank which also holds information about the pool of persons upon whom they expect to draw regularly for particular tasks. Information about the others in their social world is stored in a remote memory bank where it does not impinge upon daily thought or activity. If for some reason someone must be found from outside the regular pool of actors, access is had to the remote memory bank from which an appropriate actor is withdrawn. The search procedure is based upon a storage of the surplus actors in terms of a dominant category which provides the most information about the roles for which they may be cast. This appears to be the clan category.

Such a system ensures that everyone in the social world is still defined as an actor who meets the requirements of the roles available.

Increasing population tasks even the remote memory bank and at some point no doubt a society such as that of Gwembe must develop further forms of social differentiation. As Barth points out, one solution is that of *replication*, which creates a number of quite separate social units with different pools of actors but calls for no increase in overall complexity of organization. Where geographical conditions are favorable and the newly separated units can move apart, this appears to be the favored solution. People prefer to separate and keep their social universes small, rather than to invent new social categories which define most of those they meet as having no potential for the social roles they require or which allow them to interact with others only through intermediaries.

We do not know at what point a large build-up of population bursts the organizational forms based on the premise that all those present are actors in good standing with appropriate roles to play. We do have some idea of the mechanisms by which members of such societies maintain their organizational charts. Barnes (1951) first discussed the importance of the process of 'structural amnesia' for the maintenance of social stability in an expanding segmentary order whose members kept no written records to hold the past captive. Gulliver (1955) demonstrated how the assumption that 'structural amnesia' was operative allowed him to explain the maintenance of a fiction of close kinship ties within Jie residence groups. Clearly the process allows for the elimination of structurally unimportant persons and events from the social field, while at the same time permitting people to continue to justify their choice of close associates in structural terms. I argue that it has an equally vital role of allowing people to slough off their responsibilities to living persons who have become excess actors and a drain upon their social resources. It is associated with the shift of persons who have been in the immediate cast to the remote memory bank, and with the shift of those who have been in the remote memory bank into oblivion.

The speed with which both living and recently dead can be dismissed from memory in a society such as that of Gwembe is striking. Because Scudder and I have been following the same people since 1956, we have had a unique opportunity to check our records against the memory of informants. During this period they have been subject to both an increasing population and an increasing ease of communication, but I shall ignore these facts for the moment and concentrate rather on the way they cope with those who become excess actors. People frequently comment on our ability to remember people and events they claim to have forgotten. By jogging memories, we usually can get them to recall the fact of such persons' existence, but they claim that they cannot be expected to remember those who have passed outside their social orbit. They remember immediate kin even though these be long-lost labor migrants. They forget the dead unless these are immediate ascendants or descendants (and I have had people tell me they do not remember the name of mother or father or anything about that kinsman) or unless the dead are frequently cited by diviners as the cause for particular illnesses. I am also certain that they sometimes invent ancestral shades as explanatory devices, using their knowledge that people once existed whom they have forgotten. The speed with which they dismiss those whom they define as no longer socially relevent is in striking contrast to their detailed knowledge of the current affairs of their immediate neighbors in whose activities they are interested.

The long-range study has also made it possible for us to observe how quickly people re-order their priorities with respect to those whom they still regard as socially relevant. But this may best be discussed in the context of growing population and increasing involvement in the large-scale world with which they are now integrated. During the course of our study, they have also been shifted in space, to make way for one of Africa's large man-made lakes. The shift destroyed old social units and created new ones.

We have no reason to think that birth-rates are significantly higher at the present time than in the immediate past, but both mortality and emigration have declined in the last forty years. The much diminished surface of the district, which has lost much of its arable soils to the lake, discourages recourse to the old device of village and neighborhood fission. We have yet to compute the growth of the villages we are following, but the overall impression of a massive population build-up, especially in the Lusitu Resettlement Area, cannot be an illusion. The increasing population has some outlet in labor migration or a move to the towns of Zambia where some now seek to settle. The spread of education and the large-scale national organization provide some opportunities for which Gwembe people compete along with other Zambians. Some of the increased number of potential actors are therefore absorbed into the large-scale national order and removed from the local stage. Unfortunately they are not as easily dismissed from the social world of those they leave behind, for if they are successful their kin use the increasingly available transportation system to pursue them to the towns. Part of the interest of rural people is thereby withdrawn from their immediate neighbors and invested in town dwellers. This diminishes their ability to cope with those left on the local stage.

Most people appear to cope with the impact of increasing population and the possibility of interacting with their fellows over a greater distance by a recourse to the old devices. They maximize their ability to forget past close associations when these are no longer profitable. Those who have little to offer and no potential to become 'stars' are least endangered by the increasing pool of actors, but they attempt to manage their own affairs so as to keep alive links with 'stars'. The latter are most active in initiating the extinction of linkages – they fail to attend a funeral or refuse to provide assistance for marriage or other occasions, or they refuse to share marriage payments and other dues with those who cannot reciprocate. They emphasize their separation from their fellows by building homesteads visibly distinct from the rest of the locality. They withdraw support from those they sheltered as dependents in their homesteads and discourage their continued residence to make way for the presence of a new following. They may make the excuse of quarrels, but alliances can alter quickly even though no overt quarrels occur and the only ostensible reason for a withdrawal appears to be the desire of a man to keep the number of people with immediate access to him within a reasonable limit. There is some reason to believe that homestead sizes are also diminishing as opportunities for interaction with others outside the homestead become more significant, but our data here are not yet analyzed.

Resettlement also forced people to reconsider their priorities for the recuitment of actors. In 1956 when preparing for resettlement, they were making special efforts to offset the extinction of lineage and other kinship links which they expected to result from their dispersal into different resettlement areas. After resettlement they found the physical difficulties of maintaining contact much less than they had expected as roads, auto transport, better postal services, increasing literacy, and more frequent encounters in town made it possible to keep in touch. They appear to have chosen to re-define their social fields to maintain close linkages with former associates if these live at a considerable distance in areas which offer to them some particular advantage.

Those who once formed a single very large vicinage in Chipepo Chieftaincy have been resettled in two locales, Lusitu and Old Chipepo, separated by a hundred miles along the most direct route followed by those who go by foot but many more for those who must travel by bus and train. Those moved to Lusitu have prospered because of their access to better soils, better transportation, proximity to markets, and a greater interest by Government in their advancement. This has also meant that they have available to them a larger amount of local wage work. On the other hand they have been settled among people of a different tradition with whom they have had some difficulty setting up formal links of the kind they themselves use to create claims on others, since the Sigongo residents of Lusitu refuse to accept classification according to the Gwembe Tonga clan system. The hills of Old Chipepo, adjacent to their old homes, in which the majority of their fellows were resettled, provide a less favored environment, although occasionally the area may have more local wage work available, or if weather conditions are right it may have a better crop than Lusitu. It also has the great advantage of proximity to regions on the plateau where Gwembe Tonga have old established claims for hospitality in times of hunger. People move back and forth from Lusitu to Old Chipepo on visits and in search of work. Even fourteen years after the move they are still attempting to re-enforce their links with old associates through the cult of the shades. Each person who dies has an inheritor appointed for his or her shade; kin are still summoned from Old Chipepo to Lusitu or from Lusitu to Old Chipepo to become inheritors and thereby given the obligation to remember both members of the lineage and the descendants of lineage males.

The determination to keep both Lusitu and Old Chipepo actors members of the same casting pool contrasts with the willingness of people in either area to shift their attention from old associates immediately present to allow them to begin more intensive interaction with those newly brought into their immediate vicinity. Within four years of resettlement in the hills, one group of brothers had re-defined some of their old associates as 'clansmen only' whom

159

they did not summon, while the roles these had once played as 'lineage mates' had been re-assigned to new associates who were said to be 'out true lineage'. The recasting gave them access to dominant roles in nearby hill neighborhoods. Given the presence of both sets of actors in their immediate vicinity, a choice has been forced upon them since they could not interact with all on a day-to-day basis. Continued maintenance of ties to actors in Lusitu and Old Chipepo tests the tolerance for interaction less obviously, since distance does in fact ensure that the person who interacts with both does so at different times and in different places.

A few new roles have appeared, and even perhaps several new social categories, but this is a result of the intervention of the large-scale national organization rather than due to local initiative. The local social order continues to be one of marked egalitarianism. 'Stars' have yet to create intermediating roles to shield them from potential clients. The go-between, the *ityombo*, can be used to negotiate delicate matters,[5] but the *ityombo* is chosen for the occasion and is not a lieutenant or aide who fends off clients and organizes them for his leader. Even at times of negotiation, the primary parties are usually present to face each other although the discussion passes through intermediaries. Important spirit mediums do appear to have aides who are expected to stand between them and their publics, just as the mediums stand between the spirits and the people, but even their aides appear as such only during the course of a consultation. On all other occasions the medium must operate like any ordinary individual in terms of direct one-to-one contacts. The man, or woman, who wants to exert influence must be immediately available to those over whom he hopes to exert sway and cannot protect himself through a hierarchy of aides.

No doubt this failure to achieve any major reordering of local society is due to a reliance upon the large-scale national order to handle various problems arising from the increase in population and the new ease of communication. For one thing, those who find the local order unsatisfactory and lacking in opportunity can shift to the larger community of the towns. They then seek to continue to interact with their kin and old associates only on their own terms, which is usually during an occasional visit on holiday. Those who remain physically within the area seek to withdraw a little in space and build apart: they withdraw from village activities and spend their time rather with those who share their ambitions and links to the larger world.

The second solution points the way into the future and makes it possible to predict how Tonga society will change as its members continue to cope with the implications of growing demand on limited social resources. Already those present in the same local space are learning to segregate themselves in terms of training and interests which make them no longer interchangeable units in the social world. There is a segregation into separate pools of actors. So far this is on an informal basis, with no concomitant development of formal structural explanations for the segregation, although eventually such explanations should emerge as people seek legitimate explanations for why they do not participate in the same interests. Local men of influence still depend upon an immediate following, which limits their appeal to only a small portion of the local community. If they are to extend their influence to encompass the great majority of those present within their local sphere, as did their predecessors, they will have to develop a system of intermediaries who can serve as channels of communication and buffers between them and the mass of their followers.

A differentiation in terms of social categories or classes and in terms of a set of ranked offices will then have taken place. The net result should be an increased capacity of those who are in close proximity to minimize actual contacts and live in different social spaces. The way will then be clear for them to treat the majority of their fellows as objects rather than as demanding personalities.

My argument throughout this paper is that social differentiation is a process which permits people to minimize their contacts with their fellows and to exclude the majority of those they encounter from access to the stage upon which they act. It is this process of exclusion which enables people to continue to cope as the number of those they must meet increases while their stock of social interest remains constant. The dynamics of the process of exclusion arises from the pressure of competing others rather than from a conflict in roles, although role conflict has its own influence on the social process.

Much of modern technology has been aimed at increasing the speed of communication and thereby making all places and persons equally accessible. But as geographical limitations on interaction decrease, social restrictions increase. Persons of high visibility become unreachable by the many who would seek them out and are more isolated in their world of limited contacts than the Gwembe Tonga in their neighborhoods. Private telephone listings, batteries of secretaries and aides, locked doors, and shielding walls re-enforce the definition of roles as isolated from the larger world. The ordinary person may not need to go to the same ends as 'stars' in maintaining their isolation from their fellows, but they too are forced to make choices among those who shall be recognized as having right of entry to their personal spheres. Only these are recognized as rounded persons with a claim upon sympathies and a right to a full measure of time.

We are forced to make such choices because we are unable to tolerate the strain of interacting with large numbers of others whom we must see as persons with likes, dislikes, and the right to define our encounters with them in terms which bear upon our vision of ourselves.

An increase in population creates a larger and larger number of superfluous actors. Eventually new roles must be created for them to fill, but the new roles solve the problem of an overcrowded world only if they relegate the majority of those encountered to walk-on parts or membership in the crowd or to another stage entirely. Scale therefore implies organization and an ordering of relationships.

My thanks are due to Dr. Thayer Scudder for reading and commenting on the first draft of this paper and for discussing with me the ideas which helped to reformulate the argument in the final draft. He has suggested that a further coping method used by Gwembe people to minimize conflicting claims lies in their insistence on maintaining accustomed routines while ignoring strange events which provide them with new opportunities. While I was writing this paper we watched the response to the invasion of one of the villages by a large number of doctors and medical students. Despite their concern for their own health, people showed very little interest in the presence of the doctors and continued to behave as though they were not accessible. To our knowledge, none of the doctors was given a name or identified as a person, with the exception of one who worked at a nearby hospital already patronized by villagers. People seemed to assume that because they knew us they could reach the doctors if they wished to do so and that their link with us was sufficient. Field research in 1972 was supported by Grant GS-3295 from the National Science Foundation. Earlier work in 1956–57 and 1962–63 was supported primarily by the Rhodes–Livingstone Institute, now the Institute for African Studies in the University of Zambia, which also assisted us on later visits. In 1965 I had a grant from the Joint Committee on Africa of the Social Science Research Council and the American Council of Learned Societies.

FREDRIK BARTH

Scale and Network in Urban Western Society

1. General discussion

Our own Western, cosmopolitan society inevitably stands for us as the epitomy of large-scale society. Consequently, we tend unthinkingly to construct whatever typology of scale we employ from our image of the outstanding special characteristics of urban Western society, investing the opposed small-scale pole with a series of opposite characteristics. It is therefore especially important for an analytic clarification of the variable of scale both that we make explicit those stereotypes and features which constitute our image of Western society, and that we confront this image with systematic and balanced data from our own social environment which can falsify it, to sharpen, diversify, and correct our description of the actual social organization of this case of a, no doubt large-scale, society. In the following I shall present a brief argument on theory, method, and fact, and introduce a miniscule body of data with which to confront my argument.

What image of society does the term 'large-scale' evoke in us? In this context of implicit contrast with small-scale, I think most of us fall back on that syndrome of traits so vividly depicted in classical urban sociology (cf. Wirth 1938), perhaps with a dash of Orwell's *1984* added. We see a city where persons are anonymous, alienated, and fractionated; where social networks are open-meshed; where relations are instrumental, single-stranded, impermanent. To this we add the autocracy and impersonality of bureaucratic administration, the uniformity of mass communication and persuasion, and our own individual powerlessness in the face of centralized political and economic corporations and organized collectivities. To persist as it does, this image doubtless depicts something we experience as real and true. But as an empirical description of social organization it suffers from a weakness which it shares with other macro-oriented characterizations: its degree of completeness and area of relevance are unspecified. Complex society is indeed so complex and diverse that it offers the possibility to construct a great diversity of different representations, each of them capable of some degree of documentation but none of them

163

adequate as a model of the system as a whole. Thus, we are in danger of having our preconceptions merely confirmed, rather than disconfirming and modifying them. Concretely, I submit that in accepting this image of our society we have allowed ourselves to be mesmerized by certain visible physical features of mass society; and that we wrongly isolate, exaggerate, and blame them for a plethora of social ills, while ignoring essential realities of large-scale society with which we are, subjectively, equally familiar. What we need is a discovery procedure whereby we can record the essential, combined characteristics of the society in which we participate.

The strength of social anthropology, as practiced in societies exotic to the fieldworker, has been its focus on the *human* scale, its attention to the balance of customs, activities, or decisions which together constitute the life situation of real, whole people in their society. We can achieve the same in our portrayal of modern complex society only if we retain the same concreteness in recording the aggregate system as it unfolds itself in the real life of whole persons.

2. Methodological problems

A description of social organization must represent a record of the actual relations connecting persons in a society. The difficulties in providing such a record for a complex, large-scale society are mainly twofold: (1) Vast numbers of relationships are involved. Between a mere 100 persons there are potentially 9900 dyadic relations (Barnes 1972) – how then can we handle mass society? (2) Great diversity in the kinds of relations and kinds of groupings characterize complex society. The interplay of these, in persons and events, is staggeringly complex – but may be essential to the course of actions, and their consequences. We need to base our descriptions on the micro-level of network specifics. But network studies of complex societies, aimed at representing features of the system as a whole and not just its component parts, have foundered precisely on these difficulties. The amount of material on a real-life network that *might* be important, even to the most gross generalizations of structure and process in complex society, is unmanageable. It must consequently be self-defeating to seek *first* to map an empirical sector or network, and *then* to extract or distill from such data, by computer or otherwise, a pattern or form from which generalizations of structure and process can be deduced. A drastically different methodology is needed; and a generative type model may provide the required simplifications. If we can start with an idea of the processes at work whereby social networks are built and maintained, then we can deduce something about the form or pattern of network that would result from these particular processes. In that case, our model gives us clear criteria for what, in the myriad of potential data, is relevant to our procedure: (a) We shall need systematic observations of the empirical processes stipulated in our model so as to falsify, correct, or supplement those stipulations; and (b) we shall need sufficient empirical data on aggregate networks to falsify or confirm our predictions as to their form. Both these kinds of data are feasible to obtain. What we need is a fertile representation of how social networks are built and maintained to induce into our model.

Let us begin introspectively, by stepwise approximation. If we observe ourselves in our pursuit of the whole daily round of our activities, we certainly need to distinguish sociologically between the mere presence of others, and our having any kind of interaction with others. Most people participating in the major events of mass society do not concern us at all: or rather, they affect us as does weather, or day and night, as ecologic premises for our activities. Our interactions we might group as follows: (i) Social encounters where information and prestations are exchanged (face-to-face, or by other forms of communication such as telephone or letters). (ii) Greetings and other passing acknowledgements that indicate the potentiality of social encounters to take place. (iii) Physical adaptation to the presence and purposes of others in the public environment: avoiding bumping into each other in corridors or on pavements, letting cars pass, etc. (iv) Indirect or oblique relations: having mail delivered, having the office building serviced by a janitor, activating the bank by writing a cheque to the grocer, voting for a candidate.

I submit that it is by concentrating our attention on (iii) and (iv), and confounding them with the bureaucratic, single-stranded character of some of our type (i) encounters, that our stereotype of urban life is constructed. In reality, our social activities are comprised of a full measure of all four kinds of interaction, and we need to understand *their* place in our own, large-scale society.

Nor should we prejudge the issue by saying that small-scale, private, or personal worlds persist also in large-scale societies. Surely all our interactions are part of our society; many of the type (i) encounters have, on closer inspection, the qualities of long distance, macro-relevance, and impersonality, while many type (iv) ones may involve quite small-scale subsets of people. Our problem is to conceptualize all of them in such a way as to capture their diversity, yet make them amenable to coherent and connected representation.

The mode of conceptualization most suited for this would seem to be that of *networks*. All interactions or encounters may be represented as taking place within relationships, and the whole network os such relationships comprises the stuff of society. Since relationshipf obtain both between persons and corporate groups, this should enable us to depict a broad spectrum of features of social organiza-tion. It also allows us to focus as well on the whole system as on the individual actors. Social relations form networks, and not just chains or paths, precisely because each person and group consti-tutes a meeting-point, or knot, of many relations. Thus each actor may be regarded as the centre of a 'first-order star' (Barnes ibid.) of relationships. The complexity of the whole network within which a number of such stars mesh is great; but the image allows us at least provisionally to speak of whole societies in these terms. My purpose in this essay is to find a way to represent the characteristics of the network-building activities of social persons in our society, in such a way as to allow us to analyze the consequences of such activities for the over-all network form in Western society.

How then might we imagine that social networks come about in our society? Network analysis is concerned with choice in social action (Barnes ibid); what are the choices in our daily lives that have network consequences? Quite simply, those which are in our hands and directly concern the *building* of links are (i) whether to acknowledge another person as a social alter, (ii) whether to widen one's relation with an alter from a single-stranded to a multi-stranded relationship; and (iii) whether to facilitate an alter's con-tacts with a third person. The *dismantling* of network links, on the other hand (which presumably must be distinguished from the latency of such links), is the result of (iv) explicit rejection of, or gross and irreparable failure to give transactional satisfaction to, alter. Which options a person chooses, as between a number of alters and the alternatives (i)–(iv), will be fundamentally con-strained by his 'interactional capacities'. By this I mean those socially recognized competances which he can be seen to possess or can signal that he possesses, and which can articulate with matching competances in others to provide a basis for predictable and success-ful interaction in a social relationship. Some such competances are readily conceptualized as statuses; others are more diffuse resources of knowledge and skills, interests, ambitions, and inclinations. Interaction, and the relationship it embodies, may be based on any such standardized element which members of a society can recog-nize as present or absent in a person: encumbency in a formal office, sex, membership in a political party, reasonable competence in playing bridge. The presence or absence of any one of these makes a person a potential choice, or not, for a particular kind of activity or encounter.

We can conceptualize every social person as composed of a finite *repertoire* of such interactional competances: and how these are delimited and constructed, and how they are combined in different persons, will severely constrain the patterns that can emerge in social networks. In other words, to understand the processes and constraints in network building, we are led to investigate these features of the construction of social persons (cf. Barth 1972).

Concretely, however, these processes must be observed in *encounters*, which also exhibit certain cultural constraints in their form. The focus of encounters may be described as 'tasks'. [This term is used merely as a convenient label for all the various kinds of ends, recognized in a culture, towards which activities are directed as far as the actor himself is concerned. It thus subsumes a wide range of ends, as various as 'having fun' and 'doing a job'.] It is the performance of such tasks which brings persons together in instituted relationships. Potential alters are also offered up by the proximity fortuitously imposed on persons involved in disparate tasks; but relationships arise between such persons only from an agreement on some joint end or 'task'. Clearly, each person's recognized capacity to participate in tasks is ordered by his statuses and other competences, or may at least be described as being organized with reference to statuses in the sense of being imposed or allowed in terms of them. Systematic features of the network-building activities of a person should thus arise from the particulars of his, and the field of potential alters', repertoires of statuses and other competences.

2.1. *Some features of person and network*

With our large personal repertoires in Western society we have a large number of conventionally defined and delimited tasks in which we may separately engage; and for most of these we need, or we become involved with, partners to elaborate sequences of encounters. There are of course suitable and unsuitable partners for different tasks, most simply differentiated in terms of the presence or absence of the required reciprocal statuses for that task in their repertoire. It is surely a persistent experience from our life in Western society that for most joint tasks there are many candidates, some more and some less desirable, between which to choose. Our 'choices in social action' are thus concerned both with choice of task and choice of alter, and our 'first order star' reflects both kinds of choices. The particular choices we make in each particular case may be fateful to us as individuals; yet, though their consequences may be retrospectively explained in terms of sociological facts, I see no way of *predicting* them from such facts. But I do argue that the aggregate form of our social organization should be predictable from such facts: that both our range of choice in action (i.e. tasks), and the field of possible alters for each kind of interaction, are highly patterned in every society, and that this pattern reflects constraints laid down in the structure of social persons, viz: their repertoires. Let us try to pursue this further in the circumstances of our own milieu.

Note in this connection another feature of our complex Western society. Although there seem always to be multiple potential alters to each of the statuses in our repertoire, these statuses differ drastically in the range and density of options they provide. Some statuses are so specific, and the tasks they organize so esoteric, that suitable alters may be very few and far between. A scholar of Ugric languages wishing to discuss his latest paper on the structure of conditional clauses cannot go next door: like the lonely whales of Antarctica searching for a mate, he must seek a suitable partner for his task widely through the seas of society. Other statuses, like marriageable male and female, abound in potential alters to the extent that next door usually proves adequate, despite an ideology that greatly emphasizes the idiosyncratic and unique.

In the structure of the person in Western society – his large repertoire of diverse and variously specialized and generalized statuses – we may have isolated a feature with extensive implications for the structure of networks in this society. It should follow that each person's first-order star of relationships will tend to be very large, and to contain strands of highly unequal length, in terms of the physical and social distance to alter. But in disagreement with those who emphasize the stark impersonality of our modern world, I would further argue that this same structure of the person also provides the base for a proliferation of *multiplex* relations – such as indeed constitute a significant fraction of every person's first-order star. This is most simply visualized developmentally: Most partners with which our tasks bring us into contact in single-stranded relations also have additional, alternative statuses with which we might articulate. In other words, in the next instance they present themselves as potential alters among whom to choose partners also for some *other* tasks. For a great number of our purposes we do not use random methods, or classified directories, to locate suitable alters; on the contrary, we turn precisely to those persons about whom we already have information incidentally obtained in other connections, i.e. those we 'know', to provide us with a range of potential candidates. As a result, we will progressively turn a number of our single-stranded relations into increasingly multiplex relations – an option which presents itself precisely because of the large and diverse status repertoires of most persons. Some very important kinds of relations, such as 'friendships', can presumably *only* be built this way. But we also see the same tendency in a multitude of relations in our own life history and that of others: how a fleeting chance to date the receptionist in a public office is seized, and leads to intimacy and marriage and an extensive enmeshment in new networks, how acquaintances between neighbours in rented summer cottages mature into business partnerships, how unpremeditated attendance at a public meeting can blossom into deep involvement in a religious or political movement; how 'connections' are utilized throughout life to arrange for favourable purchases; how the single-stranded rivalry between two office associates can organize two factions in extensive multiplex relationships.

I am not arguing that such proliferation to multiplexity is a straight-forward thing, always easy for the person to achieve; nor am I denying the loneliness which many persons – probably all of us at times – may feel, which springs from a pervasive failure thus to diversify interaction in a sufficient number of relationships. Perhaps we have a need to invest, not only a certain absolute number, but a reasonable *fraction* of our sum of social relations with this multiplex quality; and perhaps some of our frustrations with mass society arise from the impossibility of achieving this proportional balance. Be this as it may, I argue that such diversification does in fact take place, and is a fundamental feature of contemporary Western social life. Its implications for further network construction are particularly great, because it is once this widening of a relationship starts that alter also starts effectively facilitating our contacts with third persons, and vice versa. Some such ramifying effect is no doubt a normal feature of certain single-stranded relations: you will expect a stamp-collector with whom you exchange stamps to introduce you to other stamp collectors. But you do not expect a plumber who mends your pipes to introduce you to other plumbers, or others of his clientele – that is, not until you expand your relationship to him in terms of a joint interest in pedigreed cats or sports fishing, or common origin or place of birth. Thus it is mainly if a person, by developing a *multi-stranded* relationship to you, starts putting a major part of his social resources at your disposal that he will have a truly significant effect on your relationships to others.

2.2. *Problems of documentation*

If this is how it happens, then we should be able to demonstrate it. My argument so far has invited us to consider four major aspects of the social organization of our society: (1) The construction of social persons: what are their repertoires of statuses or interactional competances? (2) The person's first-order star of relationships: what is its size, range, and the qualitative characteristics (single- or multi-strandedness) of its constituent relationships? (3) The development stories of these relationships: how did they arise, how have they changed, how long do they endure? (4) Finally, the structure of the network as a whole: how do different people's stars differ from each other, and how do they mesh into an over-all pattern? If we can operationalize these questions so it becomes possible to collect relatively precise and inter-subjective data on at least some of them, even within modest sectors of society, we should be able to test the main hypotheses I have suggested about the processes of network formation, and the consequent basic features of social organization, in our large-scale Western society.

The difficulties are many and obvious. A key part of the model lies in the vision of man the network builder: of persons with a characteristic structure of interactional competances which propell them to pursue certain activities and seek particular kinds of alters, thus extending their 'first-order star' in highly patterned ways. How can this structure of the social person best be conceptualized, and how recorded? Though we have a vocabulary in our society for various components of the social person, these components seem to exhibit too wide a range with respect to organizational clarity and specificity, as well as many other relevant features. Some of them we can clearly identify as statuses, of which a person is either an encumbent or he is not, and which involve undeniable rights and duties in interaction. Others are so general, like e.g. sex, that they no doubt affect a person's style in practically all his activity but hardly can be described as rights or duties in any connection. Other bundles of knowledge and propensities – e.g. an enthusiasm for the Italian Renaissance – may suddenly turn out to be quite decisive to the forging of a new relationship and have considerable network consequences for a person, and yet one hardly knows how to designate such an 'interactional competance'. Nonetheless, it is surely very characteristic of complex Western society, and has profound implications for the patterns of interaction in that society, that its members have a great range and diversity of such compe-tances, or recognizable interests and interactional propensities, in their repertoires. Again, 'propensity' is too narrow a term for what we are seeking. Some modes of interaction are codified as duties of high priority and predictability but perhaps low enthusiasm, like a private soldier's responses to his sergeant; others have the character of a diffuse inclination, latently awaiting the fortunate occasion to assert itself. Some modes of response spring from the person's inability to protect himself, as against the advances of an enthusiastic neighbour and his community project; others represent a deep-seated ambition and drive, which propel the person to invest much time and great effort, and lead him to cast the strands of his 'first-order star' in ever new directions, thereby perhaps innovating in the very shape of the over-all network.

There is also a question of skills in a more concrete sense, as a capacity or prerequisite for interacting. Proficiency in foreign languages is an acutely experienced requirement for many kinds of interaction, if you happen to be a member of a native language community as small as e.g. the Norwegian. An increasing flow of sociological literature, largely inspired by the pioneering work of Johansson (1970) has also documented other kinds of prerequisities for 'participation' in various sectors of complex society – even welfare services, specifically designed for the socially weak, are not readily extended to persons incapable of putting their case clearly and rationally in a bureaucratic interview, writing a letter or filling out a form correctly.

In view of this range of components in each person's repertoire, it seems hopeless to attempt to record complete repertoires from informants. A radically different approach is called for. If we observe the person in action, in depth over a period of time, we should be able from the encounters in which he is involved and the definitions of situations that he participates in sustaining, to record those components of interactional capacity activated in that period of time. This may perhaps serve us as a discovery procedure, so we may learn what the significant units are in the construction of the social person.

A similar procedure is indicated for the recording of networks. Rather than depending on the informant to enumerate his relationships, we may seek to record the relationships as they are called upon through the course of normal activities; thereby we may discover their place in the life of the person, their relative frequency of activation, and the balance between them. Qualitative and developmental features of each relationship, on the other hand, can then be elicited at leisure, and to some extent checked against the character of the encounters in which they were activated.

A special problem is the recording of linking persons, where a relationship is in fact sustained by virtue of relations to a third person, or where such a person has been decisive in initiating the relationship. In the case of affines this is straight-forward; where friends introduce you to their friends again it is less clear, since in a sense they have only the marginal role of providing the parties with an option to a relationship, not a commitment. And what about the people you meet because someone in authority has hired you for a job, or appointed you to a committee?

A fourth problem in mapping first-order stars is the time factor. What is the difference between latency and decay of a relationship, and how can latent relationships be discovered by the investigating anthropologist? I have friends with whom I have not communicated for years, yet I consider them to be very close and true friends still; and we have been taught that kinship can never disappear. There are clearly great cultural, as well as personal, differences here – I have sensed a contrast between on the one hand an African opportunism about strangers who quickly become friends, and friends who are equally quickly forgotten, and on the other hand the irrevocable character of friendship according to Middle Eastern values, and even practice. Anything like an exhaustive record, even of a person's crucial relationship, is probably unattainable. This being so, what indices of turn-over, or other statistical measures, might be developed?

Finally, a major process in the formation of networks – that of accumulating information on others – has largely been ignored in this discussion and seems unrecordable in practice. Quite clearly, persons prepare themselves for possible encounters by accumulating such information; and their choices and interactions when occasion arises are significantly affected by what information they have. Any superficial scrutiny of the messages that pass during an encounter will indicate how prominently information about third persons figures in these messages. Nor is the information at all solely about mutual acquaintances – persons known only to one, or to neither party, are also conspicuously favoured topics of conversation. The amount and intimacy of such information that circulates seems sometimes so staggering that I am tempted to deny any degree of anonymity, even in the largest urban aggregations! More seriously, the difficulties of ascertaining its presence or absence, and handling its volume, are so great as to be technically entirely unmanageable. So I am forced to ignore the patterning of circulation and accumulation of information, regardless of the importance it may have.

3. Some data on two network extracts

To try out some of these thoughts, and the practical possibility of recording different kinds of relevant data, I did a small exercise in 1972 on the recording of an egocentric, first-order star. Subsequently, the same year, I asked a graduate student to replicate my procedure and provide comparable data on his own network star.

172

The material was collected by careful autobiographical recording over a 14-day period. Cards were compulsively written for every alter to an encounter, including the receipt or writing of letters, but not the reading of reports, articles, etc. A cumulative record of encounters with each person was noted on his card. I carried a tiny notebook to assist me when away from my desk and cards. In due course I accumulated a box of filing cards. Each contained on the top line: name of alter, and the date, and kind of relationship in which I first met him (as far as I could recollect). For each encounter in the 14-day period I noted down one line specifying: date, mode of interaction (face-to-face, telephone, letter); place of encounter, number of others present; type of situation (seminar, coffee-break, party, friendly chat on a corner, shopping, etc.); and whether the encounter was initiated by me, by alter, or was essentially caused by circumstances we had not controlled. At the end of the 14-day period of recording, I composed a small biography of our relationship at the bottom of the card, again from memory: how first contacted (through whom, if known), and the course of development of the relationship, especially the additional statuses or interests progressively made relevant to our interaction, and the major common experiences we shared.

Such a record should be replicable from any literate, highly co-operative informant. I am still somewhat unsure of what it shows, or could be made to show. Let me first make some reservations and note some difficulties that arose.

Firstly, this 14-day period covered a very a-typical condition of life – third month in a sabbatical in which I was making every effort to avoid as many encounters as possible. From other points of view it was a critical period. However, I suspect that *any* 14-day period will be felt by the informant to be a-typical in some respect or other, so perhaps this can be ignored.

Secondly, I had unforeseen difficulties in defining or distinguishing encounters. Greetings were not counted; paying bus-fare without any verbal exchange was not counted; making a purchase involving choice and verbal exchange *was* counted. As I was on sabbatical, the issue of which *persons* I 'encountered' in a faculty meeting or large committee meeting did not arise – but how to count a coffee-break with 10 persons present where I engaged in direct conversation with 3 or 4, heard snippets of conversation between others, and was myself in part listened to by some of the others? I tried to be strict, counting only clearly consummated person-to-person interactions. This raises two questions: (1) Is it possible to agree on criteria here that are stable and comparable between informants in different life-situations? (2) Does this restriction of the record eliminate fields of social activity which are in fact large and important? It certainly eliminates all those fields of indirect interdependence referred to above as 'oblique interactions' – i.e. unilateral or mutual services without direct communication. To understand the workings of our society, and the circumstances of our individual lives, these are of course essential. But in a record of social interactions they do not figure, and to the issue of pattern and quality of our social relations they would seem relevant only as background 'ecology'. As far as I can judge, the record did in fact embrace what *I* had of social activity; but I am prepared to discover the procedure to distort the picture of some other life-situations.

Thirdly, I had difficulties classifying relations in terms of the distinction single-stranded/multiplex. These concepts seem to depend on a simplistic conceptualization of persons and statuses. I thought if two persons related to each other in terms of one status only, the relation was single-stranded; if in terms of two or more statuses each, it was multiplex. Kinship largely relates persons in terms of one status only, yet the relationship is presumably multiplex in terms of its consummated interactional content. More problematic in the present case, the imprecise status of 'friend' or the element of 'friendship' in a relationship proved difficult to pinpoint. My relationship to a number of students was a case in point. Clearly, the professor–student relationship is in its minimal definition a single-stranded relationship. Yet it allows or invites a diversity of possible encounters and definitions of situation: lectures, seminars, coffee-chats, private conversations, confidential counselling on even quite personal topics, tendencies by the teacher to take on role aspects of colleague, father, guru, friend. At what point can we say that a single-stranded teacher–student relation has become a multiplex teacher/student–colleague–friend relationship; how can we tell this from the concrete encounters that take place; what degree of agreement in the diagnosis will there be between the two parties? The intuitive character of the discriminations I tried to make between single-stranded and multiplex relations reflects a fundamental lack of clarity and precision in my concepts of 'strandedness' and status in general.

Given these sources of imprecision, what were the findings? During these 14 days of sabbatical seclusion I interacted in this genuine social sense with 109 different persons. Of these encounters, 59 were face-to-face (and a few over the telephone); with the other 50 persons distributed over 15 countries I sent or received one or several letters. With 60 persons I interacted only once, with 12 I had more than 10 encounters in 14 days. Perhaps most striking: while I had known 29 of them only one year or less (15 of them I had contact with for the first, and perhaps in some cases, the last, time), 39 were acquaintances of 1–5 years' standing, and no less than 41 – i.e. more than a third of those with whom I had any kind of social encounter – I had known for more than 5 years.

The other person for whom I have data gives a picture similar in some respects, drastically different in others. He interacted with somewhat more persons, the large majority of them face-to-face, all resident inside Norway; and there were far more single encounters and fewer persons with whom he had many repeated interactions in the 14-day period. The proportionate distribution between single-stranded and multiplex relations, on the other hand, comes out about the same in the two extracts.

Below are some tables summarizing the data with respect to duration of relationships, strandedness, frequency of encounters, and medium of interaction.

Ego – Alex

No. of encounters with each person:

	Ego	Alex
1	60	124
2	14	24
3	8	8
4–5–6	7	12
7–8–9	8	5
10+	12	2

	Duration of relationship	0	½–1	1–4	5+	Sum
Ego	Single-stranded	15	13	24	10	62
	Multi-stranded	0	1	15	31	47
45 yrs	Total	15	14	39	41	109
Alex	Single-stranded	63	15	24*	0	102
	Multi-stranded	0	20	48	5	73
28 yrs	Total	63	35	72	5	175

*Affines	1–2 yrs	0/15
Others	1–2 yrs	15/11
	2–3–4 yrs	9/22

What kinds of statements about network form and process can we make from such data? Some things seem to stand out immediately, others can be extracted or deduced.

1) *Stability* in the network is much higher than I expected. Doubtless it is even higher in small-scale societies, and there are differences between the two extracts and no doubt a greater range of differences between persons in Western society, both in terms of different walks of life and different national patterns. Nonetheless, a high proportion of our interactions in large-scale, complex society seem to take place in enduring social relations; an urban style of life does *not* entail any preponderance of fleeting and short-lived relations. This comes out also in the data from the network of the younger of the two informants, recently and unstably resident in a new encironment.

2) *Multiplexity* emerges as a characteristic of a considerable fraction (more than 40 %) of all relationships; in terms of interaction frequencies, most interactions in the course of the 14-day period were between persons in multiplex relations. The probability of multiplexity is greater, the longer a relationship has lasted: while single- to multi-stranded stands at 28:21 in the first $\frac{1}{2}$–1 year, it is 10:36 in relations of more than 5 years' duration. Three obvious hypotheses might explain this: (i) Multi-stranded relations are more easily established in younger phases of life, so they preponderate in relations dating from earlier phases. (ii) Single-stranded relations are less stable, and so do not accumulate over time as do multiplex relations. (iii) Single-stranded relations tend in time to be enlarged to involve further aspects of ego and alter, i.e. become multiplex. All three hypotheses seem plausible, and may be true. The contrast between the $\frac{1}{2}$–1 and 1–4 year columns of the 45-yrs and 28-yrs informants supports hypothesis (i); hypothesis (ii) sounds highly plausible though no particular aspect of the present data can be called on to substantiate it; hypothesis (iii) is supported in the biographies: of the 47 persons in my 14-day sample with whom I felt I had a multiplex relationship, all but 5 cognatic kin started in a single-stranded relationship to me which only slowly developed its present multiplexity.

3) *Density* in the network cannot be read from one egocentric extract alone; but without knowledge of density we can say little to characterize network form. The task of following up all the 109 or 175 persons in one of these extracts, and cross-checking their knowledge of each other, would be formidable. However, the cards already include information which, interpreted by a participant, gives some indication of density: I refer to the notes on *locality* of the encounter, and the *social situation* in which it took place. In my own case, of the 54 persons with whom I had face-to-face encounters, 43 had at least one encounter at the institute in the university; but some of these persons (9) were *only* involved in consultations or

conversations in my office. The other 34 participated in social situations characterized by collective interaction, indicating mutual acquaintance. As a participant, I can confirm that between them (and also most of the 9 who only visited my office) there is in fact comprehensive interconnection, i.e. maximal density.

The additional criterion of interaction frequency in my network extract also gives a clue to another aspect of the network, in that it singles out a group of 7 staff and students with significantly higher frequencies of encounters. This correctly reflects their participation in an inner core of higher intimacy and more comprehensive multiplexity.

Network connections mediated by writing are more difficult to describe on the basis of an ego-centric extract. Of the 50 persons included in this sample, I had single-stranded relations with 37, multiplex with 13. A typology of who they were gives some indications of density, in four characteristic spheres. (i) Family and family friends certainly know each other. (ii) English-speaking anthropologists above 40 years of age make up a small world of high density. (iii) Scandinavian anthropologists and anthropology students have relatively high mutual visibility. (iv) Finally, Norwegian 'public' persons in arts, sciences, and mass communication are largely known to each other. This takes care of 44 of my 50 correspondents, of whom I can venture the confident guess that we articulate with many mutual acquaintances in at least one of these four spheres.

The other personal extract shows similar, but not quite as marked, features of sectorial density. Face-to-face encounters took place with persons from apparently five clusters of higher or very high density, but this still left some loose ends of persons without known relations to others.

In the two 14-day periods on which the two informants respectively report (separated by c. 6 weeks) both informants had their daily work in the same institute. Yet if I go through my graduate student's card file, I find I am acquainted with only 46 of the 175 persons he lists – most of them located in the one dense cluster of persons directly associated with the institute.

In other words, the picture that emerges quite consistently in this material is one of participation by the person in a certain number of internally quite dense clusters, between which the person himself, and in some cases a scatter of others, can be described as 'bridging' persons.

4) *Involvement and dismantling*. While the graduate student informant seems to participate more marginally and in a greater number of such dense clusters than I did in my period of recording,

he also reports on a problem possibly related to this which was not noticed subjectively by me: pressures to identity more fully (i.e. full-time) in mutually exclusive cliques, and the need to withdraw consciously from involvements and dismantle parts of one's network. My own innocence of this may in part have arisen because the process was overlaid for me by the more 'impersonal' effort of protecting my free time by referring to my sabbatical condition. But I also suspect that we see in this a reflection of life cycle differences, representing rough stages through which the person tends to pass.

5) *Information* which circulated during these 14 days of encounters remains elusive. But within the dense network clusters here uncovered we would expect high levels of information, and high speed of circulation. Observing my own participation, I also noted the frequency with which I engaged in passing information obtained in *one* of the dense clusters in which I participated, to the members of *another* of those clusters. This was true between all the clusters named, but most apparent in the recurring way in which I funnelled information obtained through correspondence with English-speaking and Scandinavian anthropologists into the institute network. If not a genuine basis for power in that network, such information-passing certainly seemed to provide recurring opportunities for exhibiting a leadership position.

6) *Size* of a person's total network extract can never be properly ascertained in this way. Over a truly long period of recording, the frequency of activation of previously unrecorded relations will surely decrease, but never reach zero. Obviously, different clusters or arenas have characteristic and different rates of turn-over: almost any 12-hour period is sufficient to activate all household relations; 14 days was enough largely to cover the cluster of persons associated with a small teaching institute; while I imagine several years would be required for a fair sampling of my anthropological colleague network.

On the other hand, if the 15 new persons encountered during the period of recording indicate the rate of accretion that can be expected to my first-order star, this would give an accumulated total of c. 15,000 persons by my age, if there were no loss or decay. Considering the detail of census-type material which can be elicited from mature members of towns of 15,000 inhabitants, I feel there is nothing improbable about this figure for a network extract; but even the order of magnitude remains a pure guess.

7) *Development* is also apparent in these data. My own network extract bears an overwhelmingly clear stamp of my life career. The places I have studied, the groups and cliques I have associated with,

the minor interests I have pursued – all have had effects retained in network concentrations – i.e. they seem decisively to have affected the structure of the network, not just the particulars of its personnel. A comparison of the two network extracts obtained, on the other hand, suggests features of phase development. Comparative material is needed to differentiate the 'life cycle' patterns from the less standardized idiosyncratic developments that arise from the cumulative consequences in a person's network extract of other, less ubiquitous, factors than age and life stages.

I have a few afterthoughts about this particular material which it might be useful to formulate. On the one hand, a variety of additional data could easily be included in the same basic procedures, but I don't know to what purpose. Conversely, items were included for which I found no subsequent use (*who* initiated interaction) or very limited use (no. of persons present; the detailed course of development of each particular relationship.) In these respects, the procedure could be made both simpler and more incisive. On the other hand, the question of rhythm or cycle in the different types of network clusters should be given more attention: to extract such rhythms from the data and in turn let them guide the collection of data – both so as to cut out redundant collecting, and to give criteria (with reference to variations in the 'ecologic year' of seasons, vacations, etc.) for the timing of data collecting. Perhaps the most important finding was my own surprise at the results: what a poor informant I would have been if an investigating anthropologist had asked me to generalize about my own network – because I simply did not know, and imagined some incorrect things.

4. Generalizations

The type of data exemplified here seem to give a glimpse into aspects of social organization poorly covered indeed in normal anthropological descriptions. I imagine that such data from housewives, wage-earners, businessmen, and local politicians; persons of different sex, different class membership, different subcultures, etc. would show extremely different patterns, revealing the existence of dramatically different subjective 'worlds' and life-situations. If so, can these data also provide insight into basic social processes? I believe so: a systematization of such data should clarify to us various important aspects of the construction of social persons in a society, so we can look at these aspects of the person and say something about the kind of society of which he is a member. It is both a question of identifying the precipitate of a certain overall social organization *in* persons, and identifying the causes of this social organization – not the final causes, but a level of efficient (and hopefully illuminating) causes – in structures laid down in persons which *propell* them to generate this society between themselves.

 With respect to the social organization of large-scale Western society, I suggest that during the preceeding discussion we have identified some features from which we can construct a rough model.

 1) Persons in Western society are characterized by large personal repertoires: both in the crude sense that they combine a wide range of distinct, separable statuses, and in the more subtle sense that they command a great variety of recognizable 'interactional capacities': distinct and identifiable bundles of skills, interests, and knowledge, each of which can provide the sufficient basis for organized inter-action in a distinct relationship.

 A consequence of this structure of persons is a capacity and propensity for each person to form a large first-order star. While there is usually no structural embargo on a person's involving him-self with a great number of different alters in the same kind of relationship – e.g. having a thousand (classificatory) brothers – the probability of, and interest in, many relationships is increased where a person seeks many different *kinds* of interaction with alters. Thus, large size in the repertoire of persons will be a factor favouring large scale in society.

 2) Diversity between the repertoires of different persons increases the complexity of networks and the minimal requirements of scale. The more diversity between repertoires, the more persons will *not* be possible alters for certain kinds of interaction. In that case, a comprehensive multiplexity cannot be achieved in the relationship to an alter: others must be sought for the consummation of those parts of one's repertoire which do not match up with particular alters. This results in a considerable increase in the complexity of networks: a particular ego can have broadly multiplex relations with certain alters whose repertoires are constituted roughly com-patibly to his own; but (a) most persons are not candidates to this kind of relationship because they are not sufficiently compatible in their repertoires, and (b) some interactions can be consummated only outside of this select circle of compatibles, since complete fit (? a 'total' relationship?) cannot be expected with any particular alter. The aggregate network which this generates, given an in-clination in people to realize multiplexity in relations, would be one of numerous relatively dense clusters of relationships, connected by a scatter of bridging persons. Looking at my own network, I have remarked both how this seems to be the empirical picture, and how my different interests and activities during my life have produced

identifiable sediments of network concentration, i.e. the reflection in my extract of existing dense network clusters. If each of these my activity fields is identified in terms of the tasks or purposes for which I participated – as they generally can – then clearly the values which define tasks, purposes, or goals can be given conceptual primacy, and we may claim that my network position reflects a multitude of choices made with reference to these values. It should follow that the greater the diversity of values, accepted goals, and differentiated tasks, the greater will be the differences in the network positions of different members of society.

In other words, the diversity which provides the premise for this factor of complexity may be formulated either in terms of values or personal repertoires. The organizational implications will be the same in either case.

3) Western society is characterized by a uniquely rich development of specialized statuses, capacities, or interests in persons, fitting the encumbent to interaction with very particular kinds of alters. These features of the structure of persons have direct implications for the scale of the society which is generated: the greater the specificity of such specializations, the wider in social and geographical space will particular network contacts be sought, and the greater will be the scale of the aggregate system. I am referring for example to the kind of esoteric interest, and the matching kind of specialization and excellence, which once as a graduate student sent me looking for a social anthropologist who could teach me primitive economics; this led me to Raymond Firth, and London, and much of what has happened to me since. The consequences of this one, decisive initiative are laid down in many hundreds, probably several thousands, of network strands; the precipitate of the opportunities and demands which that move produced have in turn propelled me to other initiatives with further unfolding results. Without claiming any world-shaking consequences for my action, I would have no difficulty documenting by enumeration that quite a handful of the uncounted multitude of network strands that tie together disparate parts of global Western society have indeed been spun as a direct consequence of what in 1951 existed only as an unrealized potentiality for specialized interaction: a rare competance in a rare speciality in a few persons in the world, and a rare eagerness in myself to be allowed to consummate certain kinds of interaction with one of them in a single-stranded relationship over these interests, propelling me to cast that first, 'long' strand in a sector of my developing network star.

In precisely this way, I would argue, we can see the scale of any society as the aggregate consequence of the networks the different members of that society spin in their pursuit of culturally codified ends. Increased scale results equally from the labour migrant seeking a job in Zambian copper mines, a South Indian father seeking a satisfactory son-in-law, or a revivalist preacher seeking souls to save. But the codifications of ends, and the means available to achieve them, differ greatly between different societies; and so gross differences in the resultant scale will obtain between them.

4) Most relations in Western society are first established with some particular, limited end in mind – in contrast to many other societies where relations arise from ascription or propinquity, and have a multiplex character from their very inception. But we have observed that people still establish multiplex relations and create dense networks in urban Western life. The main difference between small-scale and large-scale is not in the presence or absence, but in the different location and linking, of these dense areas. In urban Western society, they are focussed on certain kinds of arena, most easily identified when named as institutions: a university department, a club, a profession, a family. I suggest that large-scale depends not at all on the reduction of the number of multiplex relationships and their fragmentation on many distinct alters, but to the contrary on the participation of each person in *many* multiplex relations, distributed in a number of distinct dense network areas. The greater the variation between persons in how these relations are distributed (arising from factors 1–3 above), the greater the scale of the aggregate society they generate. As for multiplexity, there is much to indicate that the most distinctly multiplex of relationships, viz. friendship, is positively associated with large scale. Perhaps the pleasures of friendship arise largely from the experience of progressively discovering and exploring the diversity of potential articulations between two large and compatible repertoires of interactional capacities.

These features of the structure of the person in large-scale society can perhaps best be highlighted by contrast to the smallest-scale society I know: that of the Baktaman of New Guinea (Barth 1975). The Baktaman form a community of 183 persons; between them there is maximal network density. Until four years before my fieldwork, warfare had severely restricted social contacts outside this community; but adult men were propelled by a desire to establish ceremonial trade relations to seek partners in adjoining communities for such trade. The total social world of the Baktaman thus consists of 6–8 such local communities, with a population of roughly 1000. A few persons (through change of residence due to rarely practiced exogamy, or other special circumstances) are members of two communities and thus form bridges between two dense network clusters;

all other members of a cluster have essentially identical network stars, with the occasional addition of 1–5 single-stranded gift exchange partnerships. Only a few dyads of men could be described as friendships, connecting brothers or age-mates within the community; most persons are never involved in a relationship of this quality. Thus, in the structure of the person among the Baktaman we see the absence of precisely those forms of complexity which I have argued generates large scale: we see a minimum of interests and specializations that could propel the person to forge new network ties; and we see a simple aggregate pattern of cellular communities loosely connected by ceremonial trade partnerships. The contrast to the life-situation described in the preceeding pages is as staggering on the level of the construction of the person as it is on the aggregate level of social form; and it is as poorly depicted by the nostalgic construct of a community based on the cozy multiplexity of small-scale relations as by the obverse construction of the anomic single-strandedness of large scale.

If indeed large-scale society is characterized by the features of integration, multiplexity, and density emphasized here, then where do the insecurities and ills of modern Western urban life arise? I think in features not so directly entailed in scale. New Guinea material should serve to remind us of the dangers and insecurity people can experience in small-scale societies; and rich historical materials on slavery and other forms of tyranny document the ruthlessness of exploitation possible within certain kinds of multiplex relationships.

Perhaps many of the ills of modern life are connected rather with our situation as the subjects of bureaucratic regimes. Though we are instructed to regard bureaucracies both as legitimate and benign in their intent, their existence means that we must live constantly in the shadow of entirely unequal assailants, with the disorienting experience of total impotence which that implies. Some of those single-stranded – and even some multiplex – relations in my 14-day sample involved me with agents of bureaucratic organizations so massively stronger than me, and so dehumanized, as to be insensitive to any suggestion of compromise. The Baktaman of New Guinea may have lived in constant fear of ambush; but in the company of 3 or 4 others they stood a chance of defending themselves. For us, there is no defence against the ambush of a bureaucratic letter or telephone call, playing havoc with our interests. No doubt also bureaucracy is somehow connected with scale: but in a more indirect way than often assumed, and at least in a way that needs to be distinguished for analysis and not confounded with other features and qualities of modern life.

DAVID JACOBSON

Scale and Social Control

1. Internal and external controls

Society has been described as a 'nexus of relations', the boundaries of which may be represented by interactional discontinuities (Wilson 1945, Barth 1972). The organization of these relations has been described as social structure or as a social network (Wilson 1945, Mitchell 1969). Order in both structure and network has been related to the ability to exert pressure on or control over those groups and individuals who participate in them (Wilson 1945, Mitchell 1969). Scale may be defined as those factors which influence the application of social pressure or the working of social control. This paper analyzes the means by which people maintain social control, and therefore social order, particularly when confronted by changes in scale.

This conception of scale and its relationship to social control are incorporated in both anthropological and sociological analyses. It is apparent in the Wilsons' *The Analysis of Social Change* (1945), an early and notable study of the relationship between scale and social organization. The Wilsons argue that 'Social structure is the application of *social pressure*' (1945: 49, emphasis in original); that social order derives from a system of social control; and that as scale increases, the ability to exert social pressure decreases. This argument is based on the assumption that control is effective only within small, local groups characterized by frequent interaction and multiplex relationships. Scale, as the Wilsons use the term, is a composite of both demographic and sociological criteria: specifically, scale is measured by the 'number of people in relation and the intensity of those relations' (1945: 25). Intensity, in turn, is measured by the differential frequency and complexity of interaction inside and outside a group. (The Wilsons do not explicitly deal with the question of a group's boundaries, although it seems that, for 'promitive societies' at least, they have in mind small, local populations [1945: 26–39].) Social control is described as effective within a group because within it individuals are known and subject to sanctions; outside the group are strangers who cannot be held

184

accountable for their actions (1945: 35). An increase in scale means a decrease of interaction within the group and an increase outside it; it also means a breakdown in social control, since individuals are freed from the constraints of encapsulation (1945: 114–115). For the Wilsons, then, an increase in scale – in population size and in complexity of relationship – is significant for social organization because it brings about the dissolution of small, local groups within which control is effective, resulting in a mass society composed of atomized individuals, no longer accountable for their actions.

This perspective is also basic to Wirth's classic analysis of urban life (1938). Wirth, in constructing a theory of urbanism, was concerned with both the anonymity of cities and with the related deterioration of social control in them. Wirth's definition of a city in demongraphic terms provided a basis for his analysis of the sociological implications of anonymity. The size, density, heterogeneity, and geographical mobility of urban populations – his components of scale – separately or in combination, make it impossible for any individual to know all of his fellow urbanites. All this thereby makes a city a world of strangers. Individuals who are unknown, who can disappear into a faceless crowd, cannot be held accountable for their actions. They are not subject to social control.

A theory of social control is implicit in the work of Wirth and the Wilson's. A more detailed and more explicit account can be suggested as follows.[1] It assumes, initially, that social life is ordered in terms of rules. These rules may be said to guide, govern, organize, or express the expectations which constitute social relations. Secondly, it postulates means by which individuals are led to comply with such expectations. The means may be classified as internal and external aspects of control. The internal aspect of control is usually described in terms of morality or moral behavior; the individual monitors his own actions; his behavior is self-regulating; and compliance is achieved through the identity of social norms and individual beliefs, which, in turn, are the product of observable socialization processes. From this perspective, control is a moral issue, not necessarily affected by external conditions, including the anonymity generated by those factors in terms of which scale is conventionally defined.

An external system of social control, on the other hand, implies that the sactions associated with compliance are located outside the individual and are brought to bear upon him. It is this feature which apparently attracted the attention of both Wirth and the Wilsons and which they saw threatened by the changes of scale in social life. This form of social control is threatened because it depends upon two features: surveillance and implementation. Surveillance is important in the first place in restricting recruitment to social relationships. It suggests the maxim: avoid relationships or transactions with others who are irresponsible or who for other reasons will not or cannot comply with the rules of the relationship. This judgment can be made accurately only when the other persons in a social relationship are known. Surveillance is also important in another way: given that transactions take place, it is necessary, in order to apply sanctions and to achieve compliance, that rulebreakers be noted and brought to the attention of those charged with enforcement. Again, an increase in scale is assumed to interfere with surveillance.

Implementation, in contrast to the detection function of surveillance, involves the effective application of sanctions to insure compliance. If we assume that sanctions are sufficiently severe to deter disobedience, control is possible when the sanctions can be applied with some degree of certainty. That is, sanctions, no matter how severe, are effective only when it is known or believed that their execution is certain, that there is no possibility of escaping them. If individuals are either anonymous or mobile, then they cannot be held responsible for their behavior, regardless of the sanctions available. It is in this sense, then, that factors of scale undermine the implementation of sanctions and thus the effectiveness of a system of social control and of the social order which it supports.

2. Social circles

In the ideal typical analyses of Wirth and of the Wilsons, an increase in scale detaches individuals from groups and undermines traditional means of social control. These isolated individuals are then subject to predatory relationships, exploitation, and the various forms of disorganization characterized by Durkheim as a state of *anomie*. While Wirth postulated the potential disorder associated with an increase of scale, he also described the means by which individuals coped with it. These include both psychological and sociological mechanisms. Psychologically, individuals respond to these conditions by developing 'schizoid' personalities and a degree of sophistication and rationality which distinguishes them from others who have not been confronted by changes in scale.[2] These personality characteristics are manifest in people withdrawing from relationships, or at least selectively activating only a fraction of the relationships now possible; the discrepancy between the actual and the potential number of relationships is taken as evidence for the decrease of solidarity associated with the increase of scale.

Sociologically, Wirth suggested that formally organized groups were the means by which social control and social order were to be achieved in the face of changes of scale. Thus, Wirth concluded that an increase in scale would result in a proliferation of groups within which control would be effective and through which order would be maintained. Although Wirth emphasized groups as the units of social order, it seems clear that these were seen as the locus of social control, and that other forms of social organization through which control might be exerted would not be inconsistent with his theory. That is, Wirth implies that social order is to be found where individuals are subject to social control. This happens when individuals are incorporated in groups, but it may also occur when individuals are otherwise encapsulated.

Encapsulation may be analyzed in terms of 'social circles'.[3] Social circles may be localized or not. If localized, they may be described as place-related phenomena. The exercise of social control over individuals tied to particular places is illustrated in Rothman's study of 18th century American towns (1971) and in Suttles' study of a contemporary Chicago slum (1972). Social order in colonial American towns was maintained through a system intended to facilitate the implementation of sanctions by making urban residents subject to them. A primary problem in maintaining order then, as now, derived from the transiency of urban populations: those who were geographically mobile could not be held accountable and were a cause of social disorder. The colonial solution to this problem came in the form of 'settlement laws'. These laws served both surveillance and implementation functions. In the first instance, they were used by the citizens of a town to screen out or restrict those allowed to take up residence: only the reputable and responsible were acceptable as neighbors. On the other hand, strangers, those who did not belong to the community, were especially closely watched and, at the first sign of misconduct, expelled in accord with the provisions of the settlement laws. Each town became a haven against the potential danger of strangers.

This same theme of safety in a well-controlled place is evident in Suttles' description of the 'defended neighborhood'. In his view, the defended neighborhood protects against the dangers, actual and potential, associated with strangers and others not regulated by formal control mechanisms. The defended neighborhood is policed by local vigilantes, in the form of youth gangs and men's groups. They maintain control by restricting the movements of outsiders within the neighborhood. Control is not problematic among the neighborhood's residents because people are known, can be identified, can be located. In short, given available sanctions, it is not difficult to apply them since the residential stability of those who live within a defended neighborhood does not interfere with the exercise of social control. Both colonial settlement laws and the contemporary defended neighborhood are attempts to manage the (potential) danger of urban anonymity by encapsulating individuals in a locality, thereby increasing the effectiveness of social control among them.

But effective social control may also be established through the encapsulation of non-localized populations. Social networks exemplify this process. Inherent in the concept of a social network is the idea that individuals are linked or are linkable to one another – that is, they can reach and be reached by others directly and indirectly. It is this characteristic of 'reachability' which facilitates social control by exposing individuals to social pressure, that is, to social sanctions (Mitchell 1969: 17).

A social circle is a part of a total network. But what part? How is it bounded? There are essentially two approaches to this question. The first is that a circle is an objective construct. That is, the observer or analyst defines the boundaries of a social circle with reference to a given Ego, and the analyst draws the boundaries for his convenience and in terms of his analytical problem (see Mitchell 1969: 13 and Barnes 1969: 69). It may include those with whom Ego is directly in contact, his 'first-order star', or it may include higher-order stars (Barnes 1969: 58–59). The problem is that from the objective point of view, all individuals in the population of the total network, including those of whom Ego is unaware, are possible contacts and may be important for some problem of interest to the analyst. From the perspective of social control, however, it is those individuals who are known to Ego, directly or indirectly, and who can reach and be reached by him that are significant. In this respect, a social circle is a subjective construct, bound by Ego's perception of those with whom he is able or likely to come into contact. (See Katz 1966: 201, 203–204; Mitchell 1969: 26, 40.)

The idea that a social circle is a subjective construct is evident in several studies. Travers and Milgram, for example, in writing of social circles as 'small worlds', describe units of social organization which are composed of 'acquaintance chains' extending or reaching at least one remove beyond the direct contacts of any specific starting point or Ego. In their study, they asked one set of individuals (the 'starters') to contact another individual (the 'target'). Contacts were permitted only when an interacting pair of individuals knew one another on a first-name basis. Thus, the 'starters' were instructed to contact someone whom they knew personally and whom they thought might personally know the target individual.

188

This procedure suggests that the small world is subjectively defined, since the starters were aware of or suspected the paths, direct or indirect, by which they could reach the target.

The subjective aspect of social circles is also illustrated in Boissevain's description of the characteristics of personal networks (1968). Boissevain describes 'concentric zones' of social relations radiating from Ego; some of them include direct contacts and others indirect contacts. The two innermost circles (the 'intimate' and 'effective' networks) include individuals directly in contact with Ego and known personally by him. The third zone out (the 'extended' network) contains individuals not known personally by Ego but 'of whom he knows and whom he very easily can get to know' (1968: 547). There is also a fourth zone (unnamed by Boissevain) which consists of individuals 'unknown to ego, although he is aware of or suspects their presence' (1968: 547); those are individuals from the extended networks of persons in Ego's effective network. Boissevain claims that Ego 'can come into personal contact' with those in his fourth zone 'via the links' in his other inner zones. Beyond the fourth zone presumably are individuals of whom Ego is unaware and with whom contact is objectively possible but subjectively improbable.

An interesting feature of subjectively constructed social circles is that the individuals who compose them are often described in an idiom of friendship. Moreover, that idiom is used, regardless of the 'content' (Mitchell 1969) of the relationships or the 'different institutional activity fields' (Boissevain 1968: 546) from which they are recruited. This is evident in Boissevain's concentric zones. The first zone contains 'friends and relatives'; the second zone, 'acquaintances'. The third zone includes the 'intimates of intimates', or, in other words, the friends of friends. Those in the fourth zone are acquaintances' friends' friends.

There is some evidence that actors as well as analysts see the links of their social circles as constructed primarily out of friendship. In the 'small world' study Travers and Milgram collected, through tracer cards, data about the relationship between pairs of individuals directly in contact with one another. In describing the characteristics of the chains which constitute a small world, Travers and Milgram note that '86% of the participants sent the folder to persons *they described* as friends and acquaintances; 14 percent of the participants sent it to relatives' (1969: 440, my emphasis). These categories were used by the actors in identifying those in their social circle, despite the availability of alternative terms for them, including neighbor and business associate or colleague. Friendship is the idiom of reachability and effective social control.

If friends are known, accountable, and trusted, they contrast with strangers: those who are unknown, uncontrollable, and, correspondingly, potentially dangerous. That danger is associated with the stranger, the individual not subject to control, is illustrated in a recent study of street prostitutes in Boston.[5] The prostitutes categorized the men with whom they routinely came into contact as ranging between those they considered 'dangerous' and those they did not. At the dangerous end of the continuum were their clients or 'tricks'; at the other end were their pimps. Underlying the continuum is their idea that the dangerous man is the one they meet in a fleeting relationship, the one who is anonymous and therefore not subject to the sanctions available to them. (In most cases, the prostitutes are unable or unwilling to call the police or others representing the formal, legal control structure.) The pimp is known, reachable, and subject to social pressure. The prostitutes do not equate danger with violence: pimps often beat them, or threaten to, and are considered violent; clients are not, in that sense, violent, but are described as dangerous. Danger, in this case, is a function of uncertainty about probable (future) association and the corresponding capacity to effectively implement social control mechanisms. (See Douglas 1966, chapter 6.) Strangers are dangerous; friends and acquaintances, those with whom interaction, directly or indirectly, at a future time is thought probable, are not.

The prostitutes' opposition of known and unknown, reachable and unreachable, safe and dangerous, applies to places and situations as well as to persons. Asked to describe dangerous places, they mention places where they do not know anyone: certain areas of Boston and its (middle-class) suburbs. They consider the places where they work, and to a lesser extent where they live, places where they know others (including some places which by objective standards are high-crime areas) as either less dangerous or 'manageable'. They also describe busy city streets as less dangerous than empty suburban or country roads.

Faced with these kinds of perceived danger, the prostitutes attempt to employ a series of strategies to manage it. They try, when working, to stay in their own neighborhood: they go to a local 'trick house' (usually an apartment building controlled by criminal interests, in which rooms are rented to the prostitutes or their pimps on a regular basis). If they leave their pick-up point with a client, they ask another girl or friend to note his car's registration number or license plate. The prostitutes will also try to obtain something that will identify the client (a home address, for example) and give it to a friend as collateral until their safe return.

190

While the prostitutes are thus trying to identify their clients, most of whom apparently have a number of counter-strategies, they also try to conceal their own identities. They do so primarily because they want to rob their customers, if they can, with impunity. Such theft includes stealing property, but also includes other fraudulent actions as taking payment for and then not rendering agreed-upon services. The basic courses of action they use to escape the reach of a short-changed and irate customer is to quit work for that night, change places of work (by moving to another bar or street corner), and/or to alter their appearance (by changing clothes and/or by putting on, taking off, or alternating wigs of different color and hairstyle). Unless the client is a regular customer (whom the prostitutes see as midway on their danger continuum and who is less likely to be a target for theft or fraud), one who knows, travels in, or has some link to their social circles, the prostitutes usually succeed in maintaining their anonymity, their freedom to escape the client's ability to enforce sanctions or bring pressure to bear, and their option to engage in predatory behavior.

3. Uniplex and multiplex

Within social circles, social control is effective and order is possible. What, then, is the relationship between social circles and scale, and between scale and social organization? The analysis of social circles, whether as local communities or as non-localized networks, supports Wirth's contention that an increase in scale is associated with an increase in the number of social circles. The potentially disruptive effects of increasing scale on social relations are neutralized to the extent that individuals are encapsulated within these circles which are the contexts of routine and regular social activity. This conclusion is not new to anthropology: it is a reworking of the familiar theories of segmentary societies and repetitive change.

A somewhat less familiar point may be that the internal structure of social circles appears relatively constant, regardless of the size of the population they encompass. There are some data which suggest that the number of links in a circle varies only a little with significant variations in scale. Travers and Milgram, for example, report an average of about 5 links in completed chains between two individuals randomly selected in a large (approximately 200 million) population. Boissevain (1968) also provides two examples of reachability within circles which closely resemble the experimentally-induced 'small world' of Travers and Milgram. In the first example, Boissevain notes that in Malta he has a small (unspecified) number of close friends and a fairly large (about 300) number of acquaintances. He further estimates that, 'using no more than three intermediary links', he could 'arrange a personal introduction' to any randomly selected Maltese adult within Malta's population of 314,000 (1968: 547). Thus, from Boissevain's viewpoint – and in this case he is both actor and analyst – the entire population of the island constitutes a fourth-order 'small world'. His other example depicts network mobilization in Sicily: one individual wanted to contact, by means of a personal introduction, another man and was able, in a population of some 4,700,000, to do so using four links. A remarkable feature of these examples is that within three populations of widely differing magnitude (314,000; 4,700,000; 200,000,000), the number of links required to connect any two individuals, personally unknown to one another, lies within an extremely narrow band of 3 to 5; i.e. it varies around a constant of 4.

These circles composed of a relatively fixed number of links may be seen as examples of social control in single-strand or uniplex relations. They include contacts which are equal to or more distant than acquaintances' friends' friends. If such indirect contacts are assumed to be the kind which are mobilized only infrequently and for limited purposes, they may be described as uniplex relations. They contrast with multiplex relations, which, according to Gluckman, serve 'manifold purposes' (1962: 26). In a multiplex relation, the same individuals interact with one another in a variety of roles or contexts and, implicitly, do so relatively frequently.

The effectiveness of social control in uniplex relations has a bearing on the 'multiplex theory' of social order. This theory is not an uncommon one in sociology and anthropology: it underlies many of the urban/rural, *Gemeinschaft/Gesellschaft*, and similarly constructed typologies. Multiplex relations are described as strengthening social control and by implication, uniplex relations are thought to undermine it (see Mitchell 1969: 23, including his reference to the work of Nadel). Individuals in multiplex relations are allegedly more accountable than those whose relations are uniplex, because they are thought to be not as free to escape sanctions and therefore are supposedly more responsibe to normative rules of behavior. (Mitchell writes: 'people in a multi-stranded relationship interact with one another in many different contexts and are therefore less likely to be able to withdraw completely from contact with one another as people in a single-stranded relationship are able to do' [1969: 23].) Furthermore, in the multiplex theory, an increase in scale is thought to correlate with an increase in uniplex relations, and so an increase in scale is thought to undermine social control. As the examples of Boissevain and Travers and

Milgram suggest, however, control operates within large-scale societies through uniplex relations.[7]

There is, moreover, further evidence which does not support the multiplex theory or which, at least, requires its modification. Some cases demonstrate that social control may be rendered ineffective despite multiplex relationships. Bailey's description of Pan Untouchables in Bisipara is one illustration (Bailey 1960). These Indian villagers were able to reduce the control their clean-caste co-residents held over them by invoking the rules and sanctions of the larger encapsulating structure of the modern state, rather than those of the smaller enclosed structure of the traditional caste system as it operated locally. In this case, control was weakened not because the Pan Untouchables were anonymous or unreachable, but because the sanctions of the traditional system were neutralized.

Other studies of village fission and schism also suggest that social control can be ineffective even between those who interact frequently and in a variety of roles and contexts. This occurs not because the sanctions themselves are weakened, but because their enforcement is. This typically happens when one party to the relationship moves away, beyond the sphere of influence in which the available sanctions can be effectively enforced (see Evans-Pritchard 1940: 169, Wilson 1945: 61). These examples suggest that multiplex relations may appear to enhance control – not because of the many-strandedness or the diffuseness of the relationship, but because they occur in situations where there is little alternative but to abide by the rules, where it is difficult to escape or avoid sanctions, and where accountability is forced by circumstances upon those in the system. The social consequences of multiplex relations ought to be differentiated from those of encapsulation, which also occurs in uniplex relations.

Changes in scale, then, may influence social organization in certain ways, but not necessarily as being disruptive of social control. This was Wirth's conclusion, if not that of the Wilsons. Its importance need not be only its implications for a hopeful optimism about the future of society. It has a theoretical significance as well: social circles occur in different types of society and among small and large populations. An analysis of the process of social control and of the context – the social circle – in which it operates focuses attention not on what constitutes differences in scale, nor on the correlates of differences in scale, but on what is *common* in the organization of social relations, regardless of the scale of society which constitutes their setting.

F. G. BAILEY

Tertius Gaudens aut Tertium Numen[1])

1. Introduction

At first sight, the simplest measurement of scale is the number of people involved. This has two attractions. Firstly, it seems to offer simple quantifying: merely counting heads. Secondly, it seems culture free. The range of behavior open to a team of one hundred is not the same as that in teams of twenty people. Decision-making by consensus may not be found in groups of more than twenty,. *whatever their culture.*

But culture cannot always be thus transcended. When we spoke above of the numbers of persons 'involved' in a contest, we ignored the vagueness of the word 'involved'. A person is, by definition, not simply involved in a situation, but is involved in it as the performer of a role or roles. When we wish to order two contest situations according to the numbers of people involved, we have to calculate that figure according to *that culture's definition* of who has and who has not a role to play in that contest. The affair gets more complicated when we take into account the fact that the definition of who should and who should not be involved in the contest can itself become a point of contest.

My interest is in processes of competition. I assume that in any culture there are 'proper' ways of having a quarrel. We can describe, in a formal 'blueprint' way, the steps to be taken and the resources to be used to arrange a marriage or to consult a healer/ curer (Metzger & Williams, 1963a and 1963b), or to install a successor in office. So also we should be able to identify limited ranges or repertoires of actions and limited sequences in which they can be arranged, when a debate takes place in a committee, or a party splits into two factions, or when a Mafia 'family' is toppled from and then regains a position of eminence (Puzo 1969).

I shall explore the connection between the numbers of people involved in a political contest (its 'scale') and the kind of claims which they use in the hope of winning the argument. Alternatively — to put the question in a manner more attractive to those interested in political strategies — what claims does an adversary use to cause more or fewer people to be involved in the contest? Also, what claims invite intervention by third parties?

Our conclusions will concern scale and its connections with the kind of language involved in a dispute, with the possibility of a compromise settlement, and they will concern the crucial effect of patterns of value distribution. In general, we are exploring the connections between scale on the one hand, and on the other claims to be acting in the public interest matched alainst accusations of self-interest or partisan interest.

2. The personnel committee

To launch the discussion, I will describe one exemplary situation.

There is in my university a committee which advises the Chancellor about personnel matters: about appointing, dismissing, promoting and rewarding faculty members on the basis of their achievements in research, their capacity as teachers, and the service they have given to the university and the community.

The committee certainly belongs to that category which some years ago (Bailey 1965) I called 'elite'. Although the members are drawn from the various departments and disciplines they are in no way seen as representatives of the interests of any particular department, but rather as guardians firstly of academic standards and, secondly, of what might be called 'natural justice'. They deal with the interests of individuals in the face of their several departments, adjudicate between one department and another, and represent the interests of the collective academic body against possible threats from the university's administrators.

In fact, immense care is taken both by the administrators and by the committee members to see that there are no unnecessary confrontations between them. Both parties endeavor to suppress the political (that is, adversary) element in their relationship, behaving rather in the manner of rational administrators, for whom every problem has a rational solution. Such behavior is possible only because at present neither party openly questions the validity of the criteria for academic excellence in use. The harmony and the Administration's care to avoid confrontation with the committee are all the more remarkable, in that according to the laws of the university the committee's recommendations to the Chancellor are no more than that: mere advice and not in the least binding.

My interest is not so much in the genesis of this situation, as in the *mechanisms* by which harmony is maintained; and secondly in the *strategies* open to the committee, when it suspects that its advice might be disregarded.

The committee is small: it has seven members and four constitute a quorum. Consequently, it does not provide a setting for the rhetorically inclined. Furthermore, the ethos of the committee leans towards the style of reasoned argument appropriate between experts (lawyer to lawyer, so to speak) rather than the appeal through slogans and symbols towards stirring the emotions (advocate and jury). Problems are discussed, certainly and inevitably in the adversary mode of argument and counter-argument, but always with a view to the administrator's 'reasonable' solution, balancing the rigor of the law against the interests of persons. Only rarely are problems construed as political contests in which the outcome should be a victory for one side or the other.

This self-image of 'statesmenship' is bolstered by a very strong rule of confidentiality. This is formally required since some of the information with which the committee operates consists of confidential references. But the effect of the rule of secrecy is to allow a relatively free discussion of most of the alternative courses of action without the speakers having to worry about the political effects of their statements in other arenas. There is no television, so to speak, and there are no constituents at the other end of it.

The Chancellor and his immediate subordinates are, of course, within the circle of confidentiality, in that both they and the committee have exactly the same body of material on which to base their decision. But the ethos of secrecy is carried further into the negotiations and confrontations between the committee and the administrators. As a general rule, advice and information are conveyed in a highly formal fashion by letter. When the Chancellor receives advice which he thinks unwise, it is usually the practice for him to initiate an exchange of letters in order to clarify the situation, and if possible so adjust matters that he will be seen to be following rather than disregarding the committee's advice. If such a compromise cannot be reached by correspondence, or if the matter requires an urgent decision, then the practice is for the chairman of the committee and the Chancellor or his representative to meet and to exchange ideas: in other words, to bargain, always in the direction of lessening the disagreement between them.

In the course of one such dispute, evidently a particularly difficult one, the chairman of the committee returned from a meeting with the administrator concerned and said, in the tones normally reserved for a declaration of war, 'This time we may have to go public'. The announcement was received with due gravity. (In fact, a very ingenious solution, which left everyone's honor intact, was later found and the committee did not have to go 'public'.)

That phrase sets some of my question. 'Going public' was evidently considered a more potent weapon than any used up to that point in the negotiations. It was also thought to be a dangerous weapon, potentially highly destructive, and certainly not to be used unless absolutely necessary.

What are the implications of 'going public'? Obviously, it did not mean that confidential material in the files would be open to everyone. But it did mean that the negotiations between the administration and the committee would no longer be conducted privily; and that the adversary and political aspects of the exchange would be made to predominate. Such a move was considered dangerous because, with more people involved, the risk of all-out conflict was increased, not only for this but also for future cases. On the other hand, there was also a feeling that the committee's hand would be strengthened by involving the mass of its constituents (that is, all the members Academic Senate) in the dispute. The implication is that while the administrator might resist the chairman and the small committee, he would be less inclined to stand out against several hundred of his fellow-academics.

So we have come to the far-from-momentous conclusion that the individual who fears he might lose a contest tries to increase the size of his support.

I doubt that any member of the committee would have been willing to leave the description in quite those terms. Getting the mob into the street was far from the committee's style. In fact, 'going public' was not so much a matter of mobilizing constituents in defense of their own interests, but rather a presentation of the justice of the committee's opinion to a third party whose moral influence might be brought to bear on the offending administrator.

But such an explanation leaves us still with a problem about numbers. Justice is codified in the book of rules and standards by which all members of the university are guided. 'Going public' must mean not merely an appeal to these standards, but also to a collection of people whose importance lies not only in their acceptance of the standards but also in the fact that they are numerous. So we are back at the proposition that the contestant in difficulties endeavors to increase the numbers of people involved in the dispute, to escalate it, because in this way he strengthens his case.

In what follows I will show that such situations cannot be so simply described.

3.1. *The third man*

Not all political situations follow the sequence described above, in which one of two contestants invite a third party to intervene. The intervention may be at the initiative of the third person. One form which such a person may take is already well known: the first part of my title, *Tertius gaudens*.

Tertius gaudens [lit: the third man rejoicing] benefits by intervening (or failing to intervene when he should) between two contestants (Simmel 1950: 154ff). He stays neutral and grows rich in a way by selling arms to both sides. He allows the contestants to exhaust themselves and then annexes them to his empire. From a position of established power, he manipulates his followers so that they fight one another and do not pit their combined resources against his authority: 'divide and rule'. *Tertius gaudens* is a manipulator, who keeps his head and refuses to commit himself to 'causes': he looks to his own profit and not to the good of the collectivity.[2]

Tertium numen is quite another personage. *Numen*, according to Lewis' dictionary, means first a 'nod'; hence 'command, will, authority'; then 'the divine will, supreme authority, divine majesty'. The person who comes between the contestants and in the public interest puts an end to the quarrel is *tertium numen*. The traditional *panchayat* in India has this sacred quality: the notional five men who make it up stand for the collectivity; for a principle of orderliness in opposition to chaos and disorder, for cooperation rather than the individual, for stability rather than change, for the man who obeys the rules rather than the man who manipulates them: in short for altruism as against egoism. In that indirect debate a few years back Gluckman (1968) spoke for *numen* and Barth (1967) for *gaudens*.[3] The personnel committee, described earlier defines itself as *numen*, standing between the individual and his department, between one department and another, and between the academic faculty as a whole and the university's administration. Others do not always see it in the same way.

3.2. *The third 'man': claims to define action*

Competitive processes consist largely of messages and claims: matters of interpretation and dispute rather than agreed facts. Even the presence of a third person, let alone his characteristics, may be a matter of disagreement. In the Losa elections of 1968, when the bishop was persuaded to issue a statement that one party had misappropriated the sacred phrase '*spes una salutis*' and that it was most improper to take a religious truth and use it as a political slogan, their rivals accepted his act as *tertium numen*: an intervention in the interests of decency and high standards of public behavior. The offenders, whom the bishop had condemned, did not say that he had done it for his own interests (which would have been *gaudens*), but simply that he was mistaken: as one pious old lady put it '*il vescovo e bugiardo*' ('the bishop is a liar'). For her, the intervention was void because the occasion did not call for a third party: there was no occasion for the collectivity to intervene, in the person of a bishop or anyone else, because the collectivity's values and standards had not been violated (Bailey 1973: 191).

When we look at contests and at the intervention of a third party, the latter is not in any objectively recognizable fashion either *gaudens* or *numen*: he may be both at the same time, because he is recognizable only in the statements he and others make about his behavior.

So there is nothing to be gained by searching for indices which might enable us to give an objective meaning to the styles of third man. Consequently our inquiry has to be reformulated to take account of this subjectivity. We can no longer ask whether differences of scale produce one or other of these roles, but rather whether differences of scale can be connected with different *claims to define the situation* and the third man's role in it.

3.3. Numina *and their collectivities*

To be acknowledged as *numen*, the claimant must disconnect himself from certain other roles, which are partisan. He must identify himself with a group to which both contestants belong and/or with some transcending value to which they both subscribe. Between the Kellys and the Cohens mediation may be offered by Jones, who is neither Irish nor Catholic nor Jewish: but he mediates not as the Welsh Protestant Jones clan but rather as the embodiment of the collective reasonableness and collective interests of all the clans acting together. The personnel committee mediates between individuals and their departments, or between the administration and the academic personnel in the name of the larger institution to which they all belong, the University. A *numen* claims to represent a larger collectivity[4] than either of the contestants, and his intervention apparently may enlarge the scale of involvement.

There are many ways of disaffiliating the human person who acts as *numen* from his other roles. Deities are born from other deities; but if their origins are thought to be partly human, then there is a clause which exempts them from partisan affiliation. God puts horns on the human husbands of human virgins, with the effect that the divine child is without human paternity and therefore without paternal affiliations.[5] The same effect is achieved by ordeals or drawing lots: the determining agent is a divinity and by definition cannot be *gaudens*. In such cases no human agency has to bear the responsibility for the decision; this happens with Frankenberg's (1957) English outsiders in a Welsh village, who, by being invited to take decisions, are relegated or elevated to a category of apparently superhuman but actually subhuman. Uniforms and the insignia of office have the same effect: they represent some kind of collectivity or transcending value and absolve the wearer from his everyday allegiances to other smaller groups. The uniform of a Roman Senator required A. Fulvius to execute his own son. Popular stereotypes have it that uniforms strip away humanity and bestow a rigid adherence to principle and reluctance to listen to 'reason'. The ultimate form taken by *numen* is the mask, which conceals and thus removes the partisan identity of the wearer. The personnel committee's ethos of secrecy is in effect a form of mask.

The mask invites the other person to perform an act of simplification: if it conceals completely, the mask compels him to do so. He is to disregard other identities than the one indicated by the mask. This situation has the same characteristics as Barth's (1972) intermediate type. The relatively unmasked identity, which offers the actors a range of roles from which to select, resembles Barth's elementary situation: you require an all-round knowledge of the other person's identities before you can act. The mask or the uniform permits interaction in situations where nothing else is known about the other person. Such interactions, so to speak, are mass-produced: 'in the round' interactions, by contrast, are craftsman-made and therefore not so easily replicable. Thus, an increase in scale goes along with a simplification of the perceptual clues for interaction. That *numen* must represent either a group to which both contestants belong or a value to which they both subscribe is a matter of logic, arising from the moral component contained in the word. (We are not talking of situations of force, where the third person bangs together the heads of the contestants, but rather one where the third man is granted the status of *numen*: of someone who has the moral right to intervene.)

To recapitulate: No man is a hero to his valet. To achieve the status of *numen*, the claimant must set himself above the contenders by representing some group to which they both belong or some value to which they both subscribe, or usually both. It is the more difficult to do this if he interacts with them every day in a variety of different identities: if he was playing cards with them the night before, and was drunk the night before that, and they were at school with him for many years, then it is rather unlikely that they will take him seriously if he gets up one morning and announces: 'Be still and know that I am God'. To do this he needs to achieve

200

some degree of anonymity: he needs to simplify the other people's perception of him, so that they perceive only his numinous qualities and not his rounded humanity. By simplifying his message (putting on a mask, either literally or metaphorically) he enlarges the scale of his congregation. In short, it is both true by definition and it follows from the constraints of communication and practical politics that a claim to intervene as *numen* is likely to require an enlargement of scale.

But, as I shall argue, the extent of this enlargement is regulated by the distribution of values.

3.4. Numina *and normative themes*

The claim to act as *numen* and its counter-accusation of *gaudens* repeat the distinction between altruistic and egoistic behavior. These words acquire meaning only with reference to some identified collectivity. *Gaudens* attaches to someone who serves a collectivity more circumscribed than the accuser thinks proper. It follows that the same act seen from below is altruistic and, seen from above, is egoistic.

A simple way of representing this hierarchy is a pyramid. Each contour is *numen* from the point of view of the contour below, and *gaudens* in comparison with that above. Each level of the hierarchy has the familiar paradoxical characteristic of both being smaller (having fewer items) than the one below it and yet containing it. If the pyramic represents groups, this is a simple nesting system in which large groups are subdivided into smaller groups and so on. The higher up the pyramid, the fewer the groups from which to choose, and the lower the possibility of choice: entropy decreases as scale increases. The same is true if the pyramid represents values, or, as they are better called in situations of contest, 'normative themes': themes which contestants can use to justify their actions. The higher up the pyramid, the more general the themes, and the less the choice: at the top one finds such cards as 'God's will' or 'it says so in the Bible' or 'it is written in the Koran', which cannot be trumped by any other card *in that game.*

It follows that the claim to be *numen* and the accusation of *gaudens*, while they refer to motivations, constitute actually a debate to define the collectivity or level of values relevant to that situation. The *numen* statement pushes towards a higher contour: the *gaudens* accusation pushes downwards.

Suppose a pyramid of five levels, representing either collectivities or hierarchies of value. Assume that all the actors agree that the welfare of, for example, the nation comes before that of any state within it, the welfare of the state is more important than that of a district, the district before the village, and so on. The center level is called x: the top is x+2: the lowest segment is x—2. T is the third man who claims the right to intervene as *numen* in a contest. His antagonist [A] may be one or both of the contenders or someone hitherto not involved in that contest.[6]

A accuses T of *gaudens*. A makes his accusation specific, by saying that T is profiting at the expense of, let us say, x. By doing so he claims to define x as the relevant collectivity and he argues that T is serving the interests of either x—1 or x—2.

What ripostes are then open to T?

(1) He may counter with a *gaudens* accusation. He does this by accepting x as the relevant collectivity: but he accuses A of representing x̄—1 or x̄—2. For example, he agrees that the interests of the district are paramount. A has accused him of speaking for his own village [x—1] or his own family [x—2]. T then attempts to destroy A's credit by pointing out that he [A] is speaking on behalf of *his* village [x̄—1] or *his* family [x̄—2].

(2) Whether or not he does this, T may also argue that the interests of x—1 are in this situation identical with those of x. 'What is good for General Motors is good for . . .' (This may be particularly useful if our initial condition about general agreement on values does not hold, and T suspects that some of the audience disvalue x and value x—1 more highly: which may have been the case for that famous sentiment about General Motors.)

(3) Alternatively, T may respond by raising the level of collectivity. He then argues that his actions serve the interests of x+1 or x+2 (the state or the nation) and he thus implies that A is *gaudens* because he is looking to the interests of a collectivity smaller than the one relevant in that situation.

When T has finished his justification, the same range of counter-ripostes is open to A.

I summarize the pattern that is emerging:

(a) We are assuming that both T and A agree on a hierarchy of collectivities or values.

(b) One stage of debate concerns the level of this hierarchy to which the contest should be connected.

(c) At the second stage of debate, the contestants agree about the relevant level of the hierarchy but differ as to whether T's claim (or A's accusation) is consonant with or antithetical to the values of that level or the interests of that collectivity.

If conviction and agreement are achieved at the first stage of debate (the relevant level of hierarchy), the subsequent argument about whether or not T's action is in accordance with that level need not increase scale. It is only when T (or A) judges that he is likely to lose the second stage of debate, that he becomes tempted to throw into doubt the level of hierarchy, with the effect of increasing scale.

These are abstract speculations. Notice that they are no more than the rules of the game. They identify legitimate moves and link these moves with changes in the scale of the contest, but they tell us nothing about outcomes. Nevertheless, the model does have use in suggesting further questions. For example:

(1) What governs the speed at which a contest may rise up the pyramid?

(2) Must the movement be step by step, or can one jump from the lowest to the highest level in one move?

(3) As one rises in the pyramid, entropy decreases and there are fewer themes to select or collectivities with which to identify. Does this mean that the possibility of compromise and bargaining decreases (because the normative themes get progressively more to be matters of faith than matters of reason, ends in themselves rather than means); or, alternatively, is the possibility of an amicable settlement increased as the issues and principles are progressively more clearly defined?

(4) In what circumstances does a move down the pyramid take place? (Hogg versus Powell in the immigration debate – see below.)

(5) Finally, what happens if we remove the assumption that all concerned agree upon a transcending, all-trumping $x+2$ at the top of the pyramid? Suppose there are several pyramids?

In the following, I discuss some of these questions in relation to debates which I have recorded at various times.

3.5. Numina: *accepted and disputed*

Sometimes both parties accept the moral right of a third person to intervene: the status of *numen* is beyond question and an accusation of *gaudens* would be ineffective.

In less well ordered times, in parts of India there were Brahmans who made a living as security guards. They guaranteed hostages or parties traveling across dangerous territories, by undertaking to commit suicide if the hostages were harmed or the travelers were attacked. The attacker would then be responsible for killing a Brahman, the gravest of sins.

What the potential victim and the Brahman himself think is not relevant; but the would-be attacker has to believe that the cost of violation is too great. He must believe that the Brahman will carry out his threat: and that he will be punished in this world or the next, or in both. We need not assume that in every case the would-be violator calculates the cost of future discomfort against the benefit of present gain: he might simply believe, without giving a thought to the sanctions and as an ultimate moral imperative, that it is wrong to kill a Brahman.

There is an analogous instance in *The Godfather*:

> The Bocchicchio Family was unique in that, once a particularly ferocious branch of the Mafia in Sicily, it had become an instrument of peace in America. Once a group of men who earned their living by savage determination, they now earn their living in what perhaps could be called a saintly fashion. (Puzo 1969: 276–277.)

Their assets were a high sense of honor, an unbridled ferocity and determination, and a very close-knit family loyalty. If a member of one family went to the stronghold of another in order to negotiate, the Bocchicchios would provide a hostage. If the envoy was killed, his family had the right to kill the hostage and this death, as with the Brahman, would be the responsibility of the offenders. The Bocchicchios would then take vengeance on the family which had violated the truce: 'Since the Bocchicchios were so primitive, they never let anything, any kind of punishment, stand in their way of vengeance.' (279) This instance, at first sight, lacks the mystical overtones of Brahman sacredness. But the very institution of the Bocchicchios as hostages indicates a moral acceptance of the principle of social order; from this point of view the murder of a Bocchicchio is a sin, and a sign that the murderer has renounced his acceptance of the values of that moral community in which he formerly lived.

The use of a Brahman or a Bocchicchio occupies the $x+2$ space at the top of the pyramid, and *within that system of values* this card cannot be trumped. If the hostage is killed, there is no conceivable justification within the normative themes of the system. Such an offender has two possible courses. One is to deny that the murdered hostage was in face a Brahman or a Bocchicchio. The other one is to assert that this particular pyramid of values was inappropriately used on this occasion, that a different set of values really applied.

An instance of this is that of the bishop in the Losa elections, already described. So far as the people of Losa were concerned, the bishop represented an $x+2$ space when he proclaimed that use of a sacred phrase for political purposes is wrong. The supporters of List One, who were hurt by the Bishop's pronouncement, evidently thought it more prudent not to start an argument with him, but rather to define the phrase (*spes una salutis*) not as scripture but as the motto of the Losa *comune*, and therefore appropriately used by those who styled themselves *Lista Civica* (the Town List).

The activites of Vinoba Bhave in Orissa, and the reaction against him by local politicians, provide another example. Vinoba, dubbed by one of his English admirers 'the saint on the march', inherited Gandhi's mantle of popular sacredness. He lived a life of extreme austerity. Much of his time was spent on devotion and on preaching social reform, not through legislation but through morality – a change of heart. In this period (1959) he made long and very well publicized pilgrimages through the countryside, asking landowners to give him one-fifth of what they owned so that the property might be distributed among the poor. He had many devoted followers, including some of high political rank and a skilled propaganda machine. How much effect he had upon the peasants and the poor is another question: but they did come to his meetings in sufficient numbers to cause him to be taken seriously by the political elite, to whom, I suspect, much of his preaching was directed.

On his own ground Vinoba was invulnerable. He was, if not the sole, certainly the outstanding heir to that charismatic political Hinduism so well developed by Gandhi. Moreover, I never heard about Vinoba those irreverent sexual speculations which sometimes threatened Gandhi's reputation. In his person, and as a saint, Vinova could not be faulted.

Nevertheless, some Oriya politicians found him a nuisance and an embarrassment. He did not, so far as I know, attack any of them personally, but his message and his way of life proclaimed them and their policies to be ineffective, wrongheaded, and ultimately immoral. Many politicians, and more administrators, considered him to be a mere visionary, preaching a Gandhian utopia of small communities peopled by virtuous men, whereas realists knew that people were not virtuous, and a nation made up of small communities, given the climate and resources of India, could hardly be prosperous.

The import of these attacks was not that Vinoba intervened as *gaudens*. There were a few attacks of this kind, but these were directed more at Vinoba's entourage than at the man himself. Occasionally it was argued that he was the unwitting tool of the Congress Party, turning the minds of the peasants towards pie in the sky, when they should be directed towards revolution.

Those hostile to Vinoba did not usually cast doubt on his sainthood, but argued rather that sainthood was not the appropriate instrument for dealing with present difficulties. Prosperity must come before the conversion of individual souls to a new morality. Moreover, the critics were able to indicate an inextricable confusion which followed upon gifts of land to Vinoba, failure to redistribute the land effectively, doubts about the title to such land resulting in difficulty in raising loans, and not inconsiderable areas where the only effect of a gift to Vinoba was to put that land out of cultivation. All these are arguments not to the effect that Vinoba is *gaudens,* but that his *numen* is being invoked in an inappropriate collectivity.

Let us recapitulate. In this section I have given some cases in which the status of *numen* was unassailable. The person cannot be attacked and, as the last two examples illustrate, *A* must cast doubt not upon the credit of *T* as *numen* but upon his appropriateness in the present context. This is not a claim to move up or down a pyramid, but to move to another pyramid altogether. In both cases, the point at issue is competition to define the connection between a *numen* and some kind of context.

4. Powell and his accusers

A few years ago English public life was enlivened or contaminated, depending on how you look at it, by the speeches of a Conservative Member of Parliament, Enoch Powell, whose constituency lay in the industrial midlands at Wolverhampton. In this area many colored immigrants from the West Indies, India, and Pakistan had settled. The majority found manual work (although many of the Indians and Pakistanis had white-collar qualifications) and they provided much-needed labor for transport, steel, textiles, and a variety of secondary enterprises. They tended, especially the Indians and Pakistanis, to live in the same region and work at the same kind of job, if not in the same plant; partly because they were *de facto* employable only in those jobs, partly because they came on a chain-migration sponsoring system, and partly, for the Indians and Pakistanis at least, because that is the way they wanted it to be. Indians and Pakistanis, segregated socially in Britain, did not find the situation so inexplicable as did the West Indians. Of course they resented their lowly position, but they had no wish to assimilate to British society and culture.

Other Conservative politicians, notably Duncan Sandys, had been campaigning to restrict colored immigration. Early in 1968, Powell entered the arena, and within twelve months he had made a mark. He had transformed the color question from being a matter of localized grumbling and occasional small-scale disorders in a few of the poorer areas in some industrial cities, to being a matter of national debate, which day after day filled the columns of the newspapers and occupied a large part of feature programs on the radio and television. Powell himself, once a professor of Greek and a wartime brigadier hitherto known, if known at all, for his role as the party's conscience in matter of primitive Toryism (free market, low taxes, no government is good government, and so on) became in 1968 a ranting politician of the streets, detested by most intellectuals, a source of fear and embarrassment to moderate conservatives, an inspiration to petty demagogues, especially in areas where migrants lived, and the darling of spontaneous grass-roots protesters. Dockers marched on Parliament in his support and, encountering a Kenyan diplomat on the way, roughed him up, telling him to go home to Jamaica. 'In Ambergate, Derbyshire, the entire staff of a gas plant, including twelve coloured men, staged a half day demonstration'. (Smithies & Fiddick 1969: 12.) The occasion for these outbreaks and the grass-roots support was Mr. Powell's sacking from the shadow-cabinet: the party leader felt that a speech which Powell had made at Birmingham went far beyond Conservative policies on race. People in the streets said he had been sacked for speaking his mind.

This is a spectacular example of an increase in scale, from several points of view. From being an eccentric and minor member of the party's elite, very much his own man and apparently with nothing more than such a politician's usual following, Powell became a national figure, eclipsing, at least in the news media, the leaders of his own party. Secondly, the issue which had been the concern of a relatively few people living in depressed areas in industrial cities in the midlands, parts of London, and a few Yorkshire towns became a national question, filling the correspondence columns of newspapers and eliciting anger even from those regions which had never seen a colored man. (Brighton, which hardly had a colored inhabitant, became the home of the 'Sussex League for Racial Purity'.)

All this was accomplished through only three formal speeches, delivered in February, April, and November of 1968. Of course Powell, being a politician, did not keep his mouth shut in the meantime, but his pronouncements were in the nature of explanations and justification. Nor, so far as I know, was there any kind of organization working to spread Powell's message, other than the ordinary news media.

How was such an expansion of scale possible? At one level it may be said that the British working class, like most people in the world, is racially prejudiced. It is interesting that Powell himself consistently denied that he was motivated by racial prejudice and claimed rather to be concerned with standards of living and of culture. In fact, the anecdotes presented in his speeches would by most people be interpreted as prejudice: the overt language is that of culture, but symbolic codings in terms of blood and purity suggest racial themes.

But, even if the audience was already racially prejudiced, to understand what happened we need to examine the speeches themselves for the way in which Powell claimed the status of *numen*. We will also look at some statements made against him, to see what use they made of *numen/gaudens*.

Powell throughout claimed to be doing nothing more than presenting facts, facts which were willfully ignored by other politicians, by 'leader-writers of the same kidney and sometimes on the same newspaper which year after year in the 1930s tried to blind this country to the rising peril which confronted it, or archbishops who live in palaces, faring delicately with the bedclothes pulled right up over their heads.'

He presented his 'facts' in two ways. 'Numbers', he said, 'are of the Essence', and his speeches are given the appearance of objectivity by statistics on immigration, on the relative size of the white and the colored population, and on how this will be affected by projected relative population growth. Secondly, his message is conveyed through homely and immediate anecdotes: Powell's meeting an upstanding, loyal, modest and hard-working Englishman who tells him that Britain is finished because of the blacks, and he proposes to migrate elsewhere; the old lady left alone in a street populated entirely by blacks, who deliver excreta through her letterbox; the widow with two children, persecuted by blacks; and so on. All these anecdotes suggest a small and defenceless person, but one who has served his country well and who has high standards of decency and probity: both the person and the standards are in dire need of a defender (like Powell) who will speak out on their behalf. If there are to be laws against discrimination, Powell suggests in one of his speeches, they should be aimed at those who discriminate in favor of black immigrants against the defenceless white natives.

These statements, and others like them, provoked three kinds of answer. The first simply denied the facts. Powell's opponents produced counter-statistics and counter-projections, arguing that his figures were false and made out the situation to be far more serious than in fact it was. Similarly, there was an air of 'folklore' about the stories which he told (particularly the fate of the old widow and the turds through her letter-box) and Powell was invited to say when and where and who told him.

The second type of answer was that Powell was making a mountain out of a molehill, in order to serve some other end (*gaudens*). If not Powell himself, then others in neighboring constituencies were using the same themes in order to win elections. Furthermore, Powell had his eye on the leadership of the Conservative Party, if not of the country, and he had done nothing more than seize upon the theme which he thought would give him maximum publicity and a maximum following. The implication of these arguments is that the race argument has been located too high up the pyramid, and that it is in fact a matter of vote getting in constituencies, or at most winning the leadership of the Conservative Party. Powell has no right to speak of the interests of the nation, this criticism says, because he is in fact intervening only to improve his position in his constituency and in the Conservative Party.

The third riposte goes completely in the other direction. Those who make it speak in the interests not even of the nation but of humanity at large. These were the criticisms which spoke in terms or orderliness and decency and humanity, and accused Powell of fomenting disorder and of being a racist.

In answer to the first kind of criticism, Powell continued to throw statistics against statistics and to produce anecdotes in corroboration for earlier anecdotes. Against the second criticism he made no direct denial; instead he used the themes both of *numen* and of *dolens*. He presented himself, before all else, as a patriot, a defender of the English way of life, the ordinary man. He was not, he said, a racist: he was merely pointing out the fact that racial differences led to disorder and in the case of Britain would lead to a lowering of cultural standards and of the standard of living. Politicians did not understand the importance of what he was saying (*dolens*). Those who accused him of being a racist either did not know what was going on (faring delicately, like archbishops, under the bedclothes) or were unpatriotic, ready to abandon their national heritage like the appeasers of Nazi Germany in the 1930s.

Making due allowance for the skill of the rhetoric and for the use of symbols of blood and purity, Powell succeeded in vastly expanding the scale of his operations and of this question by linking the alleged persecution of old ladies with the future of the nation. At this point the debate had gone beyond reasoning into slogans and had reached the stage where only simple drastic solutions seemed acceptable: Powell himself proposed to send the migrants home again, or at least to encourage them to go away.

Powell's activities caused considerable embarrassment to his Conservative Party, then in Opposition. He had achieved an enormous mass following, which might be made to serve the party's interests. On the other hand, what he said and the way he said it was repugnant to many of his colleagues. When the Labour Government brought in a Race Relations Bill in April 1968, it was left to Mr. Hogg, the Conservative spokesman on Home Affairs, to make the Party's position clear. Hogg opposed the bill, but did so on the grounds that it would not serve to produce racial harmony. In effect, and with all the appearances of friendliness and respect, he ditched Powell. He made no accusations of *gaudens*: he hardly talked about racism. In place of the thundering metaphors which resonate throughout Powell's speeches, Hogg made a lot of feeble jokes and pleasantries and in effect defined the so-called 'race problem' as one which had nothing to do with race but everything to do with housing problems, job opportunities, and so on; in other words, the kind of problem which can be settled by reasonable men, making reasonable compromises, using their common sense. Powell's level of *numen* is quite inappropriate: the nation and its heritage are not in any danger and no intervention at that level is called for. From the level of x+2 (the nation) Hogg relegated the problem to the level of x—2, questions of housing and jobs in those particular areas of those particular towns in which immigrants had settled. He thus attempted to reduce the problem in scale (in every sense of that word), to a level at which it could be dealt with not through sterotypes and simplification, but by a rounded and comprehensive consideration of particular situations and particular interests. To use an analogy, he reduced the problem (or tried to) from Barth's 'asset' level to his 'elementary' level.

The story of Enoch Powell, since it was a slice of life, inevitably went beyond the single pyramidal model outlined in earlier sections. In these I suggested that we begin the analysis by looking at situations in which the contestants shared a common pyramid of values. A claim to be *numen* is an invitation to agree upon common values, just as an accusation of *gaudens* is a statement of incompatible values. The normative themes of patriotism and racial prejudice were both attempts to find a common agreed ground from which to begin settling an argument: an attempt to define the end which would settle the means. (In this particular case, probably neither Powell nor his opponents hoped to make the other side change their minds: rather, both wanted to persuade an audience to adopt their viewpoint.)

How do these two normative themes, patriotism and racial prejudice (humanity at large), relate to one another?

Let us recall an assumption made early in the essay: as the level of generality rises in the pyramid, so the scale increases. The higher the claimant to *numen* goes, the more people are involved. This contains a simple utilitarian idea (obviously of practical use in electoral situations) to the effect that issues are more important as more people define themselves as likely to be affected by the outcome. This simple assumption now can be questioned by introducing the equally simple notion that the type and degree of involvement is no less important than the numbers involved.

The point to note is that Powell's opponents failed to reduce him by the accusation of 'racist'. What is the significance of this?

The claims failed because the audience would not accept as relevant the level of value offered as *numen*. They did not reject the value absolutely. The accusation of 'racist' was made from the level of common humanity, and not even the most primitive of Powell's supporters would have publicly denied such an ultimate Christian principle. But they did implicitly deny the speaker's definition of humanity. They were like the Greeks whose *ecumene* comprises not all men, but only civilized mankind, only those who have been civilized according to Greek standards.

We began with a model in which the generality of accepted values and the size of collectivities increased together, step by step. According to this, a claim to be *numen* was stranger insofar as it involved a larger number of people. This turns out now not always to be the case. Beyond a certain size of collectivity, the strength of the normative theme may diminish: thus in the Powell case a claim made from the level of all of mankind was noticeably not stronger than a claim made on the level of patriotism. The higher collectivities, identified by more generalized values, tend to lose their potency, and people operate a value-scale which is linked not with the mere size of the collectivity but with communities morally defined.

5. Propositions and speculations

Small-scale 'elementary' societies exemplify most perfectly shared values: in them there should be the least uncertainty about the validity of a particular claim to *numen*, and it should be that much the easier for *numen* intervention.

On the other hand, these are also the societies in which people know one another 'in the round'. They possess the maximum amount of information required to make an accusation of *gaudens*. Therefore, it is most difficult to sustain a claim to be *numen*, and this fact is noticed in everyday common-sense in phrases about prophets in their own country, heroes and valets, and so on.

This apparent contradiction is resolved if it is the case that the strongest values are those which are not enunciated, which do not require discussion and justification, and which therefore do not require a prophet (*numen*) to stand up for them. The emergence of a prophet is, perhaps, already a sign that values are in doubt (Burridge 1969).

If this is the case, then we still have intact the proposition that a claim to *numen* will be acceptable to the extent that it is made from a non-partisan position. This 'anonymity' makes it the more difficult to pin an accusation of *gaudens*, because it is not the man but the mask on his face or the god within him that speaks. We can suggest, therefore, that the larger the scale, the harder it is to make an effective accusation of *gaudens*: the mask gets in the way.[7]

It is also likely that the larger the number of people involved, the lower becomes the possibility of compromise in a contest. This seems to be a matter of experience, but it can also be deduced from propositions made above. So long as the leader accepts the accusation of *gaudens* (that he stands for the interests of his own group and not for some larger collectivity) he keeps open a relatively larger number of options and remains in a position to compromise without being bound by the interests of a higher collectivity. Compromise is a 'swings and roundabouts' business, giving here in order to gain there, and the more enterprises you take into account, the greater the possibility of reaching a compromise.

Out of this discussion emerges a picture of 'elementary' societies. Not only do the members of a moral community know one another from every aspect, and take into account the whole man when they interact, but also they are unwilling to grant the anonymity required for leadership – at least to one of their own number. This has several consequences. Firstly, the tasks carried out within the moral community, the kind of activities within their competence, must be such that strong leadership, in particular, innovative leadership, is not required. In other words, such communities are competent to handle only those activities which can be brought within the sphere of their common values. Their apparatus fails when circumstances face them with other kinds of decisions and actions: this is amply shown in *Gifts and Poison* (Bailey 1971).

Secondly, if there is to be a *numen* in such communities, he needs to be totally masked to be effective: he needs to be like an oracle, a mere mouthpiece of some higher wisdom. Again, such a *numen* cannot in practice be, or cannot afford to be seen as, a leader of men, himself interested in political power. Thus, the Bocchicchios are 'primitive' and 'not intelligent' and unable to make any realistic bid to be among the leading Mafia families. In the same way the Braham is not stereotyped as the wielder of political power and as a competitor for it, but as the impersonal repository of divinity. To quote a well-known example, such figures resemble the Nuer Leopard Skin chief rather than the Nuer Prophet (Evans-Pritchard 1940). Finally, it follows that a claim to be *numen* within an elementary society is essentially a conservative position: an appeal to the highest values which are thought to define and hold together that particular type of social system. I do not mean by this that he is always an active defender of the status quo: rather, he may be like Dumont's 'renouncer', a man who represents the ultimate values of a society by separating himself, in terms of day-to-day obligation, from the 'man-in-the-world' (1970: 33–60).

Renouncers sometimes become prophets of a new social order, either something entirely new or a return to a former 'state of grace' (Dumont 1970, Burridge 1969, and others). This comes about when the 'elementary' society is compelled by some change in its environment to have greater contact with a larger and less personalized social system. In such circumstances the man claiming to be *numen* represents not merely the repository of accepted wisdom and morality, but also the innovator, teacher, and interpreter of newer values: a synthesizer. To be successful he must have had, metaphorically speaking, a period in the desert which separated him from values and affiliations relatively low on the pyramid and identified him firmly with its apex. He represents not any particular group or particular value but the ultimate and eternal verities, This point is crucially important: to paraphrase Dumont, he renounces obligations in a particular world, the better to represent its ultimate values.

If he fails to do this and remains contaminated by particular affiliations, his moral intervention will be interpreted as *gaudens*. In this way Vinoba's association with the Congress Movement during the Freedom Fight left him slightly vulnerable to accusations of serving the interests of the party in power (Congress) in Independent India.

The prophet also fails in his claim to be *numen* if he goes too far in either direction. If his activities are such that he cannot maintain the image of being the embodiment of the ultimate values of the world he has renounced, he loses his capacity to provide acceptable interpretations of novelty. Such a man walks a tight-rope. Gandhi, compared to any other Indian politician, kept the connection with the ultimate values of the status quo and commanded a credit among peasants which was more than that of all the other politicians put together. Yet, at the same time, he was himself ensnared by those values and propounded a form of society which could not be brought back into existence in the middle of the 20th century. The act of synthesizing was beyond him, perhaps beyond anyone.

Finally, inverting Enoch Powell, numbers alone are *not* of the essence. Cultures have rules defining involvement. If numbers increase beyond the 'proper' collectivity, then the claim to *numen* becomes weaker. This fact undermined the campaign to brand

Powell as nothing more than a racist. Mere humanity, the collectivity against which the accusation of racism is made, has gone beyond the level where ordinary people in England at that time were willing to acknowledge moral responsibility. The man who claims to speak on behalf of humanity is not directly accused as *gaudens* (for not enough is known about him), but rather discussed as irrelevant. He is put beyond the bounds where compromise and argument are possible, because he has gone beyond the boundaries of the ultimate values which his opponents would accept. He becomes one of 'them' rather than one of 'us', and it becomes easy for Powell to brand such critics as intrinsically evil by associating them with those guilty and improvident (and self-interested) men who thirty years before had attempted to appease Hitler.

6. Conclusion

In forecasting the effectiveness of the political use of normative themes, numbers are certainly part of the essence, but that phrase must be used in a sense different from Powell's. Up to a point, God is on the side of the big battalions, but the contestant attempting to enlarge his support has to make the most delicate use of those normative themes which appeal to standards of righteousness (*numen*).

He first must separate himself from partisan identification with lesser groups. If successful, he enlarges the congregation of his believers; he also simplifies the language of discourse; he sharpens the adversary edge in his exchanges with his opponents; and he lowers the possibility of a compromise settlement. He can do this only to the extent (1) that he identifies the collectivity which is relevant in the sense that it can give him power (Englishmen and not all humanity in the Powell case); and (2) that he makes himself acceptable as the embodiment of the dominant value of that collectivity. The larger effectiveness of his politics depends, of course, also on other things: in particular, the dominant value (Gandhi's small community ethic) may be an ineffective guide to action in the present circumstances.

THEODORE SCHWARTZ

The Size and Shape of a Culture

1. Introductory remarks

This paper is a conceptual exploration of various dimensions and effects of cultural and societal scale, particularly with respect to the variation and commonality of culture as it is distributed among the individuals of a population, however delimited. A distributive model of culture is employed. In this model, culture is conceived of as complexly distributed among the individuals, groups, categories, statuses, and other segments or designates of a society. A society – a population marked by some degree of interdependence and inter-communication – is here taken to be a cultural artifact or system. I believe that a distributive model of culture is needed for conceptualizing culture over the entire range of societal scale and evolution.[1]

Durkheim (1893, 1933) will serve as my point of departure. Like many others, Durkheim assumed that early, technologically primitive, or small-scale societies were far more homogeneous than later complex societies. And certainly with reference to the division of labor (number of specializations), that is true. But Durkheim further assumed that the culture of small-scale societies consisted only or largely of the collective representations all members held in common. Such representations could not differentiate one individual from another. The consciousness of the individual was a collective consciousness. One person was like another and the solidarity of society was based on likeness. This was Durkheim's familiar 'mechanical solidarity':

> The first [collective or mechanical solidarity] can be strong only if the ideas and tendencies common to all the members of the society are greater in number and intensity than those which pertain personally to each member . . . But what makes our personality is how much of our own individual qualities we have, what distinguishes us from others. This solidarity [mechanical] can grow only in inverse ratio to personality. There are in each of us, as we have said, two consciences: one which is common to our group in its entirety which, consequently, is not our self, but society living and acting within us: the other, on the contrary,

represents that in us which is personal and distinct, that which makes us an individual. Solidarity which comes from likenesses is at its maximum when the collective conscience completely envelops our whole conscience and coincides in all points with it. But at that moment our individuality is nil. It can be born only if the community takes smaller toll of us. (p. 129)

One further quotation will show the contrast with organic solidarity:

Whereas the previous type implies that individuals resemble each other, this type presumes their difference. The first is possible only insofar as the individual personality is absorbed into the collective personality; the second is possible only if each one has a sphere of action which is peculiar to him; that is, a personality. (p. 131)

Durkheim pointed to the trend toward a diminishing of intercultural variation even as intracultural variation increases due to specialization.

The view of primitive or small-scale societies as homogeneous has been prevalent in anthropology. The typical monograph has described homogenized cultures, with the individual rarely seen as having any importance. The reader is usually denied whatever diversity, if any, the ethnographer encountered among his informants. We catch glimpses of such diversity even in some of the so-called 'simpler' societies, as when Spencer and Gillin mention differences of opinions and innovations under debate in the planning of Arunta ceremonials (Spencer & Gillin 1899). But the notion that anthropologists deal with relatively homogeneous cultures – abstracting that essential homogeneity from the background noise of insignificant diversity – has greatly affected our very concept of culture. For some time, our definitions of culture have centered almost exclusively on the sharedness of rules, beliefs, and practices among the members of a society. In terms of this conception, variation has meant deviation.

My interest in distributive models of culture stems from my first field work in Manus. In response to my most conventional inquiries, I encountered diversity – the conspicuous individuality of informants, their characteristic styles, their stubbornly individualized viewpoints, the lengthy discussion, both where my questions were concerned and where their own problems of action were concerned. In short, I found what I had long experienced in my own society: *the constant litigation of culture*. Were these all the effects of acculturation in Manus? Obviously, the situation in the area had become more complex than it was prior to involvement with Europeans.

Must we reckon that the pre-contact situation would have brought us back to the Durkheimian collective consciousness and solidarity of likeness? That is possible, but I have come to doubt it. Accounts of the then much less acculturated horizon of Manus culture (as, for example, in Fortune's [1935] classic study of Manus religion) present the same strong and distinctive personalities, the same diversity of approaches, the same small innovations and individual styles competing in the shaping of events. A search, with this problem in mind, through the ethnographic literature would probably support the view that this degree of diversity within the limits of a culture is not unusual. I believe even the most minimal community would reveal a comparable distinctiveness of personality and cultural variation *when measured against the scale of the culture, and by the concerns of its members.* The cultures of relatively small-scale societies were much more complex than I had been led to expect, and they called for new models and methods if I was not to discard the bulk of my observations in favor of some highly filtered and homogenized ethnography. However it might fit small-scale societies, our concept of culture certainly seemed inadequate for application to the obviously diverse, stratified, regionally differentiated, ethnically complex, pluralistic, national and industrial societies.

Durkheim, Compte, and Spencer were correct, of course, in stating that one of the basic means by which societies became more complex and capable of integrating larger populations was through the division of labor. Durkheim speaks as if there were some initial, unified pool of functions into which each individual of a small-scale society was dipped, so that all exercised the same functions with mimimal differentiation for sex and age. A society such as Manus, regardless of the small size of the individual communities, was far from being as simple as Durkheim might have envisioned. There were already many specialized crafts, as well as groups specialized in particular ecologies and in mediating between or controlling access to other groups. There were many specialized manufactures; certain persons of only one or a few villages made all important goods, which were traded throughout the Admiralty Island archipelago by others who specialized as middlemen. Obsidian spearheads, clay pots, baskets, carvings, shell money – all had specialized origin. There were musicians and poets whose works were usually commissioned by others. There were some who were genealogical experts; others known for canoe building or drum making; others known as warriors with a particular appetite for raiding; others with a flair for entrepreneurship; and still others who acted for clients in cases of law or illness. This differentiation was based more in personalities than in formally recognized statuses, and none was a full-time occupation. But they were all specializations nevertheless. They gave to life and to culture a distinctly individualized texture.

If one chooses to look upon culture as a body of information and of constructs derived from events, one can see also that its distribution among the members of a society is a way of transcending the limitations of the individual in the creation, use, and storage of the cultural mass. Distribution provides a means whereby a society can carry a much greater cultural inventory than it could if it were confined to a degree of likeness as posited by Durkheim for simpler societies. So in both ways – in the distribution of culture over individuals, and in the distribution of functions and cultural constructs of specialized behaviours over an increasing inventory of statuses – culture may be seen as growing in mass while society grows in scale.

If culture is not to be defined as a shared or common set of constructs held by all members of a society, how should it be delimited? We may begin by defining the 'personality' of each individual as the total set of implicit constructs derived from his experience in all the events making up his life history, as well as from new formations based on manipulation, combination, or transformation of such constructs. His personality is the individual's version or, more precisely, his 'portion' of his culture. The personalities of the individuals of a society constitute the individualized texture of a culture, its distributive locus, and its social units.[2] Between the extremes of total homogeneity and total heterogeneity we may speak of a 'structure of commonality', which consists of all the intersects among personalities. The social structure of commonality comprises the intersects among the personalities of sets of individuals having some common social function, attribute, identity, or accorded significance. We would expect the intersects of the social structure of commonality to contain the relative peaks of commonality. Such peaks reflect the degree of common experience among the members of a social attribute-cluster or status group, as well as socially functional standardizations.

Having dispensed with the *a priori* assumption of a given degree of homogeneity in a culture, we could define culture distributively as the structure of commonality, but this would not go far enough. There is reason for including in the culture *all* of the content of each personality – not only that which lies in some intersect among personalities, but also that which lies in the differences among personalities. This inclusiveness is important to the adequacy of the culture concept in dealing with change, innovation, creativity, and the internal productivity of new content and goals within a cultural system. *A culture, then, is the set of personalities of the members making up a society, including (but not wholly comprised by) the structure and social structure of commonality; thus it includes all the experientially derived and transformed constructs held by any member of that society.* Any one personality is not a culture. But that personality along with all others in a society as they interact among themselves in events, and along with that information stored externally in artifacts, does constitute a culture.

We have rejected Durkheim's position that individuation starts at a zero-point in small-scale societies. Such societies, even those approaching a theoretical minimum in scale, would seem to offer enough complexity of structure, or simply sufficient structure, to differentiate individuals from one another experientially. Structural differentiation, along with biological individuality, will produce a range of differentiated personalities in any society.

2.1. *Cultural and societal scale*

Before returning to the question of variability in the distribution of culture within populations I wish to explore some ways of conceiving of cultural and societal scale. The concept of 'societal scale' is relatively familiar; that of cultural scale is much less so. The intricate relationship between the two has received little consideration at all. Societal scale seems most reasonably considered in terms of sheer numbers of people integrated or identified with one another to some degree. Cultural scale may be intuited as information and representations, generated and stored within the personalities of individuals, as well as stored externally in the forms imparted to and readable from artifacts. There obviously is a relationship between the size of a society and the size of its culture. But that relationship is conditioned by the degree of social specialization, by the referential power of the stored representations, by the ratio between internal storage (in personalities) and external storage (in artifacts), as well as other factors.

2.2. *Size and scale*

We think of 'scale' primarily in terms of the sheer number of individuals in some way integrated or identified as members of a society. Large-scale societies, as I shall discuss later, contain within them many smaller segments preserving features of small-scale societies within the larger. We would miss or underemphasize this small-scale structure if we characterized the society only by its maximal scale.

Integration may be the main criterion for considering a population to be a society. It is necessary to distinguish a range of *degrees* of integration rather than trying to define a single level that we will call a society. A common identity, whether self-ascribed or imputed by outsiders, may be of varying effect and, in any case, leaves the question of social integration incompletely specified. At present, a world-wide maximal level of integration encompasses all societies. Below this maximal level, a great number of societies and sub-societies branch in a hierarchy of inclusiveness over a wide range of levels of societal scale. The degree of integration of a society at a given level depends on two things: first, the degree of interdependence, interaction, or exchange with coordinate societies at that level; and second, the degree to which functions have emerged at that level so that the level constitutes a supra-society interacting with the coordinate subsocieties (imposing control or constraint, decision, regulation, allocation, or distributive and sanctioning functions). The supra-society has identified agencies with which sub-societies interact in addition to their direct interaction with each other.

The distributive model of a culture requires specification of the societal level delimiting the set of personalities in which the culture is located. Self and other group identifications will often lead us to relatively familiar and relatively unambiguous 'societies'. As there is no one level or degree of isolation, integration, or identification to which the term 'society' should be exclusively attached, we may speak of society-designates (to include societies, 'sub-societies') at any level upon which we focus. The unspecified use of the term 'society' will be taken to mean a 'society-designate' at some level within a hierarchy of inclusion.[3] Alternatively, the ambiguity of social and cultural boundaries may be avoided or recognized by the use of the integratively neutral term 'population'.

The hierarchy of levels includes what we may call 'major levels' at which a society identifies itself and at which membership enters importantly into the sense of identity of its members. (This is in contrast with maximal, areal, sub-local, or other levels it might be useful to identify.) The importance of a given level in identifying a society or in the identities of members will vary over time and situation or frame of contrast. Thus, for a member of a Manus village at present, his village and ethnic-ecotype identification are most important while he is in his home district. Within his village, clan and lineage relations are invoked only in certain situations.

Probably no component of identity has constant salience for the individual. He is not now a member of this, now of that sub-society; he belongs at all times to a muli-level society. The shift of levels is not a change in membership, as it may be when he shifts laterally among coordinate groups.

2.3. *Scale and the function fund*

A distributive model of social structure, aside from the distribution of the cultural constructs that give it form, would involve the distribution of function over persons, statuses, groups, institutions, organizations, societies, and so forth. We characteristically encounter small groups embedded within larger groups embedded within still larger groups, finally seen as members of relatively nebulous but identifiable maximal aggregates. In some relatively small-scale societies, the number of functions at each level tends to diminish as we move upward in the hierarchy of scale; that is, in the structure of inclusiveness. For Manus, union under a single political leader never extended beyond the village, and even there it was insecure. 'Ethnic' groups of villages speaking a common language and occasionally professing a common history tended to intermarry with one another more often than not, although a significant proportion of marriages occurred across such ethnic lines. Two villages, members of the same ethnic group, were not constrained from warfare. They were not necessarily allies. They usually shared the same ecological setting, so that trade among them tended to be social-ceremonial rather than economically necessary. One of the few definite functions that I could find attributed to an overall ethnic grouping was exophagy ('eating out'): if you took a captive or killed a member of your own ethnic group, you didn't eat him. But you could send the body to be eaten by a trade partner in another ethnic group.

Although the functions of the higher-order groupings were both attenuated and sometimes vague, they did represent societal functions indicative of not fully realized possibilities of organization and integration. Sahlins has argued that the maximal grouping on one societal level is the organized functional grouping of the next in evolutionary process (1968).

Increase of societal scale may lead to the gradual acquisition of functions by higher-level societies at the expense of lower-order societies, in addition to new functions emergent at the higher level. It may be useful to develop the concept of a 'function fund'. The fund is not absolutely fixed but is open to new functions. It is divided, increasingly separated, and allocated both horizontally

221

(among coordinate societies and organizations) and vertically (among societal levels). The horizontal tends to tilt into the vertical as functions are culturally ranked. Functions may be divided, combined, transferred, usurped, and fulfilled more or less successfuly. Institutions, organizations, societies, or individuals must adapt to loss or gain of functions. Much of the literature on the family reports a progressive loss of function, leaving its residual functions poorly understood. Much of U.S. political rhetoric involves the perception of and calls for resistance to the upward flow of function. There is a discourse parallel between function and power, although the measure of power is not necessarily the number of functions but control or exercise of any vital function that could stop the system in the short run. For these reasons, change of scale, the emergence of new levels, leads to struggle for and resistance to the reallocation of function.

2.4. *Boundaries*

We cannot avoid the problem of societal boundaries. These may often amount to gradients or zones of transition rather than clear-cut lines of inclusion/exclusion. We cannot count the number of members of a society without being able to decide on its boundaries. We must accept the possibility of ambiguous membership and relative boundedness for some social entities. In some situations we may find relatively discrete, well-bounded, non-overlapping societies; but often we will find instead overlapping, non-discrete, but inclusively related societies. We may find that the maximal extension of a given society ramifies widely and indefinitely through the networks of its individuals, until such interlacing and overlapping networks include all of the geographically accessible population of an area in chains of relatedness. (Schwartz 1963.)

Maximal groupings sometimes coincide with some clear-cut geographical isolate. The Manus form a distinctive areal culture, owing to a separation from their nearest neighbors by at least 150 miles of ocean and the realistic policy of Manus sailors never to lose sight of their shores (if they can help it). Further, we may often have recourse to relatively definite political boundaries in which the publics of leaders at some levels of organizational scale may be enumerable. At other levels, enumeration may be impossible. Manus leadership was largely confined to the village level, and subject there to cleavage of the local constituency. A leader of great prestige had an aura of influence of tenuous extension and reliability within the radius of his renown. The membership of this circle could neither be counted, nor counted upon.

It would probably be desirable to distinguish size and scale. We should speak of differences of scale in reference to a difference in size that implies organizational discontinuity. Size is a continuous variable, but we want scale to sort itself into levels with differing organizational and experiential implications. We should be looking for a series of levels or break-points in scale, although of course we do not expect abrupt breaks, beyond the lower end of the size dimension. We would expect organizational differences between groups of two, three, four, or five but not between say, groups of fifty-six and fifty-eight. Rather, we would look for transitional zones marked by coeval emergent and remnant modes of organization resulting from growth of scale (escalation). Entities of higher scale will not necessarily lose all of the attributes of smaller scale, but may retain many in association with its substructures. In other words, we would expect the consequences of scale differences to 'scale' in the statistical sense, though the unfortunate homonymy of terms is confusing. (Carneiro 1970.)

Various theorists have discussed the major break between micradic and macradic relations.[4] The micradic extends through dyads, triads, etc., as far as relations can be extended in which interacting individuals may take each other into account as specific and known individuals, besides whatever categorical relations may exist between them. Beyond the transition zone, relations are said to be impersonal; individuality is not known and cannot be reckoned in interaction; relations tend to be categorical and functionally specific, oriented by relative statuses. Some micradic break-points have been developed by Simmel in his discussion of dyads and triads, a theme which Bailey developed at this conference. (See Bailey, this volume; Simmel 1950.)

3. Structural scale

I have been discussing size as the primary dimension of scale, differentiating it as a continuum from scale as a series of levels. Now I wish to consider the implications of scale in relation to social structure and culture. 'Structural scale' refers to possible measures of complexity: how much structure is there in a given social entity? We might even speak of density of structure in terms of the number of structural differentials for a given population (such as Marsh's [1967] scale of social differentiation). We might refer to the spatial density of structure in a similar manner.

We could look also at the longitudinal, temporal compression of structure in terms of structural change over time. First, such change would encompass relatively stable status structures, such as corporations having a turn-over rate or flow-through of personnel while conserving a configuration of functions. Abstraction is the basic adaptation of such corporations. And yet particular personalities in specific statuses do have their effects. Rates of personnel turn-over affect scale differently than does the size of the synchronous personnel set. Second, changes in societal states that are potential in a social structure need not represent structural changes but rather partly reversible phases. Examples would be the structural effects of war and peace, business, and domestic cycles. In these terms, a relatively stable culture could have considerable temporal complexity in sequential or alternative social forms.

Change of scale in the temporal dimension of cultures comes with the onset of accelerating rates of irreversible change that is increasingly perceptible and demanding of adjustment, measured against the lifespan of individuals. In this temporal flux, individuals and groups are differentiated into overlapping, co-existing time-limited cultures. These will be discussed in a later section.

We should also take into account the distribution of population over structure. For example, some statuses may be occupied infrequently by relatively few people, while other statuses are universally occupied or held by large segments of a population. What effect does frequency, number, and proportion of personnel occupying a status have on that status, on status relations, and on the implications for roles? It depends on the functional integration of statuses: for example, the extent to which large numbers of people rely on the occupation of certain specialized statuses by one, a few, or a small proportion of persons in a society. Where a status is both meagerly populated and simultaneously of functional importance to large numbers of people, we would expect to find a concentration of power, prestige, and set of status-qualifying attributes which very few can fulfill.

The distribution of population over a status structure suggests that with growth of scale, there would be increasingly small face-to-face ratios. This concept may be illustrated by my experience in Manus – of being 1 to 20,000 natives, all of whom felt they knew me because I had visited each village repeatedly. They expected me to know them when we met again at the town market, just as they expected me to know Jim, the American G.I., 'you know, the one with the red hair', who had been there during World War II. The small-world view does not grasp such asymmetries. One has a similar experience in teaching large classes. To each student whose attention is supposedly concentrated on the professor, the professor is intensely one to them, and there is the tendency for them to assume or to feel that the relationship should be more symmetrical

224

than it can be. The relatiohship is micradic in one direction and macradic in the other.

The situation of extreme face-to-face ratios is common in our society, culminating in the TV superstar or politician who performs repeatedly for tens of millions of persons. Perhaps one of the effects of charisma is the illusion that a face-to-face asymmetry between the leader or star and his innumerable public does not exist. The mass media, the cult of celebrity filling the avid demand for 'intimate detail' of the leader/star's life, further supports the illusion of symmetry. Here is the one to many, face-to-face relationship in its most extreme form and yet the small-scale aura of personalism still lingers. For people coming from a small-scale society (or as we all do, from small, local behavioral scenes), in which the face-to-face relations are more nearly even, people are often known to those on the small side of such a relation. In this case it is difficult to shake off the illusion of near-symmetry. For people in large-scale society, sophistication requires a formula such as 'You wouldn't know me, but I've been in four of your classes'. The notion of an omnipresent, omniscient god, aware of and concerned with the detailed behavior of each person, is obviously a small-scale concept extended to the most extreme asymmetrical face-to-face ratio. If paranoia is (among other things) based on a delusion of reference, then this is a form of positive paranoia – of the 'somebody-up-there-likes-me' variety. (See Schwartz 1973 for an extended discussion of the Paranoid Ethos.)

To continue this line of speculation a bit further, what is the opposite of paranoia as a small-scale perception amounting to a delusion of reference? Perhaps the perception that one is not a referrent for any other being in society or in the cosmos. The delusion is of non-reference, which evokes the possibility of non-being. In one extreme form, one may imagine such a person as anti-charismatic, such as the assassin achieving celebrity by the annihilation of another's charisma.

Among measures of scale of structural complexity proposed by various authors are (1) the size of the status inventory and role repertoire for an individual or for the social entity as a whole; (2) the largest status structures or organizations, measured in terms of the number of differentiated statuses organized around some function; (3) the number of echelons in hierarchic structures; and (4) the number of different event-types, each event-type having its social structure or status configuration. Further measures of structural complexity might be the ratio of status relations to statuses and the ratio of potential to actual relations among the individuals of a society. These would turn out to be significant measures because of the way they behave under growth of scale.

225

The size of a status inventory or event inventory may deviate from expectation based on some function of population size. Between societies or cultures, and between various phases of cultures, we may expect variation in structural density (in the number of distinct statuses per population size). We may refer to this distribution of statuses over a population as a 'status space'. Like the notion of a 'function fund', it implies limitation and competitive allocation. We might speak of the density of a status space as a variable. The concept is already familiar in relation to certain kinds of statuses. We speak of 'leadership space' or 'opportunity space', and the notion of expansion or contraction of opportunity space is becoming common. Expansion or contraction can relate to the number of statuses, size of and pressure on occupancy per status, and the rate of turn-over or flow-through. Such effects offer a way of viewing the familiar phenomena of status, prestige, power, and performance from the less familiar perspective of scale.

The mesh of status qualifications is not uniform, like a screen. It is variable, controlling the flow-through of individuals in statuses. The mesh must be large (that is, not narrowly defined) when the status occupancy is to be large, or when the population from which it is to be recruited is so small and fluctuating that individuals of specified personality attributes may not be present at the right time in the right numbers.[5] Where the pool is small and the mesh narrow and, perhaps, based on ascribed qualifications, we can expect wide variation in the quality of role performance. Where many are funneled toward relatively narrow status occupancy, the result will be intense competition, unstable occupancy, and structural devices for increasing the leadership or status space, as in the frequent schism and separation of leadership domains.

In much of Manus, too many aspirants are motivated to seek leadership and entrepreneurial statuses. The existence of multiple levels, each with its own leadership statuses, would be one way of increasing internal leadership space. But the echelons in traditional cultures were few. The pressure contributes to the instability of Manus communities. The credit for any feat is divided between the performer and leaders of higher echelon, to the advantage of the latter. (This applies also to bureaucracies and, perhaps to all hierarchic organizations.) A leader requires a distinctive social entity – his public – to have a group that counts for him in the prestige accountancy. His feats and those of his augmented lineage will then redound to his own credit. Fragmentation or political atomism has the effect of increasing leadership space by providing a maximum number of politically usable entities. This competitive fragmentation of social entities may be referred, not quite facetiously, to a 'fish-to-pond' ratio. Perhaps this ratio may help to describe the schismatic proliferation of entities in political, religious, and intellectual spheres of our own society. In Manus, as a concomitant of political fragmentation, integrative activities were shunted into economic and ceremonial relations, into network building rather than the control or consolidation of coherent entities.

Networks have different functions in large-scale and small-scale societies. In mosaics of small-scale societies such as traditional Manus, networks connect members of groups which may be spatially separate and ecologically complementary and which may be ethnically or culturally diverse. In spite of political atomism, quite large areas can be integrated by means of multiple, functionally diverse, interpersonal and intergroup networks. Quite large-scale integrations are attained which have tended to be overlooked because of our proclivity to see as integrated only that which is organized into a political hierarchy.

When societies are quite small, linkages through the direct personal networks of members have a greater significance for the complex of societies as a whole than would be the case in larger societies. The effective networks within a small-scale social mosaic are mainly external relations, whereas the social networks of large-scale societies are mostly internal relations. The latter will tend to substitute for corporate groups rather than being links among corporate groups. Many types of networks internal to large-scale society, of varying degrees of formality or informality, may display some of the properties and functions of corporations.

4. Cultural scale

Having considered scale in relation to societal size and structure, I would like to discuss cultural scale. While it occurs to us to think about societal scale, it may seem odd to ask, How large is a culture? Other questions follow: How much culture is there per capita, and how is it distributed? That there has been immense cultural growth is obvious, although the growth in 'mass' is partly concealed by more efficient, higher-level representations. The total stock of representations stored by an individual over the ages may be relatively constant, but the mass of referents and internal translations must have increased greatly. The change may have been relatively slight for some individuals, relatively great for others. The situation with respect to the distribution of information in a population suggests a cultural evolutionary stratification of society like that of co-existing temporal cultures that I have suggested. In a society which prides itself on its burgeoning technology, large numbers of people scarcely understand why the light goes on when they throw the switch, let alone the mysteries of their television sets.

Over the course of cultural evolution, there has been a general correspondence between the scale of human societies and the growth of culture. Cultural scale overlaps or subsumes some aspects of structural scale to the extent that we may consider social arrangements as cultural artifacts.

Some writers, notably Leslie White (1959, 1975), have suggested taking the amount of energy brought under use by a given society as a measure of cultural scale. Closely related would be the size of the inventory of tools or of artifacts in the sense of material culture. For the measure of cultural mass, however, the accumulation of information would be still more basic, if it could be measured. Information would be found in many forms – it being, of course, form itself.

There is an engineering measure of information that would have some interesting applications for us. But it views information in a relatively primitive way, mainly in terms of variance or uncertainty reduction at the code or message unit level. It does not seem to be helpful in differentiating the meaningfulness, significance, import, or referential load of a message or representation. MacKay (1952, 1959) has probed more deeply into measures of structural information and meaning, suitable as theoretical measures of culture as form and representation. (See also Garner 1962 and Attneave 1959.)

We may conceive of culture as representations or constructs that are internalized, permutated, and generated by individuals and distributed as constituents of personalities. The unweighted union of all the personality constructs of members of a society constitutes the inventory of available constructs. This union, weighted with the frequencies with which particular constructs occur across personalities, forms the informational mass of the culture. The informational complexity, density, or referential load of particular constructs will also have to be taken into account as another weighting factor if we are to compute, even in imagination, the magnitude of a culture.

We are accustomed to thinking about the distribution and stratification of wealth or power in a community; information should be viewed in a similar way. The distribution of information or constructs among the members of a society might be considered in terms of how accessible to communication, how generally available, given constructs are. What proportion is there between the disjunctive and conjunctive portions of a culture – between the structure of commonality and its complement? The growth of the cultural mass is in part accomplished by distributing this mass among the members of a society creating specialists, but less conspicuously, by simply storing the great diversity of experience in individual personalities and making this diversity accessible to some degree through communication.

Aside from the average information per capita, how significant a portion of a culture is in any given personality? What is deleted from the culture with each death? Would it, contrary to Durkheim, be greater in a small-scale society than in a large-scale one? The answer would depend on analysis of the degree of completeness of cultural transmission and the rate of culture change. Where the rate of change is appreciable and transmission relatively low, each death is a significant deletion in the phasing-in/phasing-out process. Each old man that dies in Manus now carries the past and the old culture with him. The recent death of the genealogical expert of a group of villages has left the kinship system truncated, although still functioning on the altered basis of shortened or non-specified chains of relationship. It is easy to find extreme cases, but in any culture there is some loss and some culture change with the deletion of any personality. Something comes into a culture when an event or experience is represented in any personality; it goes out of a culture when there is nowhere a representation accessible to be read by any member of the society. In large-scale cultures, explicit representation mitigates culture-loss through the death of individuals, but it does not eliminate it. Time-limited or temporal cultures are themselves constructs of the culture, perceptually segmenting the continuous process of deletion and substitution of personalities as units in the distribution of cultures in time.[6]

In addition to social distribution, external storage is also a culture amplifier. Every artifact is form or information imparted to some medium – a breath, a sheet of paper, a carved rock – in which information is stored and from which it can potentially be read. Information can be amplified as it is copied and transformed in individuals or artifacts. The amount of energy or material required has no strict proportionality to the amount of information handled. I would call the process whereby a cultural mass grows through the construction of artifacts 'exthesis'. In exthesis, man creates extension of himself and of his own capacities, thereby extending these capacities and partly separating his contribution to cultural transmission and growth from his own survival as an organism.

The cultural mass in external storage has become tremendous. As it grows, there are increasing problems of communication, of retrieval, of access, of the treatment of information as property or as a commodity, and problems of communication and the metering of information-flow across informational gradients. These problems have some significance even in relatively small-scale societies such as Manus. A culture may therefore be seen as having a communicational structure based on differential storage. It is this structure that is recognized by distributive models of culture.

Consciousness is that which is accessible to awareness, not just that which lies within the immediate awareness of the individual. Similarly, the cultural reach of individuals can be considered in terms of access, at various costs, to the distributive culture of which they are a part. The individual is bounded in his cultural reach by factors both within and external to himself. The greater the cultural mass in proportion to that stored by any given personality, the greater the lines and rates of communication must be, if the whole of a culture or some large portion of it is to be activated at any given time.

Meier discusses transaction rates as an index variable of cultural scale (1962). He sees the growth of urbanism partly in response to the need, with increasing cultural scale, for vastly increased transaction rates. He epitomizes urban life by the flow of commuters into the city, where by 5 minutes after 9 o'clock everyone can be near a telephone and opening the day's mail. The city represents high cultural density as well as high population and structural or status density. The city may be seen as having as its main function the processing of information – its generation, concentration, storage, and redistribution. Even in manufacturing, raw materials are 'informed or instructed' and then re-distributed, which is itself an informational process. Information added is a production factor often ignored except as a technological attribute of capital.

Cultural density would depend only in part on the concentration of information in space. The effect of physical space on transaction rates depends on communicational technology. Under current circumstances of electronic transmission and modern transportation, cultural density depends on access and traverse times that are, for some forms of information, relatively independent of distance.

Another measure of cultural scale might be the amount of internal variability. This could be defined in various ways. We have already spoken of the size of the cultural mass as a weighted construct inventory; but variability should also imply the existence within a single culture (a single-access system) of large numbers of alternative constructs between which the individual must choose. Berrien has discussed this measure of cultural complexity (1968). He sees increase of cultural variability as the basis for increase of uncertainty; hence of decisional space, or choice. This is not to say that choices are undetermined. Rather, branch-points occur with greater frequency, with more branches, and with only partial overview by the actor of the nexus of determinants of choice. Whether, over the course of increasing scale, there has been gain in the subjective sense of uncertainty, choice, or freedom, I cannot say. The very concepts are emergent, as is increased awareness of the determinants of choice. Simmel has noted the gain to personal freedom in mass society that compensates, in part, for its impersonality.[7] He sees this, however, largely as being the result of anonymity.

5.1. *Effects of and constraints upon escalation*

In the preceding section, I surveyed a number of dimensions, possible or imagined measures of societal and cultural scale, and indicated some possible effects of variation along these dimensions. As we undertake the study of scale, we follow a course which biologists have explored as they have considered the organization of organisms of vastly differing sizes, from unicellular animals to large multicellular organisms, and beyond individual organisms to their social and ecological coordination as species. As we are engaged in a parallel consideration of scale and organization, we may find some suggestive analogies. We are aware of the ways in which human social and cultural systems are non-commensurate with non-human organic systems. The theory of representations discussed earlier and the capacity of human systems to set goals rather than merely to pursue them in a more limited teleology are specific to human systems (Schwartz 1968).

5.2. *Disproportional growth*

I would like to explore some of the possible implications for societal and cultural scale of the principle of disproportional growth. D'Arcy Thompson in his *On Growth and Forum* (1917) has emphasized the cognitive or epistemological relativity of scale: 'There are orders of things corresponding to orders of magnitude. Each has appropriate principles of cognition'. In illustration of this principle, he states:

> The dimensions of a cilium are of such an order that its substance is mostly if not all under the peculiar conditions of a surface layer. . . . It is certain that we shall never understand these remarkable structures so long as we magnify them to another scale, and forget that new and peculiar physical properties are associated with the scale to which they belong. (p. 71)

The principle of disproportional growth is often associated with the 'square-cube law' (attributed to Archimedes): 'In similar figures the surface increases as the square, and the volume as the cube of the linear dimension'. A result of this is that a thing or an organism or a system cannot simply be scaled up yet still preserve the same form and proportions. For example, '. . . if we build two bridges geometrically similar, the larger is the weaker of the two, and is so in the ratio of their linear dimensions' (ibid., p. 26). Thompson recalls that the Lilliputians, finding Gulliver to be 12 times as tall as they were, estimated his volume and hence his ration to be 1,728 (or 12^3) more than theirs. Similarly, a fish, doubling its length, increases its volume 8 times.

It is clear that for biological systems, as well as for physical systems, one cannot simply create a giant amoeba. It would be necessary to revise the proportions and possibly also the materials. It may also be necessary to change totally the organization of the system. Thus the respiratory system of an insect would not be capable of being scaled up beyond a certain size. Berrien cites an example from architecture of school buildings which must take certain forms – elongated, narrow, and growing wings when enlarged – as long as they are dependent on windows for light and air (1968: 78). They must take the form of two rooms back to back. This constraint changes entirely with the technological possibility of artificial lighting and central air conditioning. The difference is analogous to the change of organizational principles between insects and larger animals. With reorganization, great block buildings are possible in which the surface-to-volume ratio may increase.

The important thing about the relationship between linear dimensions, area, and volume is that any force acting on or within a system will act differently with respect to these structures. Some forces act in relation to the surface area, other in relation to the mass or volume of the object, others in relation to cross-sectional diameters. For example, the strength of a supporting member varies with its cross-sectional area or the square of its linear dimension, whereas its load depends on its volume or the cube of the linear dimension (Thompson 1917: 75). The transmission of materials, gases, or heat is surface-related, while the metabolic needs of an organism or a cell depends upon its volume.

I must now cast about for ways in which the principle of disproportional growth may have relevance in the escalation of social and cultural systems. We may start with considerations of growth in size. We are seeking some suggestive derivations from the analogy to the physical or organic principle of disproportionality in growth, or simply in comparisons of structures of different sizes. We have said that scale is not simply size but differences of size that induce or require differences in structure. The structural change may be null, continuous, or discontinuous within certain ranges of the change in size. The physical and biological models mentioned may first suggest some analogies to human populations of various sizes taken in their spatial arrangements. But beyond that we are led to other, less obvious cases of disproportional growth in society and culture.

The situation is, at first, puzzling. The square-cube relation in a strict quantitative sense holds for the surface-to-volume ratio of a sphere. When we deviate from the circular and spherical, the relation of some dimension to surface or volume approaches a linear rather than a polynomial function of the dimension of the system – population size, in this case. If we want to calculate the biomass of a society, we could multiply the number of individuals by the average mass of an individual. Even if we laid all members of the society end to end, the human filament would tend to add some constant average increment of mass or volume per unit of population rather than another unit-thick outer shell of exponentially increasing volume. However, with most populations more than reproducing themselves in a certain interval, we are back to growth as measured by some exponent. Rates and patterns of population growth are well known but will not be taken up here. The implications of differing population growth rates in interaction with average longevity and population size for social organization are of extreme importance and must be mentioned.

There are ways in which some important social and cultural effects of population increase grow disproportionately to the increase of size, at rates greater or lesser than that of population growth, as functions that would involve either exponents or factorials of the N of population size. I can offer no formulae or specific exponents in this paper. Data probably exist from which some formula could be approximated (for example, in the material on size and social differentiation given in Marsh, *Comparative Sociology* [1967]). I aim only to mention a number of possible relations. The biological work of D'Arcy Thompson (1917) and Julian Huxley (1932) on heterogonic (or allometric) growth indicates that the form of systems, whether spatio-temporal or on other dimensions, can be expressed by differential rates of growth. The study of structure as differential growth rates exists as an unrealized possibility for social and cultural systems. It could shed some light on the limits of workable growth of organizational and relational schemes that might be predictive or explanatory of break-points in the discontinuum of scale.

By definition, if a growing population still constitutes a single society, then the population units, individuals, and groups must remain related to one another. They are integrated, interdependent, and intercommunicating to some extent. The 'human filament' conjured up earlier minimally fulfills this requirement. Each individual or group has direct contact with two others in the chain, as well as indirect, attenuating, transitive relations proportional to distance with all other members of the filament, whether or not its ends are joined to form a ring. We recognize in this filament the 'generalized systems' of Levi-Strauss (1969 [1949]). These systems are obviously misnamed, given the severe restraints I have indicated in comparison to 'complex' or many-to-many nets of relation and interdependence. Such rings, if they ever existed in that form, would seem to be poorly adapted to small-scale social entities, given the vulnerability to deletion of constituent groups under population fluctuation and the concentration (theoretically) of all kin of a given type in a single group. Rules of relation that produce larger rings would not be advantageous, for they would not increase the one-to-two relation of each group and would increase the vulnerability of the ring as a whole to disruption. Many-to-many related groups in diffuse and dispersed networks would be much more invulnerable to catastrophic demographic fluctuation of small local groups; also, they would have the further advantage of many more direct links and more and shorter multi-link paths to whatever resources the net covered. They also would have the advantage of the dispersion of kin of a given type over the whole net.[8]

Complex, many-to-many relations among individuals, groups, and their corpus of relations and representations lead to more than 'mere' analogy in application of the principle of disproportional growth to societies. To invoke Durkheim: 'There remains no other variable factor than the number of individuals in relation to their material and moral proximity, that is to say, the volume and density of society' (p. 339). Multiply-bound individuals and groups take on the geometry and systemics of a solid of extremely diverse parts and relationships. It is this multiplicity and multi-directionality of a variety of linkages that draws human beings into at least two dimensional relations, as reflected in the network metaphor. A society has volume (aside from literal spatial territory and biomass) to the extent that individuals are multiply connected by bonds of equal length (equality not necessary, but it enhances the sphere-metaphor): that is, bonds that are functionally equivalent and of equal transactional intensity (for example, bonds of primary relationship).

Let us consider both social and cultural complexity in terms of the number of potential relations among the elements of a society or a culture. Let N stand for the number of elements (number of persons in a society or number of representations in a culture). Then the number of potential relations among these elements increases polynomially, exponentially, or factorially under combinatoric measures of combinations, selections (indeed, of all sizes up to N), or permutations. This is indeed disproportional growth corresponding to N^2, 2^N, or $N!$ (See Gallant & Prothero 1972; Steen 1976.) However we combine or mitigate the growth of potential relations, their disparity of growth-rates probably far exceeds that of the square/cube law. Combinations in which specific arrangement or order among elements are ignored grow more slowly than permutations in which they are not ignored. Yet specific arrangement or order among elements are ignored grow more slowly of events. One of the many ways by which we reduce complexity is through grouping elements into classes, within which they can be treated as indistinguishable. We group them by abstraction into a hierarchy of classes. We create social and cultural structure. Although this drastically reduces the combinatorial growth of potential relations, individual elements remain insistently with us in the model of culture employed here. Variance in role performance, for instance, is not wholly accounted for by abstract status and role definitions.

It is evident that as the number of potential relations increases, a decreasing proportion of them can be actualized. The ratio of potential to actual relations itself increases exponentially with increase in the number of elements, and marks an important contrast between large and small societies and cultures.

Although I have chosen to speak of cultural and social size and complexity together in the above remarks, the elements and relations are obviously very different. In social relations, the ratio of potential to actual links in networks has been called the density or saturation of a network (Barnes 1969). High saturation of potential links can only be achieved in small societies or in small localities or small networks, if dispersed. As societies have grown, the overall density of actualized, non-abstractly categorical relations diminishes drastically. My remarks above on extreme face-to-face ratios indicate some of the consequences and adaptations. In culture (the elements include social forms and adaptations), the increasing ratio of potential to actual relations is that of existing knowledge and representation to their potential maximum extension, based on combination of existing elements. Growth of culture is not only combinatorial but empirical as well. Evolutionary response to the escalation of culture has produced adaptations that in turn have provided for its further exponential growth. The first knowledge revolution (if much condensation of the process is permitted) transformed knowing, in which all men have participated, to the conscious pursuit of knowledge and method – an applied epistemology. The second knowledge revolution in which we are now engaged virtually industrializes the pursuit and the training of its workers in the form of universities, research and development plants, and the accelerating production and improvement of the tools and externally-stored forms of knowledge.

The probability of connection between any two specific individuals depends in part on the spatial spread of that population. Reduction of this probability would occur where population is large, even where density is high. It is affected by other variables, such as the transaction rate and the average ambit of movement relative to the radius of the space. With other things constant, the reduction of the probability of specific encounters with increase of scale would reduce internal communication. It would affect the distribution and general accessibility of culture. Given the distribution of culture over a society, as cultural and social mass each increase, the access of an individual to any part of that mass would be greatly diminished without compensatory development of communications and organization. Such development has taken place, but it probably only partly offsets the growth of scale. Most of us have experienced this diminished access in the growth of our professional organizations and information. We are required to be more selective rather than comprehensive, though our selectivity is both purposive and contingent.

Durkheim argued that the relatively small mass of a small-scale society makes internal specialization less likely, but makes it more likely that the entity as a whole will be specialized in relation to other entities. Gallant and Prothero[9] see specialization resulting not from increased number and separation of functions, but from the disconnectedness among individuals in large-scale society making isolation and incomplete communication likely.

An interesting possible effect of scale on differentiation was suggested by Haudricourt, the French linguist.[10] He argued that we should find the greatest phonological complexity in languages spoken by small numbers of persons. In larger societies communicational gradients are such as to allow for differentiation of dialects. But with contact between dialects, internal borrowing takes place; and in borrowing, simplification or 'pidginization' results. It may hold for other aspects of culture that interaction, communication, and learning across lines of diversity may not only reduce the diversity but simplify the resulting common structures – pidginized cultures. Such cultures would be regularized, structured for relatively easy learning by adult inductees. The United States may be one such culture, but any multi-ethnic, multi-national amalgam would be to some extent.

5.3. *Analogies from 'surface-to-volume ratio': boundary effects*

We may speak of surface or boundary effects in contact between social entities. As the ratio of volume to surface increases with scale, the number of persons in border positions decreases in proportion to the number of persons in interior positions: just as, in cell division, by the time a single cell has divided six times (retaining contact), some cells are then bounded entirely by other cells so that their relation to the outer environment is a mediated one.

Haire studied a number of firms over periods of rapid growth (1959). He plotted the square root of 'surface' personnel against the cube root of 'inside' personnel and found the predicted strong relationship in all firms. Surface people were in sales, receptionists, shipping, etc., while inside people were in production, maintenance, and internal communications. There is no reason why we should expect close numerical approximatation to the square-cube law, but it is of interest to explore possible implications of interior to surface disproportionality over changes of scale. It implies that a larger society should be a more monocultural, ethnocentric, parochial society, in which a great mass of its members have contact only with other members of the same society or sub-society. The effect would be exacerbated, as in the case of the United States, where its borders bring it into tangential contact with only one other country markedly dissimilar to itself – Mexico. An identificational boundary may be relatively sharp, but to the extent that it is also a cultural or informational boundary, it is a gradient the steepness of which is variable, depending on the degree of difference it bounds. The relative steepness of outer bounds to internal subsocietal or sub-cultural bounds is also important. The low surface-to-volume ratio of large N societies is mitigated by borders with multiple flattened tangency or deviations in shape from sphericity (or circularity) which would decrease the average distance of members from a border and increase their average distance from the center. References to the distribution of a society in space usually call for a two-dimensional topology. References to sphericity or deviations from it include the relational dimension.

5.4. *Size and stability*

The growth of a system should also be seen in relation to the other systems on which it impinges or which it contains, or in which it is contained (coordinate, inclusive, and included systems). If a system is growing relative to its environment or to some source of perturbation, then the size of the system relative to the amplitude of fluctuations affecting the system would become more favorable. A small-scale society would be in the opposite situation – relatively easily wiped out by environmental and internally-generated fluctuations, like the poker player who has no reserves. The probability in a large system of a given fluctuation confronting or exceeding system limits would diminish. The increased stability of large systems can be overcome by a disturbance that affects the fine inner structure of a system more nearly on the scale of the disturbance itself. Toxicity may be an example of this effect; a minute quantity of an intrusive substance affects some small but vital substructure of a large organism. Despite the apparent disparity of scale, there is scale-matching at the internal locus of functional interference. Thus we must complicate the picture of large-scale related stability, noting that this relative invulnerability may be offset by the tendency for large-scale systems to be more internally functionally differentiated and integrated. They are then vulnerable to the disruption of functionally essential small sub-systems. This in turn may be mitigated by redundancy of essential structures and by the relatively large scale of sub-systems in large systems.

On the other hand, a system may generate disturbances of its environment which will increase in effect as its scale of intervention approaches that of the environment itself or of its critical substructures. Technology has amplified these interventions into the environment. The probability of an intervention encountering or exceeding the limits of the larger system of the environment increases with these changes.

We may speak of a set of degrees of system disturbances. First is a zone in which a perturbation is just perceptible, therefore informative of potential disruption rather than disruptive. Next is a zone of plastic recovery in which the system readily bounces back to its original form. There is also a zone of system adaptation. In this, the limits of the system are confronted, not destroyed. The system is capable of adapting or accommodating. The magnitude of a given change relative to a system may be measured by the extent of necessary system accommodation. Finally there is a zone of irreversibility, in which the system is either destroyed or transcends the perturbation that breeches its limits and reorganizes as a different system with a new set of limits. A system may maintain itself, it may be destroyed, or it may be transformed. For disturbances of relatively low degree, negative feedback may suffice for restoration. This mechanism is dependent on error or deviation

238

which provides the information for corrective response. In organic social, and cultural systems, deviation and response on the many parameters of such systems constitute much of the life or activity of the system as constant as respiration, metabolism, behavior, and communication. An inerrant system would be, if not dead in the sense of dissolution, at least in suspended animation. So essential is deviation to the life or activity of a system that organic, social, and cultural systems must be self-exciting, providing constant perturbation. Negative feedback does not ensure that disturbances of the system will remain within restorable limits. Feed-forward is also often required. In this, early warning sensors are used to detect fluctuations in the environing system before they have produced perhaps excessive changes in the system itself, thus limiting system deviations to which negative feedback will respond. But feed-forward also depends, in this case, on the detectable occurrence of environmental deviation. Again, depending on magnitude and speed, the system may not be able to respond with sufficient rapidity or adequacy. We have noted that the environmental changes may be induced by the system itself – say, the technology-amplified effect of a human population on its environment. At increasing magnitudes, such effects may not be reversible. Our capacity not merely to respond and restore but to anticipate irreversible disturbances is available, but as we know, our use of this capacity is not guaranteed.[11]

Anomalous as it seems, it may be that the smaller the group (the greater its surface in relation to its volume), the more prone it is to fission. Even a relatively densely packed status and leadership space would remain small and likely to be split between two personalities in conflict or competition over leadership or the allocation of functions or resources. This effect has been discussed earlier; the point is that here, too, smallness leads to instability. The membership is at or near the surface, not enveloped within the volume of the group. The sanction of withdrawal and schism is a constant limit on any trend to escalate through hierarchic differentiation. Smallness again appears to be self-maintaining. (Schwartz 1963, 1975c.)

Warfare is a surface effect. It was endemic in Manus with more or less constant raiding – forever scoring and evening up scores.[12] The situation could be compared to a mass of bubbles. The expansion of each (at least interior to the mass) was limited by the pressure toward expansion of all other bubbles. Each group kept up an aggressive outer posture of thrusts and raids against others in order to prevent its own contraction. Warfare was exacerbated by its integration into the system of entrepreneurial renown. The small

239

scale also meant larger alliances were either not possible or unstable. These small-scale, atomistic areas were a complex of garrison villages. Each group was virtually encircled. The encirclement fears of large nations may be relics of small-scale thinking.

The incidence and type of warfare may depend on relative scale rather than the absolute scale of the separate entities. It occurs among coordinate, autonomous social entities. It is inhibited by subordination to a higher level state, whether this is imposed by force or contract or both. Pacification of warlike Manus was accomplished with remarkably meager personnel and direct use of force. In some areas it preceded actual effective governmental control. The threat of force was there. But the perceived advantages of a superordinate state (albeit colonial) added the legitimacy of contract, the dissolution of which was feared in anticipations of decolonization.

The relatively large surface of small societies affects diffusion, rate of change, and cultural stability. It would seem that a culture is most affected by the input of information from other societies. The outward transmission of information – culture transfer – is just as fateful in the long run as it diminishes the informational gradient between societies.

Under conditions of small scale, the surface would act not as a bottleneck (a least dimension) but in a manner comparable to that of very small animals in which transpiration and heat loss are a serious problem, due to the relatively large surface-to-volume ratio. It would be critical to keep the boundary from being too permeable in either direction if cultural distinctiveness is to be maintained. The very proximity of inside to outside may make boundary and identificational problems more acute. Difference, and therefore the identity and autonomy of a society, must be maintained in spite of close contact. One way of accomplishing this is what I have called 'cultural totemism' (Schwartz 1975a). This refers to the use of a few 'small' cultural and linguistic differences as emblems of group identity. The effect is to maintain or amplify difference despite the lack of a real communicational barrier through the use of almost purely identificational barriers to assimilation.

Boundary effect also depends on the amount of difference encountered at the boundary. The multi-ethnicity of Manus greatly increases the boundary effect. The surface of interaction between two culturally differentiated groups is also increased by the dispersion of one group within another, or by the dispersion of one group over many others. The latter was the case of the Manus fishing people, each community of which situated itself in relation to other widely dispersed and culturally varied land-based groups.

240

Obviously migration also greatly increases the surface contact area of a group. Labor migration has this effect by dispersing individuals of one society into the midst of another society. This effect is offset considerably by the clustering of people of like provenance in the centers of migration.

The distributive structure of a culture could be described in terms of internal informational gradients. Such gradients are of importance in social structure, often being the basis or the rationale for status distance. These gradients are maintained by the culturally regulated metering of internal information-flow. The effect of metered flow is to maintain such distances or to reduce informational gradients gradually or suddenly. Initiation can be seen in this way, in that a society maintains and, at the right time, removes an informational gradient between novitiate and initiator. This concept of controlled informational gradients and metered information-flow in culture and between cultures can be widely applied to such diverse subjects as the theory of incest, the cultural structure of education, and diffusion between cultures, including relations of development and underdevelopment.

To speak of boundaries does not imply that a cultural system is closed. Such systems are always open: or more accurately, they are semi-permeable. Their surface of contact with their environment and with other cultures is a filter, differentially open and closed, changeable in its transmission characteristics as the culture changes. Communication across boundaries not only can take place: in a sense, it is the very point of them. There can be no communication (other than ritual exchange of tokens of commonality) without a degree of difference and independence between different points in a system. (A single individual may meet these conditions if productive thought may be understood in part as internal communication.) At the same time, where communication is most needed and possible, given differences and an informational gradient, it may be least possible in another sense because separation or independence may coincide with a lack of shared codes with which to discharge the message potential between these points, persons, or societies.

5.5 *Attribute clustering*

With increasing scale, while proportionately fewer members of the population have contact with the outside, the amount of contact that people have with others on the inside increases. The larger the group, the greater its volume relative to its surface, the higher the probability that the contacts of an individual will be with others who are similar to himself (with members rather than nonmembers). On the other hand, a greater volume-to-surface ratio de-creases the probability of any two specific individuals coming into contact by chance. However as the members of a population are of differing cultural, ethnic, class, occupational, religious, generational, and other identificational attributes, then random distribution and association of persons would minimize the level of commonality in each person's social sphere. Random distribution of persons within the volume of a large-scale society is greatly reduced, and therefore local commonality is increased by many mechanisms of assortment by attribute (attribute clustering). A social structure could be described partly in terms of such assortment mechanisms which help accomplish the vast reduction of the potential to the actual.

If we were to imagine a city like Los Angeles, in which everyone were assigned residence and other relations on the basis of some random principle, there would be a great lowering of the levels of commonality in the average encounter among persons. Attribute clustering raises the level of commonality, probably adds to the individual's sense of security, and diminishes both the need for and the possibility of actual communication. Given the growth of scale of a social entity, whatever internal differentiation arises will be amplified by assortment mechanisms that will lead to further internal structuration or cellulation of that larger entity. The situa-tion at its most extreme could lead to virtual isolation of some sub-segments of a given entity from one another. We would find involuted networks folded in upon themselves to keep even func-tional contacts within the attribute or identificational group.

Isolative trend would have to be counteracted by cross-cutting ties and contacts if the society is to remain a single entity with relations other than through the supra-system. Cross-cutting ties of intermarriage and of exchange that served to maintain contact among small-scale societies no longer fulfill this function to any great extent in large-scale modern societies. Ties of exchange or of functional complementarity can only accomplish a minimum of integration, in terms of maintenance of levels of commonality, as long as they are limited to single function, impersonal contacts. Difference-amplifying mechanisms operate to increase structural complexity and to increase the cellulation of the structure of com-monality. They tend to enhance commonality within the cells of that structure, at the same time that coordination between cells is maintained by some common orientations and constructs associated with larger entity functions.

Against the background of attribute clustering, there is another process or effect we might call 'attribute dispersion'. Perhaps an appropriate name for attribute dispersion could be the 'Nazarene effect'. Jesus was not received as the Messiah in Nazareth; only strangers could see him in this persona. 'A prophet is not without honor, save in his own country, and in his own house.' We could examine, in this respect, the role of the stranger, the foreigner, the overseas enclave – Chinese, Lebanese, Jew, traders among 'Goyim'.[13] Aside from all other aspects of colonialism, the colonists among the colonized were outsiders to all local systems. As such, the least among them could command an authority derived in part from his salience as an outsider – from his immunity to the 'Nazarene effect'. This effect entered into the 'pacification' of an area such as New Guinea where, in addition to the demonstration of new instruments of force, the outsider was useful to the native as a third force in whose name one could stop fighting.[14] Pristine states are rare; the state has most often been imposed, facilitated both by force and the externality of the alien. For some things, the person must be an inside outsider, as in the case of Manus curers treating sorcery. The European is too far outside; he is not relevant to the sorcery system. But the foreign (not immediately local) native curer is more effective than the local curer, especially if one must travel far and pay much to be treated. One often sees foreigners living on the cheap charisma of their attribute differentiation, liberated from the invisibility of their familiarity in their home cluster.

Where attribute clustering is centripetal, the Nazarene effect is centrifugal. The familiarity of the individual within his own setting leads him outside this setting, where he will be recognized as different. A new identity is automatic. In the new setting he generates an informational gradient; his potency is unknown, even if ultimately the difference turns out to be trivial or 'small' (as in the initiation ceremony in which the initiate finally discovers it was uncle, after all, who was swinging the bull-roarer). The effect is like that of the incest taboo. This taboo guarantees to each new union the full potentiation of the coupling of hitherto-avoided strangers (by cultural definition, if not in fact). But eventually there is a lapse into partial importance as this union, too, becomes literally 'familiar', hence incestuous. (See Schwartz 1975a.)

The Nazarene effect is perhaps strongest in smaller societies. There, the individual has greatest familiarity to the greatest number of people. He may gain prominence by being possessed, by being 'not himself'. Exogamy is, in part, a response to this aspect of small scale. Larger groups allow for internal externality; that is, for a person to be a stranger to the majority within his own society. Attribute clustering in large-scale societies enhances local familiarity or commonality. And as cellularization becomes more complex, it may internally replicate the interplay of attribute clustering and dispersion of small-scale societies. Under what circumstances do relatively many or few seek to enhance commonality or to exploit their own saliency outside the cluster? At times they may enjoy both, as in the foreign colony or enclave, or in the ethnic enclaves within US universities.

6.1. *Growth of cultural scale*

I have spoken of a culture as an accumulated mass of information in the form of representations distributed through a population, as well as in artifacts and event structures that can be 'read' (represented or that can inform the behavior of individuals). In culture as well, growth encounters some limiting conditions but also enjoys some peculiar privileges. These privileges arise because there is no strict conversion proportionality between information and factors of communication (such as the number of persons, amounts of matter, energy, space, and time) that creation, storage, retrieval, and transmission require. Unlike energy, it is not the case that information can neither be created nor destroyed. Any 'reading' by an individual creates new information (not previously read by anyone, or no longer stored if previously read) or at least a new copy of information in another individual at another point in space and society. Information may be increased through operations on information, not only through empirical readings from the environment.

The power of representation lies partly in the fact that it can be false. A representation may be part of a chain of transformations that may be separated from and rejoined to the task of referencing the environment. The capacity for counterfactual representation, or for representation without reference or with reference held in abeyance, is the basis for the creation of goals that go beyond present and past experience of 'the way things are'. This capacity decisively transcends the lower-order teleology of oriented behavior and the mere pursuit of goals.

Another source of the relative decoupling of information from the quantity of personnel, matter, energy, space, and time is the possibility for selecting levels of representation that possess great differences of coding efficiency. Engineering considerations of the limits of given communications systems deal mainly with the lowest levels of coding; for example, measures of channel capacity by band width and channel noise, and by the number of letters or words per minute that can be transmitted, read, retrieved, and stored. Significance (the number or importance of ideas to someone) largely escapes such measures, although a number of theoretical possibilities of approximating magnitudes of higher order information exist. The power to amplify information – to transcend lower-order limitations on complexity of representations with respect to handling capacities – largely resides in the human capacity to create hierarchies of representation. In doing so, humans represent more with less – they abstract. I call this property of representations the 'referential load'. Speed (the compression in time of operations on representations) has also been a major source of amplification in informational capacity. Energy required tends to be proportional to time. Aside from the speed of the human neural system as a requisite for relating the higher order representational capacities to action, speed is probably the main contribution of electronic computers and the first major breakthrough in this respect since man.

We do not as yet have good measures on the notions of abstractness and the power of an abstraction or a conceptualization. Those aspects of culture which grow most rapidly are marked by the kind of gain achieved through integrating information as well as through accumulating more information of the same kind. There is an analogue here to our previous discussion of integration of coordinate but non-hierarchic differentiation and of hierarchic, emergent new levels of social structure. The latter process may, perhaps, be called 'transcendence'. Carniero, Marsh, and Miller, among others, have suggested scales of social complexity that include not only population size but some count of numbers of levels or echelons of integration achieved in a particular society. Some notion of the power of such integration levels might be conveyed by the slope of the pyramid of organization. It may be that integration through superordination is the easier way to achieve transcendence, and that non-hierarchic coordination by adequate and flexible interconnection of semi-autonomous units is an achievement we tend to underestimate in comparison to the more obvious hierarchic structures.

6.2. *Escalation and resistance to escalation*

We may see two opposed tendencies, although they are far from balanced. One is the movement toward increased scale, regardless of whether we are looking at it in terms of population size and density or in terms of structural or cultural scale. The other is the tendency for some counter-trends that conserve the behavioral environments of individuals and groups at a relatively small scale even though they are contained within much larger entities. We may speak of resistance to escalation.

We hear much about scale increasing to the point that man is 'overwhelmed', where people speak of having lost the 'human scale'. The idea of a 'human scale' expresses a wish to return to smaller worlds, to lives in supposedly personal and whole relations. At a large university, one often hears complaints of the student lost as 1 among 30,000. Such statements focus on the overall size of the social entity. They do not examine the actual behavioral and inter-actional world of the individual. In the last two universities where I have worked, the anthropology department has been one floor below or above the sociology department – yet the number of contacts were very few. I don't know the names of many of the people on the adjoining floors and am not sure which departments are on the other floors. The same is notoriously true of the pseudo-neighborhood, in which one does not necessarily know the names of one's closest neighbors, let alone the 20,000 or so that live in a place that has been given a name like Westwood or Del Mar. We have gone from the notion of loneliness as in 'lonely as a cloud' to being 'lonely in the crowd' – from isolation in a spatial sense to isolation in a moral and psychological sense.

Is this picture of high-density isolation correct? For some years I have had students in urban anthropology courses doing studies of the networks of individuals. Each has been a resident of a metro-polis. Even so, it is apparent that each individual has a small interactional world of persons whom he knows, just as the members of a village know other members of their village. There *are* important differences between personal networks of urbanites and villagers. The urban network may show greater diversity of membership. The members of a network will often not have grown up together. Given the effects of attribute clustering, however, they will often have grown up in parallel. But in size and intensity, the urban personal network is usually village size or smaller. This urban 'village' will usually not be as spatially compact as an actual village, but reckoning by traverse times, the difference is reduced.

The urban network is a sphere of interaction that has remained relatively village-sized throughout the ages and against the current of increasing scale. It is true that this village has zones of intimacy, and that the size and turn-over depend on circumstances such as mobility and occupation. Yet relatively few among those studied by my students seem not to have an adequate nucleus of persons with whom they interacted in a knowing, repetitive, and multi-functional way. A somewhat larger zone exists on the periphery of the personal network, of people about whom one might know a name but not the wife's name or brother's name or anything more than a context of acquaintance. Beyond this is a zone, still not as large as one might expect, of people with whom one has repetitive service relations – a gas station attendant, a checkout clerk at a supermarket – people whose names are very often not known. And beyond this is a still more formless world of function mediated in ways transiently affected by the personalities of individuals and in which one forms impressions, likes and dislikes, flashes of intuition, and then passes on. Within the village-sized range of personal networks, there would seem to be personality and status-dependent variation in the size of personal networks and in the intensity and intimacy of relations.

Resistance to increase of scale takes many other forms. I have already mentioned attribute clustering, the complex internal sorting of relations, associations, and residence rather than the random distribution of persons in large-scale population aggregates. In cities, we also find the persistence of many nominally autonomous entities struggling with the anomaly of their valued but unreal autonomy. Greater Los Angeles has some 98 'autonomous' municipalities, some 28 of which are wholly enclosed within the territorial limits of the city proper. The formation of politically 'independent' municipalities continues to be a trend in many other large cities. The cities remain extremely large-scale, aside from those sections that have resisted or have de-annexed to avoid engulfment. The largest entities have little behavioral reality for the individual even though they have acquired large-scale functions such as regional control of water and air resources. A study of the cognitive maps which individuals have of their cities also reveals that individuals have very limited zones of fairly intensive knowledge of certain parts of the city and large *taches blanches* covering much of the rest of the map. Although I grew up in Philadelphia, the entire northern half of that city remains unknown to me and only certain small areas plus the downtown are extensively known. The familiar localities are known in the detail with which a peasant knows his immediate countryside or a Manus knows the network of trails or the reefs around his village.

The persistence and new formation of cultural entities that create a sub-structuring and internal complexity of identified groups can be seen as prevailing against the trend to larger circles of identification. Movements toward international consolidation exist, along with resurgent micronationalisms based on language, ethnicity, or religion. The recent increase of ethnic awareness in the United States is a case in point. The increase of ethnic awareness by any one group stimulates intensification of ethnic awareness in all other groups. The black liberation movement leads to a new consciousness of ethnicity among Asian Americans, American Indians, and reverberates further among women, youth, homosexuals, and others. All borrow the same kind or imagery; they see themselves as resisting cultural imperialism, resisting absorption or 'co-optation', asserting their self-determination.

The technology of transportation and communication compensates in part for the growth in the spatial scale of society. *If the radii of social entities are taken not in some absolute spatial unit but as traverse times or communication delays, then the spatial scale of society would appear constant or shrinking.* The decrease of traverse times particularly enables the spatial dispersion of productive and social functions. This decrease greatly facilitates the substitution of selective networks for spatially-determined personal groupings and renders neighborhoods obsolete as people maintain dispersed networks of friends and functional relations.

On the other hand, the reduction of traverse times has the effect of increasing social density, if density is considered not as the number of persons for a given spatial unit but rather the number of persons within a given traverse radius or communicational time lapse. Working to the same effect is the increase of transaction rates. Social density thus defined increases the informational mass to which the individual potentially has access. The new technologies, of course, permit a vast expansion of face-to-face ratios through disembodied contacts – the substitution of images for substance. McCluhan is led to speak of the return of the tribe, of the village earth. I think this is a wishful, optimistic view of the results of this new social density. Nevertheless, some contact is possible almost instantaneously over great distances, so the effect of spatial scale as an impediment to access is reduced. Despite the decrease of traverse and communication times, the personal network does not expand significantly in terms of the numbers of persons included.

6.3. *Time-limited cultures*

As the world-wide rate of culture change accelerates and massive culture transfer occurs among large-scale societies, culture is less delimited in space and increasingly time-limited. Time-limited cultural entities are to some extent replacing, or at least taking their place with, identificational and territorially-bounded entities. We may speak of time-limited, temporal, or generational cultures.[15] The definition of a generation is itself cultural: it is an identificational boundary in time rather than in space. We have all noted an accelerated proliferation of generational cultures and of the difference-amplifying effects of our perception of 'generation gaps'. The temporal scale occupied by temporally-bounded cultures is itself changing. Part of this change is an increasing longitudinal effect: the amount of change contained within a given interval of

248

time or in the lifespan of individuals has increased. It is often said that the present youth generation, rapidly becoming super-annuated, has experienced enormous change in their brief years. This experience of rapid change has been with us for some time. The generation of my parents from the 1880s to the present witnessed the development of mass production, of almost all modern means of transportation, of communications, of electrification and other new power sources, titanic world wars, and a drastic restructuring of relations in the world as well as the more recent developments they share with youth. However, perhaps what is critical are the changes to which society is in the process of adapting within a certain period of life. With which decade of their lives do people most identify? They nostalgically think about 'their' songs, dances, clothing styles, slang, culture heroes, 'their' war. The anchor-point would seem to be late adolescence – the transition to early adulthood.

The anthropologist must now study generational cultures – long after the literary critic was looking for those crucial transitions of style in critical individuals to establish (for example, the generation of the Spanish poets of the 1890s). We are subject to numerological biases such as decades and centuries. What kinds of events at what age define the boundaries of generational cultures? How disjunctive are they? Generational cultures are a part of the increasing aware-ness of internal cultural gradients. They contribute in a major way to structural complexity. Multiple sub-cultures, ethnic, regional, class, and co-existing temporal cultures amount to an evolutionarily mixed or stratified society, providing uneven internal distributions of technological knowledge and of different horizons of adaptation to culture change.

7. A summary discussion

It has been said, today one can travel further and further and have it make less and less difference. The overall convergent trend of societies means that space is less significant as a container for cultural variation. Significant variations are apt to be contiguous, co-existing, and more finely textured. The significance of inter-societal variation is not obliterated; it remains to an extent, but the trend is against it. If we consider the distribution of culture in a traditional areal culture such as that of Manus, we would find marked variation from one social entity to another in various cultural and ecological specializations, or in terms of emblematic cultural differentiation. But within each social designate we would also find a sufficiently complex matrix for the development of distinctive personalities, resulting both from common experiences refracted through different biological individualities and from the degree of differential experience that structural positions and micro-historical events provide.

Contact between societies as well as the scale of the contacting societies makes a difference in terms of the internal and the inter-societal distribution of culture. Where the surface effect is large, the prevalence and diversity of possible contacts induces differentia-tion within the social entity. Individuals are on the frontier, and the social and cultural environment is not homogeneous. The social structure of commonality within the small-scale society may be less significant than it becomes later, provided there are relatively few statuses and each one is maximally occupied. In all societies, how-ever, we would expect a certain number of more restricted statuses as well as a large number of informal statuses we would not recog-nize as formal offices. These provide greater diversity than the more meager set of formalized statuses would indicate.

The internal differentiation of personalities as distributive units of culture need not depend entirely on status differentiation. For any status-defined role, we must expect significant variations in role performance because of differences in the overall personalities of individuals. Possibly there is a universal self-enhancing or at least self-identifying motive that leads individuals to emphasize emblema-tic differences between themselves and others. These emblematic differences are comparable to what I have called cultural totemism with reference to groups. At least marginal differentiation of self seems to operate under all circumstances. I find it is not submerged even in the seemingly extreme solidarity of religious cults I have studied. On the contrary, like other events, these cults provide the opportunity for differentiation of individual styles, manners of self-presentation or assertion of the individual's version of the desired course of events. In the litigation of culture in each event, the individual brings himself into play even though he may merely settle for the sure triumph of conformity with the probable outcome. (Such is the person who is influenced to vote for the person the pools indicate is most likely to win.) The contribution of personalities to the variance of role performance remains even where there are strong ideological pressures against the 'cult of personality'.

We might ask whether the concept of culture is useful when we get beyond relatively simple and small-scale societies. When it is defined in its distributive form, we need not ask if there is sufficient commonality to justify the notion of culture. Similarly, as the scale of cultural difference on an inter-societal basis diminishes, does the concept of culture lose value if its referent becomes less variable if the differences are less distinctive? It seems to me that even if the process of cultural convergence became even more pronounced than at present, the concept of culture remains vital to our understanding of human behavior. It is applicable over the entire span of the evolution of societies. The distributive model seems an adequate conceptualization as the spatial dimension of cultures becomes less decisive than the sub-structuring of cultures, within which personalities and status-defined identificational and informal groups and networks become the significant units of variation.

I cannot see that any of the bases for the differentiation of individual personalities have been lost in the process of escalation of the maximal social entities. The increased internal complexity would seem to provide a great diversity of niches for the mix of personalities generated in a society. The expanded range of personalities does not seem to be based on an expansion of personality types. It may result from typological conservatism both in the process of personality formation as well as in our perception of personality types. It is the experiential diversity of personalities taken in their totality that increases with scale. Personalities diversify within the constraints of type. There is little point in cultural studies, in confining our interest in personality to the typological level. The personality does not exist only in its base-level, characterological constructs. It exists as a multiplicity of chains of translation toward behavior and from behavior, toward underlying interpretations and classifications, through a hierarchy of specificity in which constructs at all levels have their effect. We should not expect much variation in the basic building-blocks; rather, we should look for variations in the structures that are built on and with them.

In conclusion, then, personality does not suddenly appear on the basis of status specialization in larger-scale societies. It remains important throughout human existence as the social unit of the distributive structure of culture. The status profile of the individual and the associated normative role constructs are a part of personality, but variance in role performance depends further on the overall personality of individuals. Regardless of structural complexity and large status inventories of large-scale societies, without this personality variance we would indeed have a 'mechanical integration' based on utterly reliable role performances.

The very growth of scale has set in motion countervalent trends, resistant to the growth of scale of the individual's effective behavioral world. The individual continues to live in a relatively small world and to interact in a village-sized personal network. The larger world impinges, but it is perceptually narrowed by simplifying abstractions and magnified personalities that foster the symmetrical illusions of small scale. The process of attribute clustering, the structural complexity, and the presence of co-existing time-limited cultures – all these things contribute to the sub-structuring of society that creates relatively small, internal societies. Sub-structuring guarantees higher cell-by-cell levels of commonality. Thus far, trends toward more inclusive identificational entities seem to dissipate under new surges of local particularism, nationalism, ethnicity, and generational cleavage, although these broadening trends are supported by super-ordinate functional needs of increasing urgency. Generational cultures seem to spill readily across territorial boundaries; but the hope (if it deserves hope) that this will lead to world-wide unification may prove as illusory as the hope of an earlier generation that class-consciousness would have that effect. In any event, the emergence of one world might turn out to be meaningless as the last super-entity looks within itself to the new diversity and to the myriad small worlds that have developed within it, partly in reaction to the very process of its growth.

FREDRIK BARTH

Conclusions

How can a concept of scale best be used in furthering our analysis and depicting the properties and processes of organized social life? The essays in this collection demonstrate a number of ways in which questions posed in terms of scale illuminate the structure and pattern in social reality; and some of the essays seek to fashion the concept of scale into a truly analytical concept.

The first requirement, to my understanding, is that we conceptualize scale as a characteristic of the context of social interaction. This forces us to look for the interconnections of actions and events in natural subsystems, it asks us to pursue investigations of reality which do not spring from our conceptualizations and models. Size and numbers are empirical properties of each person's social space; networks are discoverable aspects of social fields (in the sense of institutions or domains). Pursuing these facts imposes an aspect of comparability in our descriptions of different parts of culture and society, interferes with our conventions of delimiting and abstracting from reality, and assists us in transcending our own categories and initial understandings. In the following, I shall try to explicate my bases for these statements, and thus summarize the importance and value that I see in the systematic conceptualization of scale as an aspect of social organization.

1. *What is scale?* Separated from the familiar contexts of 'large-scale' and 'small-scale', the term looks incomplete when it stands alone, and seems disappointing or perhaps mystifying if it stands only for numbers: we feel it should serve us as a concept to capture fundamental aspects of both 'size' *and* 'complexity'. I think the essays in this volume show that the use of the term simply to refer to the variable of *size* is analytically most defensible and useful; the aspect of 'complexity' lies in what it measures the size *of*. So scale refers to the numbers of something that can be counted: *size* in the sense of both the number of members or parts, and the spatial extension. It seems inevitable from the outset to include both these aspects of size: we expect a political system of 500 persons to show

different properties from one of 500,000; but a system of 500 can also be expected to show different scale properties depending on whether its members are concentrated, or spread out over 500 km². The special character of the concept of scale lies in entailing a comparison and a judgment of significance on the dimension of size: differences in scale are not just non-committal numbers, but statements about orders of magnitude: 'differences that make a difference' (Schwartz 1972). It thus provides a qualitative rendering of quantitative properties, which is a way of making these properties commensurate between systems, and coordinate with other qualitative properties of systems which we as anthropologists are used to, and interested in, depicting.

2. *Scale of what?* Clearly, scale is a property of systems – of *any* system. Though this implies that it is a property of the models which we construct, it does not follow that scale needs to become an artifact of our investigation: that we can arbitrarily represent phenomena as small-scale and large-scale according to how we choose to construct our models. The concept of scale becomes useful only when linked to a discovery procedure: it should depict properties of systems 'out there'. We can variously let the 'scale' of a social system refer to (a) a calculation of the minimum numbers/size needed for the system to operate; (b) the actual size encompassed within its boundaries; or (c) the size of the minimal region or population that embraces all types of members within a system. Of these, (a) serves to explore implications of the investigator's model, and develop hypetheses about the parameters of a system, which can no doubt be useful but are often far removed from verifiable data. On the other hand, the way social systems are generally constituted in empirical networks, (b) often becomes highly tentative or arbitrary since the operation of drawing boundaries is so subjective.

I feel that the preceding papers indicate (c) to be the most generally applicable sense of 'scale'. To elucidate the scale of Santal society (cf. Sinha, above) we need to depict its small-scale character of replicating village communities and the absence of higher-level coordination, beyond circles of villages, while the fact of a population of c. 3 million Santals is inconsequential for most purposes. Likewise, the scale of the Nuer social system seems best depicted, not by delimiting that system somewhwere among the Dinka and against the Shilluk (or by calculating how many persons are needed to run a lineage system), but by discovering the numbers and range of representative larger clans, the number of villages coordinated in initiations and feasts, the numbers of men mobilized in a war or feud, etc.

Nor should scale be conceptualized as a property primarily of 'societies'. So much anthropological thinking seems unalterably cast in the conceptualization of societies as *units* with organizational *traits*, that it is important to emphasize here again the aspect of scale in *all* orders of social systems. The social space of a person can be characterized as to scale. In some social organizations this is characteristically and uniformly small, in others it is generally much larger; often, there are highly significant differences between different interacting persons with respect to the scale of their respective social space, and this is importantly reflected in their relationship and in the dynamics of the social system in which they partake. On the level of group and social fields, different domains of activity may be organized in systems of very different scale within one and the same population and region, as documented above by Grønhaug. The integration of these disparate scales in terms of social organizations of communities and regions becomes a major focus of description of the third, higher level of social system.

In this manner, the aspect of 'complexity' that at first seemed lost in defining scale as a question of size alone, is regained. The purpose of systematic attention to scale is not that we should emerge with some sort of index which places a 'society' somewhere on a single continuum. Its usefulness lies in its making commensurate certain aspects of the structure of social persons, fields or domains, and communities and regions, thus facilitating the depiction of the intricacy and complexity of social organization. Particularly Barnes' and Grønhaug's substantive presentations illustrate this; and the social systems of the Pueblo might serve as a paradigm: despite relatively small numbers in a community, the pattern of organization and exclusion of persons is such as to produce a great difference in scale between the social space of an individual, and the aggregate of groups and social fields within a community. A person thus experiences non-participation in much of social life; he is not even informed about much which (indirectly) is considered to affect him as a person. In this way, certain qualitative aspects of large scale are generated, through the complexity of organization of relatively small numbers.

3. Scale is a property of the *context* for encounters and events. We emphasize again that scale is a property of *systems*: not of events and encounters, but of the systems in which they belong. Thus small-scale vs. large-scale should not be confounded with micro- vs. macro-aspects of social systems: large-scale systems are *also* embedded in the events of encounters of persons. In a meeting of three persons, each may act as the representative of households in a

small-scale lineage segment, or as the representative of households in a large-scale market system for employment, or as the representative negotiators of large-scale nation-states. To use the concept as I argue here, we must pursue the interconnections and demarcate the system before we can judge its scale.

Large-scale society also takes place between people. By insisting on this fact, we avoid a trap into which anthropologists easily fall: that the study of local communities is the study of small-scale systems, while large-scale society somehow exists only outside these loci and is to be discovered in the *interconnections between* communities in a region, between regions in states and supra-national alliances. (Boissevain, 1975.) No such hierarchy in fact obtains, and small-scale communities do not aggregate hierarchically into large-scale systems: the events of large-scale systems are there, under our very noses, if only we can recognize the significant contexts for these events: an exchange between neighbours may well require the context of a world market to be understandable, while a love-letter remains an event in a small-scale system, no matter how much postage is required for it to reach its destination.

4. Asking questions about scale should be a *discovery procedure*. If we agree to make scale stand for a property of empirical systems, and not an artifact of our investigation, the concept must be linked with procedures whereby orders of magnitude can be ascertained. We have chosen the deceptively simple view of scale as a question of relative size, entailing the procedures of quantification and judgment as to whether differences in number make a difference. What happens when we apply this to concrete social systems? We are forced to pursue the interconnections of events, to define the system in which they belong. We are forced somehow to delimit the extent of each system, so as to be able to count. We are forced to make it comparable to other connected or similar systems, so as to judge their different orders of magnitude. In short, we are driven to transcend our initial understandings and preconceptions and provide answers about further aspects of reality: i.e. to 'discover'. The question of scale confounds our conceptualization of 'society', it interferes with our freedom to abstract and theorize – it forces us to 'find out'. How then do we start?

Grønhaug's essay is perhaps the one which most clearly explicates a procedure. In its simplest essentials, this involves tracing patterns – not by constructing structural models at this stage, but by trying to cover fields of empirical occurrences. Having observed an action, you seek to discover the field of options to which such an action belongs, and the contexts in which these options are relevant.

Having ascertained the existence of a social relation, you place it in the context of the involved persons' network stars and how these mesh in wider social networks. Having identified the members of a social group, you then map the other statuses each of these persons occupies. A persistent concern to discover scale properties thus leads to conceptualization in terms of groups, populations, fields, and networks – which in various ways are all systems which can be characterized by their empirical size and extent.

The course of investigation is thus from the event to class, from the singular to population or aggregate. This is methodologically sound: not because micro in any sense 'comes before' macro, but because it simplifies discovery. We bring categories and preconceptions to our investigations: indeed, we cannot start without such conceptions. But in complex society, it is usually possible to achieve a selective perception so that macro-concepts can be exemplified *someplace* in real life, and one's preconceptions thus be reinforced. By contrast, tracing distributions and aggregating micro-data are procedures more difficult to control and steer than selection and exemplification; they thus more readily produce the unexpected and help us to transcend our categories. As Grønhaug points out, in the course of an investigation we must be prepared both to expand and to contract the scale of the area and population under study. But systems expand more readily than they fall apart; and going from part to whole is a simpler procedure than discovering valid wholes and then subdividing them into parts.

The kinds of aggregate units that emerge most fruitfully in these essays are found on the levels of persons, fields or domains, and regions. It is by interconnecting these levels by the relative concept of scale that the major insights in the character of social organizations can be generated.

5. *'Society' is not the largest-scale system.* This somewhat whimsical statement should be both unhelpful and unnecessary, but probably is not. A vast amount of ethnographical material has been interpreted on the holistic assumptions of the existence of distinct and separable societies, internally structured through the articulation of their parts, and mutually comparable as entities with various similar or dissimilar morphologies. To the extent that anthropologists have taken cognizance of larger-scale systems, such as a world market, these have too readily been regarded as modern disturbances which may imply change, disintegration, etc., but are without relevance to our basic schemata. Of course we know better, at least since the description of the Kula (Malinowski 1922), and even in soundly traditional schools scholars occasionally rouse themselves

to take cognizance of this (Uberoi 1962). Yet whatever social and cultural patterns we discover, we have a deeply-ingrained reflex to think of them as somehow belonging 'inside' an encompassing unit called 'society'. To my way of thinking, it seems quite reasonable to accept 'Kiriwina' or 'the Trobriands' as a 'society' despite the existence of the Kula. However, we can do this only if we do not make 'society' a keystone of our conceptualization of all things social, but mean by it merely the (ascertainable degree of) integration of various persons and social fields in a representative area. In that case, the properties of the Kula system are *not* contained as a part of the Trobriands, or Dobu, or any other 'society' for that matter.

The ethnographic literature on Africa has been cast so predominantly in the converse mold of unit societies that traditional large-scale systems have largely been obscured from view. It is ironic that the strongly sociologically-oriented British tradition of social anthropology should so completely have accepted a pattern where language groups and names impose the format of sociological description and analysis. Systematic mapping of empirical networks and interconnections, without prejudging the demarcation of units, could well lead to substantial discoveries of traditional as well as contemporary systems, and a re-drawing of our picture of African forms of social organization.

Redfield's simple formulation of a model focussing on scale, when he pointed to the co-existence of great and little traditions in India, served to open a way out of a similar impasse. Indeed, with the accumulated wealth of description that has resulted, India may serve us as a complex parable of scales, encompassing the bewildering substantive variety sketched by Sinha. I interpret his essay as indicating the potential fertility for these data, not only of polar dichotomies of large vs. small and tribe vs. caste or the networks and centres so vividly depicted for channels of communication, but of a systematic explication of scale in systems of all levels. We need to know the size of the social world of different categories of persons and the sizes of various instituted fields of relations to be able to analyze the articulations of this complex civilization.

Let me exemplify: By focussing on the Santal as a tribe, and discussing their place on a tribe-caste continuum, we no doubt say some ethnographically very true and insightful things. But at the same time we have let heavily loaded concepts influence – we might say pre-arrange – our descriptions and thoughts. Major aspects of Indian culture history adhere to the concept of tribe, and by its use certain aspects of Santal social identity are given priority over others. Structuring our investigation in terms of a general concept of scale, the obvious step would be to focus down on the level of persons with Santal identity and observe their place in the total network of their social world. We note that nowhere do they exceed 20% of the population of a district. Thus, though segregated in hamlets, they live in a world peopled largely by non-Santals. In what way does Santal identity entail a different boundary or sphere of involvement/non-involvement from that of non-Santals in these same districts? Perhaps the answer to this can provide us with an initial 'truth' about Santals, equally valid and analytically more productive than the historical 'truth' of tribe. It may lead us to a careful documentation of social fields and boundaries, to questions of boundary maintenance and change, and to identity management. Indeed, perhaps persons even purposely seek to control their involvement and non-involvement by embracing, retaining, and discarding such identities, or modifying their content?

6. Since all systems are commensurate in terms of scale, this can provide a framework for analysis and comparison and give us a key to the *dynamics of complex social organizations*. The preceding essays have shown that a mapping of the various social fields in a community and region, and of the social space of interacting persons, reveals illuminating and in part highly unexpected patterns. With regard to personal space, members of the symposium shared the assumption that scale correlates with class position, and presumably even more directly with leadership, being inherent in the representative function of leaders. Much material agrees with this; but these cases do not so readily enable us to discover whether such differences in scale are *sources* of power, or merely correlates or consequences of rank.

Occasional inversions occur which should allow us to refine our understandings somewhat. Cases that come to mind might be the local school headmaster vs. the cosmopolitan junior teacher; the migrant labourer vs. the parochial landowner dynasty of his village; local leaders vs. the shopkeeping ethnic minority e.g. of the overseas Chinese type. In the traditional Middle East, a Jewish trader in the bazaar in Smyrna could give you a credit note which held good in Baghdad and Shiraz, while the provincial governor might have difficulties securing you quarters in a government post on the outskirts of his own province. No doubt we must ask 'power for what', and distinguish domains and arenas of activity as well as distinguish the mode of relation or transaction: whether in defence or self-interest, in mediation for third parties as broker or middleman, etc. Even in the confrontation of two persons, it may be quite problematical to determine who is asserting power (rather than who 'has' it in an institutional sense) and who is being dominated, and how differences in their respective social space affect their relative chances to dominate.

The example of the husband–wife relationship in traditional Arabia (field materials from the town of Sohar in Oman) may be illuminating here. In this society, women's contacts and movements are severely restricted, whereas men cultivate wide networks. The customary arrangements of authority and responsibility, and the formal laws of Islam, further favour the husband immensely over the wife. Nonetheless, in the domestic field where they interact, they seem to feel that they meet roughly as equals, and many couples seem from the observation-post of domestic friendship to exercise fairly balanced control over each other. Nor are there effective bars against domineering activities by the wife and occasional cases of true domestic tyranny by her. Two circumstances doubtless contribute to this situation: (a) A husband will, because of sexual segregation and a strong institutionalization of domestic privacy, have great difficulties mobilizing influence from other social fields as sanctions in a domestic confrontation. (b) Since the domestic field is the main field of self-expression for the wife, but not for the husband, much more is at stake for her. She may therefore be inclined to escalate conflicts and fight to the bitter end for matters of relatively low priority to him, who has numerous other fields of participation and expression. The husband's option to terminate interaction with his wife and withdraw from the domestic scene – structurally a source of strength – may then easily serve as an invitation to escape her sanctions, but indeed lose the battle. Thus actual influence over decisions need not result, even where greater social space is combined with greater authority and greater sum of available sanctions.

In many cases, the social space of two interacting persons are not so much disparate in size as grossly discrepant in extent: they live in different social worlds, yet touch in some limited field. To me, the prototype case of this will probably always remain the nomad and the agricultural tenant in South Persia (Barth 1961: 78ff). A nomad is a member of a tribe, the local camps of which are at any moment dispersed over perhaps c. 2000 km^2 of country, constituting a part of an annual migration channel of maybe ten times that size. Parts of this geographical space are also included in the migration channels of other tribes, and most of it is also the habitat of sedentary villagers. The agricultural tenant lives with great stability in a village, the centre of a social world largely contained within a 10 km radius and peopled by other villagers, landowners, a police post, and a local court, as well as a near-perpetual caravan of nomadic camp units. For 2–3 days (choosing as our example a locality of middle altitude) a particular nomad belonging to a particular camp may pitch his tent in close proximity to the fields and village of a particular tenant and his co-villagers. Though their total worlds are highly discrepant in extent and personnel, the two have ready statuses in terms of which they may interact: they have roughly common standards of behavior towards temporary neighbours; recognize rights of various kinds to cultivated fields, pasture, drawing of water, etc.; have common conceptions of procedure in trade, the value of money and goods etc. They thus may readily enter into a relationship. However, because of the marked discongruity between their two worlds, a relationship between them must build on premises different from those taken for granted in most relationships, where the parties share significant parts of their social space.

The theoretical issues involved are discussed both in Bailey's and Jacobson's essays, above. Without the enmeshing effect of an immediate joint network, questions of social control, the underwriting of trust, and accountability arise, as Jacobson shows. In case of conflicts, each party finds it difficult to mobilize support relevant to the world of the other, and impartial third parties (Bailey's *numen*) are not readily available: the nomad's chief has no place in the tenant's world, while the village bosses, local police, or district court are no acceptable arbiters for a nomad. In this ethnographic case, the discrepancy in social space is overcome by a dramatic increase in scale: the parties interact not in their simple identities as household heads, but in terms of membership in tribes and clientage hierarchies. Only on this level of scale do the social systems to which they belong become homologous and capable of confrontation and compromise: the tribal chief and the landowner patron live in a common elite world where they can match each other's influence in the shared arenas of the court system and the political corridors of the province. But the mobilization of this administrative superstructure entails risks and costs for both nomad and tenant; it can be contemplated only if the necessary groundwork has been done in the unequal relationship to the respective patrons – and so these ephemeral temporary relations of nomad and tenant become one of many considerations involved in self-management as a weak participant in a complex and large-scale political system.[1]

I would venture the generalization that wherever the social spaces of interacting parties are highly discrepant, this interaction will be so significantly affected by systems of larger scale as to be adequately understandable only in terms of these.

7. All large-scale social systems have a precipitated constituent on the *micro-level*, in the structure of social persons. Indeed, since all social systems, whether large- or small-scale, are constituted of patterned and institutionalized behavior, it follows that all parties to such behavior must be characterized by the minimum of properties for playing *their* part in the larger system. These properties can be designated simply as having the status(es) in one's repertoire to participate in such a social system; their character becomes clearer if specified as: having criteria of relevance for one's behavior in the relationship(s) involved, having some expectations as to the behavior of others, having some understanding of some of the events of the system, and patterned ways of responding to these events; perhaps also having skills and material assets assigned to these ways of responding, i.e. to tasks, and ends and goals to pursue in the activity. No system is so 'large-scale' that it can lack these features of social anchorage; likewise I am unable to imagine any participant in a system being so constrained by forces outside himself that his actions are fully predetermined, and unaffected by his own understanding, expectations, and conceptualization of self. This being so, it must be part of our task in describing a system to identify these components of it in real persons.[2]

The importance of this part of the description lies in the insight it can provide into process. It allows us to distinguish those consequences of the operation of a system which reproduce its own prerequisites from those other consequences of the system which may be important, but lack such system implications.

The fact that a system operates exploitatively towards some parties in no way reduces the necessity of describing their participation in it; and there are yet components of that system to be found also in the structure of the unfortunates who are being exploited. Thus, e.g. in describing peasants, we cannot limit outselves to describing the macro-features of the system and decrying the exploitation of peasants – we also need to specify what makes them exploitable. As can be seen from a number of different concrete historical instances, efforts to extract tax from a rural population do not always lead to a large-scale system where that population shows the particular form of vulnerability and accommodation so they can usefully be typed as peasantry.

Berreman's material on the different phases of contact in Aleut history illuminates this. We can see an early phase of gross exploitation where Aleuts had the recurring experience of being the weaker part and so the losers in confrontations. Yet, even under extreme conditions of population decline, their situation allowed for the constant re-creation of Aleut identity and activities. The recent situation has an entirely different character: Aleuts have become truly powerless, not in the sense of being the weaker party in confrontations, but in being unable to confront at all. The gross disparity in scale between what remains of Aleut social organizations and the organizations that envelop them, and the disparity and discongruity in social space between Aleuts and the non-Aleut persons with whom they interact, impose complete dependence. Berreman briefly notes the basic pattern of Aleut response to this, and how it must fail to change the conditions of dependence.

A comparison to Barnes' 1952 material on Bremnes is instructive. In a sense, of course, any person is powerless in his relations to the agencies of large-scale organizations; but Bremnes people participate in collectivities which share a relative consensus of values and interests, and have their emissaries in the seats of large-scale decision-making (cf. Barnes, p. 22). There is thus neither the disparity or discongruity between their world and that of the city, and so they can confront what they see as the forces of darkness, and do battle with them, even if they do not always win.

8. Well-springs of large-scale systems are found in the *structure of persons*. We may pursue the case of Bremnes a bit further: How do the large-scale systems of these rural people come about? Certainly, many of the obligations and memberships ascribed to them arise elsewhere, imposed on Bremnes people as citizens of Norway, purchasers of external goods and services, etc. But others, emphasized in Barnes' description of the 'great tradition' in which Bremnes participated, have had their well-springs in the persons and chosen activities of people in Bremnes and similar communities: in youngsters studying and applying themselves and learning a particular view of life, sometimes thereby also building careers as school-teachers, clerks, and politicians; in dedicated laymen hammering the virtues of Bible, frugality, and country speech and values; in thrifty householders looking for modest prosperity from labour migration to the New World, new fishing technology, new occupational options – in other words, persons holding a particular set of Pietist values being *propelled* by these values to pursue particular goals, create assets and articulate collective representations, and forge networks of social relations. Without these countless practitioners and missionaries of the Pietist way of life there would be no resources for a 'great tradition', no ground-swell of force to organize, and no personnel standing forth to mediate and lead. It is of course highly relevant that most of these grass-roots activities are perfectly compatible with the basic economic interests of the dominant bourgeois class in Norway, and that unless this were so the many small actors would probably

not have succeeded so well in their various endeavours. But to point to such macro-circumstances is entirely insufficient by itself as a description or an explanation of the phenomena. These urban class interests could never themselves have animated Bremnes and other rural people to such activity, nor was the resultant effect ever optimal from their point of view. In a real sense, the well-springs – but not the sufficient determinants of final form – lay in the structure of social persons in Bremnes and similar places.

Those large-scale systems that impinge on Bremnes from without, or that we saw enveloping and destroying the Aleuts, are likewise being carried forth from their places of origin by a multitude of ordinary persons propelled to act as they do by how they are socially constituted, in terms of values and blindness to other values, career demands and opportunities, etc. The events of the large-scale systems are created by persons affecting the timing and shaping of these events by their ideals, interests, skills and incompetences. Likewise, the village Brahmin mediating between the Great and the Little Tradition by parochializing Sanscrit concepts and universalizing village deities, is doing so in the pursuit of ideas of excellence and truth received through those strands of communication he has been able to cast, or that have been cast to him, from the centres of the great tradition.

In other words, we can observe both the precipitate of systems in the structure of persons (as under point 7, above), and well-springs of these systems in persons; and to describe a social system, whatever its scale, we should be able to identify and depict these micro-components of it. But we must also be able to show how the events that occur between persons are aggregated into systems, and how the properties of these systems emerge.

9. The *processes of aggregation* of a system are distinctive objects of observation and description. There is no reason to rely on speculation and induction for identifying these processes when they can in fact be empirically observed and recorded. The present context is not the place to outline a whole, and personally favoured, schema of social analysis, but we may note some basic concepts and viewpoints of particular relevance to describing the scale properties that result from processes of aggregation.

Anthropology has not been particularly rich in analyses of emergent system properties. The simpler demonstrations have been favoured that either show
(a) how external constraints channel the behavior of persons by limiting their effective options, and thus produce a relatively uniform mass response; or

(b) how premises have been introduced into persons, affecting the direction in which they are propelled to act, again with a homogenizing mass result. Indeed, the paradigm explanation of pattern which shows how customary norms are inculcated in persons, who consequently act out customary behavior, combines these two explanations, since diffuse sanctions are also assumed to operate to enforce compliance with custom. Even when the aggregate pattern is revealed to be evil – as in much recent Marxist anthropology – the same explanatory model is appealed to by identifying some partisan advantage in the pattern and imputing the insight and power to that party to mystify others into accepting false standards.

While acknowledging both the paradigm and this particular variant as sometimes true, I would argue for far more attention to the *emergent* properties of aggregate systems. Large-scale patterns of behavior frequently seem far from optimal from *every* partisan view and the population as a whole; and the aggregate result of the individual pursuit of excellence is frequently not the greatest sum of excellence. An example of relentless deterioration in a small-scale system, despite the desires and reasonable efforts of all participants, has been brilliantly analysed by Goffman (1971: 335–390) in his portrayal of families with a mentally disturbed member. We need to refrain both from the traditional functionalist optimism and from the easy assumption that every pattern must directly reflect somebody's purpose, and rather make more systematic efforts to uncover both unsought and unseen emergent properties in systems. To do this, it is essential to identify the scale of systems, and to identify correctly the peculiar properties associated with each system and each order of magnitude in scale (cf. Schwartz, citing D'Arcy Thompson).

We can observe the process of aggregation of a system whenever we see cases where events are connected and influence each other. The most obvious way in which human acts connect with each other to form a system is as steps in a plan. Through the process of planning, the result is created, not piecemeal with each step and as a simple summation of the parts, but from the emergent properties of the *whole plan*. But often, the results of a plan do not in fact eventuate, since behavior is rarely autonomous and solitary, and events also become connected in larger systems through interaction with others and their (changing) plans, and confrontation with the realities (and chance occurrences) of nature. In other words, in the processes of *interaction* guided by planning, manipulation, and strategy we observe a complex aggregation of system in connected events. And there can be no doubt that such processes are indeed empirically observable: in the unfolding sequences of interaction, in the decision-making processes of collectivities, in the commentaries and justifications of persons, in the exultant or agonizing reanalysis and recounting of strategies, etc.

As essential as the recognition of these processes of aggregation is the recognition that actors and only actors (in the sense of persons and the coordinated collectivities of corporately organized groups) are capable of engaging in them. The systematizing effect of these processes on the aggregate can be claimed only if, and to the extent to which, persons or corporate groups are capable of decision-making and coordinated action – singly as plans and severally as interactional outcomes. The value and attraction of these analyses naturally are that, while the processes of aggregation may be complex, the outcome – i.e. the system properties generated – may be simple (e.g. 'stalemate'). And though the actors in such systems may be very large-scale (e.g. nation-states), the models we can use for their interaction may be of the same general kind, except insofar as their decision-making processes constrain their strategic options. The number of actors, on the other hand, entails highly significant and variable scale properties – from the fundamental differences between unity, two, and three exercised in Bailey's paper to the situation of actors embedded in uncounted multitudes explored by Jacobsen.

A very different order of system is that referred to by concepts such as arena, situation, ground rules, or forum. The connection these establish between events is that of congruence from contiguity in space and time. The constraints are partly physical, but mainly those of cultural conventions, which mark off such frames for action and ascribe to them their characteristics. The source of patterning, i.e. the process of aggregation, lies as much in what is elicited by the opportunity an arena offers as in what it discourages. Arenas etc. cannot be found or created at will by actors; they must be sought, and activities cannot be consummated unless they exist. So what actually unfolds of behavior depends on the presence or absence of such structures; and that which does unfold has effects on what emerges in the way of further options.

I feel that much insight into exotic societies can be achieved by pursuing the same simple observations we make along these lines in our own society: How the absence of suitable arenas for a variety of collective activities impoverishes the life of rural marginals, or underlies many of the difficulties of self-realization experienced by teenage youth; how profoundly modern politics is shaped by the arena provided by modern mass communications, etc. To exemplify what changes in the physical components of such an arena may entail, let us consider the very small-scale system of a family household as it is familiar to us from Western society. In three successive generations, such families have been provided with very different technologies; yet the values that propelled them, the kinds of fellowship they have wished to consummate, have changed relatively little. Observe then the actual interaction that takes place: in one generation gathered around the single focus of the oil-lamp, in the next generation provided with multiple electric light points with consequent dispersal of activities and personnel, and in the present generation drawn together as a pacified agglomeration around the TV set. My understanding is that very significant emergent properties are generated by such processes of associating disparate activities in one arena.

Colson's paper provides us with a perceptive demonstration of the changes effected on such arenas in a village by changes in numbers. These clearly involve changes in scale in the system she analyzes, arising from the various individual accommodations to arena circumstances such as withdrawal from public access, entailing deep changes in the system.

Whereas the processes which aggregate activities on an arena are largely those of choice and management by actors, other types of processes are also prominently at work in aggregating institutional systems. Some of these are automatic, arising from physical causes and interconnections, others are culturally predicated but no less compelling and relentless for that. The 'fields' empirically depicted in Grønhaug's paper each seem to be dependent on one or several such processes, e.g. the hydraulic interdependence of all the activites connected with one large irrigation channel, or the common (but very unequally advantageous) subjection of all labourers and employers of a region in a labour market. Thus, once an irrigation canal is constructed, there is an inescapable inverse relationship between how much water is drawn in its upper course and how much is available in its lower course; this entails 'systematic' relations between irrigated area, agricultural pursuits, and political interests in its upper and lower reaches. Needless to say, this does not mean that irrigation, agriculture, and politics are thereby specifically determined by this systematic factor alone – but its role in affecting these aspects of life along the canal should be demonstrable. Likewise, once certain forms of labour-contract and a minimal level of personal security in movement are instituted in an area, a labour market emerges with certain system properties affecting opportunities, wages, and other essential aspects of the cultivators' life-situation. These system properties have under early capitalist institutional forms seemed so autonomously emergent and so compelling that they were conceptualized as iron laws, until an awareness of their component processes made systematic counter-measures possible.

10. What *kinds of systems* are we concerned with when analyzing scale in social life? Obviously, any number of different kinds; but I have urged strongly for a focus on processual analyses of systems, and attention to their emergent properties. This also would entail the expectation that certain ubiquitous and important processes will generate widely or universally occurring systems of particular importance. Without prejudging either their universality or their boundaries, one may accept the usefulness of a procedure whereby one does not project on the material, but nonetheless searches for, such major systems. Above the level of social persons, those which I would particularly point to may be labelled politics, economy, local community, and group image. Each of these can be identified with a key resource or other subject of transaction which shows a patterned distribution, and indeed through its circulation constitutes the system in question, in a way analogous to the water in the hydraulic system mentioned above. But how these systemic processes affect life in a region depends dramatically on the scale properties which each system develops under varying cultural conditions: therefore the need to give them our attention in the present context.

I would thus expect to find, in any population of co-mingling persons, that transactions about support, rallying, and alliance become systematically related to each other so that these forms of prestation or social goods constitute a political system in their distribution and circulation. This would seem to arise regardless of actors' intent or even recognition, since support given to one is thereby necessarily no longer freely available to others, and so an ordering of priorities is imposed and a set of consequences induced. An alliance entered and honoured likewise orients the two or more who entertain the alliance in their relations to third parties as well, and thus tends to have 'real-political' implications in ever-widening circles. Even where participants culturally insist that it is otherwise – as in drawing distinctions in the kind of submission due to God and to Cæsar, or to Church and State as Europeans have at times attempted – there seem to be systemic pressures at work confounding that which actors try to keep separate.

If this is so, what might be the constraints on the expansion of scale in political systems? Gellner treats one such constraint inherent in the basic constituting process of rallying support. Though many means have been used to mobilize collectivities, most of them depend directly or indirectly on the interests, obligations, and values shared by members or entertained by followers: i.e. they depend on ideologies. We can then readily see that different and differently constituted ideologies have very different potentialities for sharing and generality, and thus entail dramatically different scale properties of political systems.

A second system of some degree of universality may be the economy. Given the cultural mechanisms of money and explicit market institutions, a whole variety of specific system properties emerges as described in Western economics. But the ubiquitous necessity which persons face to allocate time and resources, and the variously instituted options they have to offer exchanges, go a long way towards producing a degree of systemic distribution and circulation of goods and labour in all societies. In view of the accusations sometimes made (O'Laughlin 1975: 353), I should state explicitly that I see nothing inherently natural or moral in an imagined condition of full exchangeability of all forms of goods; as always, it is the emergence of any degree of system which must be demonstrated and explained with reference to its specific extent and kinds of interconnectedness.

Within such systems, scale is a vitally important property, since the mode of operation of monopolies, oligopolies, or mass interactions of coevals are so very different; since a number of characteristics of markets such as e.g. elasticity are affected by it; and since only by demarcating scale can the full range of endogenous variables in a system be discovered.

A third kind of system of wide occurrence and profound importance is that of the local community, if we invest this concept with a reasonably precise meaning. It does not have the limited character of an 'arena', it lacks the analytical distinctiveness of 'a political system', it may be insignificant or absent in the life of some populations: yet anthropologists will probably feel that it constitutes the truly focal social system in many ethnographic situations. Of what is it constituted, and what are the empirical processes that are operative in aggregating it as a system? Its essence seems to be a particular distribution of information: one where persons, whether actually involved in direct relationships or not, have a surfeit of information on each other: their whole status repetoire, their assets and inclinations, their past performance in a number of relationships. The processes which generate such a distribution of information are gossip, intensive and dense interaction, and high mutual visibility. Where this collective surfeit of information exists, certain system-properties seem to emerge: collective identity and solidarity, pressures towards a variety of forms of equality, difficulties in pursuing collective strategies. These system properties seem to emerge whether ideologically favoured (as in many peasant villages) or contradicted (in Nuer villages, as distinct from lineages).

Scale is an essential variable for the very emergence of local communities. Obviously, the processes mentioned above can become prominent only where a relatively small population regularly co-mingles; experience from European towns suggests a few thousand as the upper limit of population that can attain these system-properties to marked extent. Much work needs to be done with an analytic rather than descriptive purpose to explore the forms, and conditions for emergence, of local communities of varying structure and size.

Finally, how shall we handle the apparent fact that modes of self-representation and group conceptualization, though taken into account in all the social processes mentioned so far, also seem to affect scale properties directly? I am thinking of how an ideology of nationalism as sketched by Gellner is reflected in a person's actions, also in the absence of a nation; I recognize how Bailey's *numen* becomes so, merely (and only) if people say he is so. Even more strikingly, I imagine how the presence of a Brahmin in a small Indian village gives a great number of unchanging activities in that village a new context of meaning – and thereby a new scale? – by elucidating their symbolic place in Hinduism, the Great Tradition, and Cosmos. Surely, it is such a symbolic apparatus which the Aleutians lack, to judge from Berreman's description, which gives them their subjective experience of powerlessness and small scale – whereas a Himalayan hermit in his cave, communing with a pantheistic Godhead, in a sense that is real at least to him, participates in something highly complex and large-scale with deep joy and none of the bewilderment of powerlessness.

There are problems here which have not been pursued in these essays, but which may well prove tractable in the same framework of social-event analysis and system aggregation as exemplified in many of the essays and discussed in this summary. Essentially, we need to search for the processes that could be generative of such symbolic apparatus, to identify events of the system on micro-level where it will have its precipitate and where it arises from the activities of persons, and then to seek to observe its aggregation and its emergent properties. In such a way we might hope to build a sociology of knowledge for these forms of symbolization.

11. The *quality of life* for the individual varies under different conditions of scale. Recently, there has been a resurgence of public and political awareness of this effect of the scale of social systems on the life situation of participants, from the *ujamaa* ideologies of Africa to

the drive for community and neighbourhood involvement and realization in many urban Western circles. Some of the bases of these ideas are perhaps a nostalgia for a past not personally experienced and consequently not realistically envisaged; indeed, the life qualities desired are perhaps less directly linked to smallness than to other factors, such as a slower rate of change. Nonetheless, these ideas express a growing awareness that social planning can and should concern itself with fundamental parameters of social existence and not merely with the sectorial implementation of a development dictated by technological change.

The present essays share the view that such a connection exists between the scale of social systems and the characteristics of persons and activities; but this is a highly complex and dynamic connection, in need of a great deal of empirical and analytic work along a number of lines suggested in these essays. Explicitly addressing myself to the notion of *quality* of life, I should like to comment briefly on the three issues of social control, freedom, and variety. In considering these, as all other issues, one may emphasize with Barnes the need to consider not merely the ideal poles of large and small scale, but mainly the intermediate levels and mixtures of scale that characterize most societies and most lives. Thus for example, Christie (1974) in an attempt to relate 150 years of national criminal statistics of Norway to an overall measure of social density, finds confirmation for a view that correlates high per capita levels of criminality both with (early) small-scale and dense social characteristics, and with (recent) large-scale and open ones, contrasting with remarkable levels of security and lawabidingness in the middle range and historic phase.

Jacobson addresses this issue directly in his essay on the forms of social control inherent in social relationships under differing conditions of scale. He clarifies the important distinction between the mutual control implicit in a multiplex relationship (where A can sanction B's behaviour in one context through the control of prestations desired by B in another context), from that entailed by dense networks or social circles (where A and B both have relations to common third parties, who can be induced by A to sanction B for his failure to act fairly towards A). Having identified the various dense networks in which a person in one form of large-scale society participates (cf. Barth, above), we should be in a position to observe the forms and effectiveness of these sanctions, and the degree of moral embeddedness entailed by different forms of social organization.

The view that high density of relations and tightness of social controls are characteristic of small scale and entail a denial of personal freedom is deeply engrained in the folk sociology of the West. Generations of youth have yearned to be free of the stifling smallness of town or village, artists and intellectuals have fought the constraints on their individuality, whenever possible escaping to the freedom of great cities and cosmopolitan centres. Somewhat similar views are known in the Middle East; they seem far less pronounced in the great civilizations of China and India; while few tribal societies are reported to subscribe to analogous ideas, except for the Australian 'walkabout' and a few similar institutions. Freedom is most readily understood as a subjective concept; and it seems reasonable to expect a clear conceptualization of it, and a longing for it, to arise most readily where persons have experienced individuality and autonomy in one sector of activities while being denied it in other sectors. Perhaps the mixture of scales in different fields – from global to very small-scale – characteristic of life in traditional Europe, was one which particularly could serve to foster such frustrations and associate the experience of freedom with large-scale social systems.

The actual, objective extents of pressure to conformity or conversely freedom of individuality and creativity in different societies are perhaps even more difficult to judge and measure. But my own field experience with the Baktaman of New Guinea (Barth 1975), a society located towards the extreme small-scale pole, convinces me of the absence of any close and direct correlation between conformity and smallness. Moreover, to discover the character of interconnection, it is not enough to search for such correlations between gross variables, however cleverly conceptualized. What is required is a truly dynamic and empirically valid model of the entire process of cultural transmission and behavioural enactment, capable of showing how encounters both reflect and generate culture. Components of such a model may be found in the analyses of great and small traditions cited by Sinha, in the distributive model of culture developed in Schwartz' essay, as in a number of other sources in part touched in the preceding essays; but an adequate model has yet to be assembled and constructed.

Finally, with the label of 'variation' I refer to the co-existence of a plurality of cultural forms and options, as a quality in the social milieu obverse to the freedom and individuality of persons. Subcultural variation characterizes a number of ascriptive groupings, such as sex, age-group, descent category; it is characteristic of regional units and social classes, and may also be associated with other social circles constituted by dense networks. An increase of freedom is particularly, but not exclusively, associated with the existence of such groups with optative membership, while ascriptive membership in e.g. regional sub-cultures may easily be experienced as constraining and is often associated with a feeling of marginality, of exclusion from the important centres of other, larger-scale networks. Modern welfare states seem increasingly torn by a policy dilemma regarding such participation – as between the value for persons to assert themselves and have real influence in decentralized, smaller networks and neighbourhoods, vs. being allowed access to the benefits of large centres and collectivities where their individual impact is much smaller. My own value-position tends to the view that both kinds of participation are important, that freedom and individuality of persons are positive qualities, and that these are increased by a person's participation in optative systems exhibiting a wide mixture of scales but including several dense networks of discrepant social and spatial distribution.

However, our understanding of these circumstances, and their effects on the quality of life under different cultural regimes, is so incomplete that any value-position must be highly tentative. More importantly, I see no necessity for such value-positions to affect our ability to describe different combinations of scale in different empirical social organizations, to measure the part they play in the different sectors of the lives they shape, and to analyze their pre-conditions.

There is an immense potential for humanly very important insights to be gained from such analyses of the comparative range of social organizations accessible to anthropologists; and it is my hope that this collection of essays may stimulate further exploration of such themes.

References

Antropova, V. V. 1964: The Aleuts, pp. 884–888 in M. G. Levin & L. P. Potapov, eds: *The Peoples of Siberia.* Chicago: University of Chicago Press.

Asad, Talal 1972: Political inequality in the Kababish tribe, in Ian Cunnison & Wendy James: *Essays in Sudan Ethnography.* London: C. Hurst.

Attneave, Fred 1959: *Application of Information Theory in Psychology.* New York: Holt, Rinehart and Winston.

Bailey, F. G. 1960: *Tribe, Caste and Nation: A Study of Political Activity and Political Change in Highland Orissa,* Manchester: Manchester University Press.

Bailey, F. G. 1961: 'Tribe' and 'Caste' in India, *Contributions to Indian Sociology 5,* pp. 7–19.

Bailey, F. G. 1963: Closed social stratification in India, *European Journal of Sociology 4,* pp. 107–124.

Bailey, F. G. 1965: Decisions by consensus in councils and committees, in M. Barton, ed: *Political Systems and The Distribution of Power.* London: Tavistock.

Bailey, F. G. 1970: *Stratagems and Spoils.* Oxford: Blackwell.

Bailey, F. G. 1971: *Gifts and Poison.* Oxford: Blackwell.

Bailey, F. G. 1973: *Debate and Compromise.* Oxford: Blackwell.

Bakken, Erling & Olav Dragesund 1971: Fluctuations of pelagic fish stocks in the northeast Atlantic and their technological and economic effects on the fisheries. Paris: Organization for Economic Co-operation and Development, Direc-torate of Agriculture, Fisheries Division. (Mimeographed, iii, 26 pp. FI/T (71) 1/6).

Barnes, Harry Elmer & Howard Becker 1938: *Social Thought from Lore to Science* (Vol. I). New York: D. C. Heath.

Barnes, John Arundel 1947: History in a changing society, *Journal of the Rhodes-Livingstone Institute V,* pp. 48–55.

Barnes, John Arundel 1954: Class and committees in a Norwegian island parish, *Human relations 7,* pp. 39–58.

Barnes, John Arundel 1957: Land rights and kinship in two Bremnes hamlets, *Journal of the Royal Anthropological Institute 87,* pp. 31–56.

Barnes, John Arundel 1968: Networks and political process, pp. 107–130 in M. Swartz, ed: *Local-Level Politics.* Chicago: Aldine.

Barnes, John Arundel 1969: Networks and political process, pp. 51–76 in J. Clyde Mitchell, ed: *Social Networks in Urban Situations.* Manchester: Manchester University Press.

Barnes, John Arundel 1969: Graph theory and social networks: A technical comment on connected-ness and connectivity. *Sociology 3* (2), pp. 215–232.

Barnes, John Arundel 1971: The righthand and lefthand kingdoms of God: a dilemma of Pietist politics, pp. 1–17 in Thomas Owen ed: *The Translation of Culture: Essays to E. E. Evans-Pritchard.* London: Tavistock.

Barnes, John Arundel 1972: *Social networks.* (*Module in Anthropology 26.*) Reading, Mass.: Addison-Wesley.

Barnett, Homer G. 1953: *Innovation: The Basis of Cultural Change*. New York: McGraw-Hill.

Barth, Fredrik 1960: The System of Social Stratification in Swat, North Pakistan, pp. 113–148 in E. Leach, ed: *Aspects of Caste in South India, Ceylon and North-West Pakistan*. London: Cambridge University Press.

Barth, Fredrik 1961: *Nomads of South Persia*. Oslo: Universitetsforlaget.

Barth, Fredrik 1954: Competition and symbiosis in North East Baluchistan. *Folk 6* (1). Copenhagen.

Barth, Fredrik 1966: *Models of social organization*. Royal Anthropological Institute of Great Britain and Ireland, *Occasional Papers 23*.

Barth, Fredrik 1966a: Sociological aspects of integrated surveys for river basin development. Paper presented at the ITC–UNESCO Centre for Integrated Surveys, 4th International Seminar.

Barth, Fredrik 1967: On the study of social change, *American Anthropologist 69*, pp. 661–669.

Barth, Fredrik 1969: (ed.) *Ethnic Groups and Boundaries*. Oslo: Scandinavian University Books, Universitetsforlaget.

Barth, Fredrik 1972: Analytical dimensions in the comparison of social organizations, *American Anthropologist 74*, pp. 207–220.

Barth, Fredrik 1975: *Ritual and Knowledge among the Baktaman*. Oslo: Universitetsforlaget.

Beccaria, Caesar 1819: *An Essay on Crimes and Punishments*. Philadelphia: Philip H. Nicklin.

Benedict, B. 1966: Sociological characteristics of small territories, in M. Banton ed: *The Social Anthropology of Complex Societies* (ASA monographs 4). London: Tavistock.

Benet, Francisco 1963: Sociology uncertain: the ideology of the rural urban continuum, *Comparative Studies in Society and History 6*, pp. 1–23.

Berreman, Gerald D. 1955: Inquiry into community integration in an Aleutian village, *American Anthropologist 57*, pp. 49–59.

Berreman, Gerald D. 1960a: Cultural variability and drift in the Himalayan Hills, *American Anthropologist 62*, pp. 774–794.

Berreman, Gerald D. 1960b: Caste in India and the United States, *American Journal of Sociology 66*, pp. 120–127.

Berreman, Gerald D. 1962a: Pahari polyandry: a comparison, *American Anthropologist 64*, pp. 60–75.

Berreman, Gerald D. 1962b: Caste and economy in the Himalayas, *Economic Development and Cultural Change 10*, pp. 386–394.

Berreman, Gerald D. 1962c: *Behind Many Masks: Ethnography and Impression Management in a Himalayan Village* (Monograph No. 4, The Society for Applied Anthropology). (Also, Bobbs-Merrill Reprint A-393. Indianapolis: Bobbs-Merrill.)

Berreman, Gerald D. 1964: Aleut reference group alienation, mobility and acculturation, *American Anthropologist 66*, pp. 231–250.

Berreman, Gerald D. 1966: Caste in cross-cultural perspective, comprising: Structure and function of caste systems (Ch. 14), and Concomitants of caste organization (Ch. 15), pp. 275–324 in G. de Vos & H. Wagatsuma, eds: *Japan's Invisible Race*. Berkeley: University of California Press.

Berreman, Gerald D. 1967a: Stratification, pluralism and interaction: a comparative analysis of caste, pp. 45–73 in A. de Reuck & F. Knight, eds: *Caste and Race: Comparative Approaches*, London: J. and A. Churchill.

Berreman, Gerald D. 1967b; Caste as social process, *Southwestern Journal of Anthropology 23*, pp. 351–370.

Berreman, Gerald D. 1968: Caste: the concept, pp. 333–339 in David Sills, ed: *International Encyclopedia of the Social Sciences*, Vol. II. New York: Macmillan Co. and The Free Press.

Berreman, Gerald D. 1969: Women's roles and politics: India and the United States, pp. 68–71 in R. O'Brien, C. Shrag, W. Martin, eds:

Readings in General Sociology (4th ed.)
Boston: Houghton-Mifflin.

Berreman, Gerald D. 1971: Self, situation and escape from stigmatized ethnic identity, pp. 11–25 in 1971 Yearbook of the Ethnographic Museum, University of Oslo. Oslo: Universitetsforlaget.

Berreman, Gerald D. 1972a: Hindus of the Himalayas: Ethnography and Change. Berkeley: University of California Press (2nd edition).

Berreman, Gerald D. 1972b: Social categories and social interaction in urban India, American Anthropologist 74 (3), pp. 567–586.

Berreman, Gerald D. 1972c: Race, caste and other invidious distinctions in social stratification, Race 13 (4), pp. 386–414.

Berreman, Gerald D. 1973: Caste in the Modern World. New York: General Learning Press.

Berrien, F. Kenneth 1968: General and Social Systems. New Brunswick, N.J.: Rutgers University Press.

Bertalanffy, L. v. 1973: General System Theory. Harmondsworth: Penguin University Books.

Bloch, Herbert A. 1952: Disorganization: Personal and Social. New York: Alfred A. Knopf.

Blom, Jan-Petter 1972: (ed.) Extracts from discussions. Burg Wartenstein Symposium No. 55 on 'Scale and social organization'. Wenner-Gren Foundation for Anthropological Research, New York.

Bloomfield, Leonard 1933: Language. New York: Henry Holt.

Blumer, Herbert 1937: Social disorganization and individual disorganization, American Journal of Sociology 42, pp. 871–877.

Blumer, Herbert 1969: Symbolic Interactionism. Englewood Cliffs, N.J.:

Boissevain, Jeremy 1968: The place of non-groups in the social sciences, Man 3 (4), pp. 542–556.

Boissevain, J. & J. Friedl (eds.) 1975: Beyond the Community: Social Process in Europe. Dept. of Educational Science of the Netherlands, The Hague.

Bose, N. K. 1968: Competing productive systems in India, Man in India 48 (1) pp. 1–18.

Bose, N. K. 1971: Land-man ratio in tribal areas, Man in India 51 (4) pp. 267–274.

Bose, S. 1964: Economy of the Onge of Little Andaman, Man in India 44 (4), pp. 298–310.

Bose, S. 1967: Carrying Capacity of Land under Shifting Cultivation, Calcutta: The Asiatic Society.

Boulding, K. E. 1956: Toward a General Theory of Growth. General Systems Yearbook, 1.

Bourne, George (pseudonym for Sturt, George) 1912: Change in the Village. London: Duckworth.

Braidwood, Robert J. 1964: Prehistoric Men. Glenview, Illinois: Scott, Foresman (7th ed.).

Brox, Ottar 1966: Hva skjer i Nord-Norge? En studie i norsk utkantpolitikk. Oslo: Pax.

Burridge, Kenelm 1969: New Heaven, New Earth. Oxford: Blackwell.

Carneiro, Robert L. 1970: Scale analysis, evolutionary sequences and the rating of cultures, in Raoul Naroll & Ronald Cohen, eds: Handbook of Method in Cultural Anthropology. Garden City, N.Y.: Natural History Press.

Childe, V. Gordon 1950: The urban revolution, Town Planning Review 21, pp. 3–17.

Childe, V. Gordon 1965: Man Makes Himself. London: Watts (4th ed.).

Christie, Nils 1975: Hvor tett et samfunn? Copenhagen/Oslo: Christian Ejlers Forlag/Universitetsforlaget.

Cicourel, Aaron V. 1964: Method and Measurement in Sociology. New York: Free Press of Glencoe.

Cicourel, Aaron V. 1968: Preliminary issues of theory and method, pp. 1–21 in The Social Organization of Juvenile Justice. New York: John Wiley.

Cicourel, Aaron V. 1973: Cognitive Sociology: Language and Meaning in Social Interaction. Harmondsworth: Penguin Education.

Claus, Peter J. 1973: Toward a structural definition of peasant society. *Peasant Studies Newsletter 2* (2), pp. 6–11.

Cohen, A. 1972: *Arab border villages in Israel*. Manchester: Manchester University Press.

Cohn, B. S. and McKim Marriott 1958: Networks and centres in the integration of Indian Civilization, *Journal of Social Research 1*, pp. 1–9.

Cohn B. S. 1971: *India: The Social Anthropology of a Civilization*. Englewood Cliffs N.J.: Prentice-Hall.

Colson, E., 1960: *Social Organization of the Gwembe Tonga*. Manchester: Manchester University Press.

Colson, E. 1971: *The Social Consequences of Resettlement*. Manchester: Manchester University Press.

Cooley, Charles Horton 1964: *Human Nature and the Social Order*. New York: Schocken Books.

Cooley, Charles Horton 1967: *Social Organization: A Study of the Larger Mind*. New York: Schocken Books.

Davis, Fred 1971: *On Youth Subcultures: The Hippie Variant*. New York: General Learning Press.

Davis, Kingsley 1951: *The Population of India and Pakistan*. Princeton, N.J.: Princeton University Press.

Deutsch, K. W. 1963: *The Nerves of Government*. New York: Free Press of Glencoe.

DeVos, George & Hiroshi Wagatsuma (eds.) 1966: *Japan's Invisible Race*. Berkeley: University of California Press.

Dewey, Richard 1960: The rural-urban continuum: real but relatively unimportant, *American Journal of Sociology 66*, pp. 60–66.

Douglas, Jack D. (ed.) 1970: *Understanding Everyday Life*. Chicago: Aldine.

Douglas, Mary 1966: *Purity and Danger*. London: Routledge & Kegan Paul.

Douglas, Mary 1970: *Natural Symbols*. New York: Random House.

Dreitzel, H. P. (ed.) 1970: *Patterns of Communicative Behaviour*. (Recent Sociology, No. 2) New York: Macmillan.

Dumont, Louis. 1970: *Religion, Politics and History in India*. Paris: Mouton.

Durkheim, Émile 1933: *The Division of Labor in Society*. Translation by George Simpson. Glencoe, Illinois: Free Press. [*De la division du travail social*. 1893.]

Durkheim, Émile 1954: *The Elementary Forms of the Religious Life*. London: Allen & Unwin [1912].

Durkheim, Émile 1951: *Suicide: A Study in Sociology*. Glencoe, Illinois: Free Press [1897].

Eggan, Fred 1954: Social anthropology and the method of controlled comparison, *American Anthropologist 56*, pp. 743–763.

Eidheim, H. 1971; *Aspects of the Lappish Minority Situation*. Oslo: Universitetsforlaget.

English, P. 1973: The traditional city of Herat, Afghanistan, in L. C. Brown, ed: *From Medina to Metropolis. Heritage and Change in the Near Eastern City*. Princeton, N.J.: Darwin.

Evans-Pritchard, E. C. 1940: *The Nuer*. London: Oxford University Press.

Fallers, Lloyd A. 1956: *Bantu Bureaucracy*. Cambridge: Heffner. [Reissued University of Chicago Press, 1965.]

Farber, Marvin 1943: *The Foundation of Phenomenology*. Cambridge: Cambridge University Press.

Faris, Ellsworth 1932: The primary group, essence and accident, *American Journal of Sociology 38*, pp. 41–50.

Ferdinand, K. 1962: Nomad expansion and commerce in central Afghanistan. *Folk 4*, pp. 123–159. Copenhagen.

Firth, Raymond 1951: *Elements of Social Organization*. London: Watts.

Firth, Raymond 1964: Capital, saving and credit in peasant societies: a viewpoint from economic anthropology, pp. 15–34 in Raymond Firth & B. Yamey eds: *Capital, Saving and Credit in Peasant Societies: Studies from Asia, Oceanica, the Caribbean and Middle America.* London: Allen & Unwin.

Firth, Raymond 1966: *Malay Fishermen: Their Peasant Economy.* London: Routledge & Kegan Paul. (2nd ed.)

Firth, Raymond 1971; *Elements of Social Organization.* London: Tavistock. 3rd ed., with new preface.

Fortes, M. 1969: *Kinship and the Social Order. The Legacy of Henry Morgan.* Chicago: Aldine.

Fortune, Reo F. 1935: *Manus Religion.* Philadelphia: American Philosophical Society.

Foster, George McClelland 1953: What is folk culture? *American Anthropologist 55*; pp. 159–173.

Foster, George McClelland 1960–61: Interpersonal relations in peasant societies (with comments and rejoinder). *Human Organization 19*; pp. 174–184.

Foster, George McClelland 1967: Introduction: what is a peasant? pp. 2–14 in Jack Michael Potter et al. eds: *Peasant Society: A Reader.* Boston: Little, Brown.

Freeman, Linton C. & Robert F. Winch 1957: Societal complexity: an empirical test of a typology of societies, *American Journal of Sociology 62*, pp. 461–466.

Frankenberg, R. 1957: *Village on the Border.* London: Cohen and West.

Frankenberg, R. 1967: Economic anthropology: one anthropologist's view, pp. 47–89 in Raymond Firth ed.: *Themes in Economic Anthropology.* (*ASA monographs 6*). London: Tavistock.

Gallant, Jonathan & John Prothero 1972: Weight watching at the university, *Science 175*, no. 4020, January 28.

Garfinkel, Harold 1967: *Studies in Ethnomethodology.* Englewood Cliffs, N.J.: Prentice-Hall.

Garner, W. R. 1962: *Uncertainty and Structure as Psychological Concepts.* New York: Wiley.

Geertz, C. 1957: Ritual and social change: a Javanese example. *American Anthropologist 59*, pp. 32–54.

Geertz, C. 1970: *Agricultural involution.* Berkeley: University of California Press.

Gellner, Ernest 1965: *Thought and Change.* Chicago: University of Chicago Press.

Ghurye, G. S. 1942: *The Indian Aboriginals 'So-called' and their Future,* Poona.

Gluckman, M. (ed.) 1964: *Closed Systems and Open Minds: The Limits of Naïvety in Social Anthropology.* Edinburgh & London: Oliver & Boyd.

Gluckman, M. (ed.) 1968: The utility of the equilibrium model in the study of social change, *American Anthropologist 70*, pp. 219–237.

Gluckman, Max, J. C. Mitchell, & J. A. Barnes 1949: The village headman in British Central Africa. *Africa 19*, pp. 89–106.

Godelier, M. 1973: Anthropologie et économie, in *Horizon, trajets marxistes en anthropologie.* Paris.

Goffman, Erving 1959: *The Presentation of Self in Everyday Life.* Garden City, N. J.: Doubleday (Anchor Books).

Goffman, Erving 1961: *Asylums.* Garden City, N.Y.: Doubleday (Anchor Books).

Goffman, Erving 1963: *Behavior in Public Places.* Glencoe, Illinois: Free Press.

Goffman, Erving 1967: *Interaction Ritual: Essays on Face-To-Face Behavior.* Garden City, N.Y.: Doubleday (Anchor Books).

Goffman, Erving 1969; *Strategic Interaction.* Philadelphia: University of Pennsylvania Press.

Goffman, Erving 1971: The insanity of place, in *Relations in Public.* New York: Basic Books.

Goffman, Erving 1974: *Frame Analysis: An Essay on the Organization of Experience.* New York: Harper & Row.

Goldenweiser, A. A. 1922: *Early Civilization.* New York: Alfred A. Knopf.

Griffith, B. C. & N. C. Mullins 1972: Coherent Social Groups in Scientific Change, *Science 177*, pp. 959–964.

Grønhaug, R. 1971: Changing community structures and intercommunity relations in Southern Turkey, *Folk 13*, pp. 149–166. Copenhagen.

Grønhaug, R. 1971a: *Macro-factors in Local Life. Social Organization in Antalya, Southern Turkey*. Mimeo, University of Bergen.

Grønhaug, R. 1976: Comment to LaBianca's review of the establishment of signs in social process, *Current Anthropology* (June), pp. 309–310.

Grønhaug, R. In press: *Micro-macro Relations. Social Organization in Antalya, Southern Turkey*. Oslo & Boston: Scandinavian University Books, Universitetsforlaget and Harvard University Press.

Gulliver, P. 1955: *The Family Herds*. London: Routledge & Kegan Paul.

Gumperz, John J. 1958: Dialect Differences and Social Stratification in a North Indian Village. *American Anthropologist 60*, pp. 668–682.

Haire, Mason 1959: Biological models and empirical histories of the growth of organizations, in M. Haire ed: *Modern Organizational Theory*, New York: Wiley.

Hanssen, B. 1953: Fields of social activity and their dynamics, pp. 99–133 in *Transactions of the Westermarck Society*. Copenhagen.

Haudricourt, André G. 1961: Richesse en phonémes et richesse en locuteurs. *l'Homme 1* (1), pp. 5–10.

Hauser, Philip Morris 1965: Observations on the urban-folk and urban-rural dichotomies as forms of Western ethnocentrism, pp. 503–518 in Philip Morris Hauser & Leo Francis Schnore eds.: *The Study of Urbanization*. New York; Wiley.

Henry, Jules 1963: *Culture Against Man*. New York: Random House.

Henslin, James 1968: Trust and the cab driver, pp. 138–158 in M. Truzzi, ed: *Sociology and Everyday Life*. Englewood Cliffs, N.J.: Prentice-Hall.

Horton, John 1964: The dehumanization of anomie and alienation, *British Journal of Sociology 15*, pp. 283–300.

Howarth, David 1951: *The Shetland Bus*. London: Nelson.

Husserl, Edmund (See Farber 1943).

Huxley, Julian 1932: *Problems of Relative Growth*. New York: MacVeagh, Dial Press.

Isaacs, Harold 1965: *India's Ex-Untouchables*. New York: John Day.

Isard, W. & T. A. Reiner 1968: Regional science, in D. I. Sills ed: *International Encyclopedia of the Social Sciences*. New York: Macmillan.

Johansson, Sten 1970: *Om levnadsnivåundersökningen*. Stockholm: Allmänna förlaget.

Jones, Dorothy M. 1969: *A Study of Social and Economic Problems in Unalaska, an Aleut Village*. Unpublished Doctoral Thesis, School of Social Welfare, University of California, Berkeley.

Karve, I. 1961: *Hindu Society, an Interpretation*, Poona.

Karve, I. 1965: *Kinship Organization in India*, 2nd ed., Bombay.

Katz, Fred E. 1966: Social participation and social structure, *Social Forces 45*, pp. 199–210.

Kedourie, Elie 1970: *Nationalism in Asia and Africa*. New York: Norton.

Kluckhohn, Clyde 1949: *Mirror for Man*. New York: McGraw-Hill.

Krader, Lawrence 1968: *Formation of the State*. Englewood Cliffs, N.J.: Prentice-Hall.

Krislov, S. et al. 1972: *Compliance and the Law*. Beverley Hills: Sage Publications.

Kroeber, A. L. 1948: *Anthropology*. New York: Harcourt, Brace. (Revised ed.).

LaBianca, Ö. 1976: Signs in Social Process: Reidar Grønhaug's Views. *Current Anthropology* (June), pp. 307–309.

Leach, E. 1961: *Pul Eliya: A Village in Ceylon*. Cambridge: University Press.

Lenski, Gerhard 1966: *Power and Privilege. A Theory of Social Stratification*. New York: McGraw-Hill.

Lévi-Strauss, C. 1967: Social structure, in *Structural Anthropology*. New York: Anchor Books.

Lévi-Strauss, C. 1969: *The Elementary Structures of Kinship*. Boston: Beacon Press. Translation: revised edition. [originally, *Les structures élémentaires de la parenté*, Paris 1949].

Lewis, Oscar 1951: *Life in a Mexican village: Tepoztlan Revisited*. Urbana: University of Illinois Press.

Lopreato, Joseph 1965: How would you like to be a peasant? *Human Organization 24*, pp. 298–307.

Lupri, Eugen 1967: The rural-urban variable reconsidered: the cross-cultural perspective. *Sociologia Ruralis 7*, pp. 1–20.

MacKay, Donald M. 1952: The nomenclature of information theory, in H. von Foerster, ed: *Cybernetics, Circular Causal and Feedback Mechanisms in Biological and Social Systems*. New York: Josiah Macy Jr. Foundation.

MacKay, Donald M. 1969: *Information, Mechanisms, and Meaning*. Cambridge: MIT Press.

Maine, Henry 1861: *Ancient Law*. London: J. Murray.

Malinowski, B. 1922: *Argonauts of the Western Pacific*. London: Routledge & Kegan Paul.

Mannheim, Karl 1940: *Man and Society in an Age of Reconstruction*. New York: Harcourt, Brace.

Marriott, McKim 1959: Changing channels of cultural transmission in Indian civilization, pp. 66–74 in Verne F. Ray, ed: *Intermediate Societies, Social Mobility and Communication*. Seattle: American Ethnological Society.

Marriott, McKim 1960: *Caste Ranking and Community Structure in Five Regions of India and Pakistan*, Poona: G. S. Press.

Marriott, McKim 1963: Cultural policy in new states, pp. 27–56 in Clifford Geertz, ed: *Old Societies and New States: The Quest for Modernity in Asia and Africa*. London: Macmillan.

Marriott, McKim 1969: Little communities in an indigenous civilization, in Marriott ed: *Village India*. Chicago: University of Chicago Press.

Marsh, Robert M. 1967: *Comparative Sociology: A Codification of Cross-Societal Analysis*. New York: Harcourt, Brace and World.

Martin, Jean Isobel 1970: Suburbia: community and network, pp. 301–339 in Alan Fraser Davies & Solomon Encel, eds: *Australian Society: A Sociological Introduction*. (2nd ed.) Melbourne; Cheshire.

Marx, Karl 1964: *Economic and Philosophic Manuscripts of 1844*. New York: International Publishers.

Mead, Margaret & Theodore Schwartz 1958: The cult as condensed social process, pp. 85–185 in Group Processes. *Transactions of the Fifth Conference, October 12, 13, 14 and 15, 1958* (Princeton, New Jersey). New York: Josiah Macy, Jr. Foundation.

Meier, Richard L. 1962: *A Communications Theory of Urban Growth*. Cambridge, Massachusetts: MIT Press.

Mendras, Henri 1972: Un schema d'analyse de la paysannerie occidentale. *Peasant Studies Newsletter 1*, pp. 79–93, 126–144.

Merton, Robert K. & Alice S. Kitt 1950: Contributions to the theory of reference group behavior, in R. Merton & P. Lazarsfeld, eds: *Continuities in Social Research*. Glencoe, Illinois: Free Press.

Metzger, D. & G. E. Williams 1963a: A formal ethnographic analysis of Tenejapa ladino weddings, *American Anthropologist 65*, pp. 1076.

Metzger, D. & G. E. Williams 1963b: Tenejapa medicine I: the curer, *Southwestern Journal of Anthropology 19*, pp. 216.

Miner, Horace 1952: The folk-urban continuum, *American sociological review 17*, pp. 529–537.

Ministry of Planning, Department of Statistics 1970: *Survey of Progress 1969–70*. Kabul.

Minogue, K. R. 1967: *Nationalism*. New York: Basic Books.

281

Mintz, Sidney Wilfred 1973: A note on the definition of peasantries, *Journal of Peasant Studies 1*, pp. 91–106.

Mitchell, J. Clyde 1969: The concept and use of social networks, pp. 150 in J. Clyde Mitchell: *Social Networks in Urban Situations* Manchester: Manchester University Press.

Molland, Einar 1951: *Fra Hans Nielsen Hauge til Eivind Berggrav*. Oslo: Gyldendal.

Nadel, S. F. 1965: *The Theory of Social Structure*. London: Cohen and West.

Odum, E. P. 1963: *Ecology*. London: Holt, Rinehart and Winston.

O'Laughlin, Bridget 1975: Marxist approaches in anthropology, in B. J. Siegel, ed: *Annual Review of Anthropology 4*, pp. 341–370. Palo Alto, California: Annual Reviews Inc.

Opler, Morris E. 1956: The extensions of an Indian village, *Journal of Asian Studies 16*, pp. 5–10.

Ortiz, Sutti 1971: Reflections on the concept of 'peasant culture' and 'peasant cognitive systems', pp. 322–336 in Teodor Shanin, ed: *Peasants and Peasant Societies: Selected Readings*. Harmondsworth: Penguin.

Pahl, Raymond Edward 1966: The rural-urban continuum, *Sociologia Ruralis 6*, pp. 299–329.

Pahl, Raymond Edward 1967: The rural-urban continuum: a reply to Eugen Lupri, *Sociologia Ruralis 7*, pp. 21–29.

Paine, Robert 1966: A critique of the methodology of Robert Redfield: 'folk culture' and other concepts. *Ethnos 31*, pp. 161–172.

Park, Robert E. 1925: The city: suggestions for the investigation of human behavior in the urban environment, pp. 1–46 in R. E. Park, E. W. Burgess, et al., eds: *The City*. Chicago: University of Chicago Press.

Parsons, Talcott & Edward A. Shils, (eds.) 1951: *Toward a General Theory of Action*. Cambridge: Harvard University Press.

Peters, E. 1972: Aspects of the control of moral ambiguities: a comparative analysis of two culturally disparate modes of social control, pp. 109–162 in M. Gluckman, ed.: *The Allocation of Responsibility*. Manchester: Manchester University Press.

Powell, John Duncan 1972a: On defining peasant and peasant society, *Peasant Studies Newsletter 1*, pp. 94–99.

Powell, John Duncan 1972b: Reply. *Peasant Studies Newsletter 1*, pp. 161–162.

Puzo, Mario. 1969: *The Godfather*. Greenwich, Conn.: Fawcett.

Radcliffe-Brown, A. R. 1968: *Structure and Function in Primitive Society*. London: Cohen and West.

Redfield, Robert 1930: *Tepoztlan, a Mexican Village: A Study of Folk Life*. Chicago: University of Chicago Press.

Redfield, Robert 1941: *The Folk Culture of Yucatan*. Chicago: University of Chicago Press.

Redfield, Robert 1942: Introduction, in *Levels of Intergration in Biological and Social Systems*. Lancastar, Pa.: J. Catell.

Redfield, Robert 1947: The Folk Society, *American Journal of Sociology 52*, pp. 293–308.

Redfield, Robert 1953: *The Primitive World and Its Transformations*. Ithaca, N.Y.: Cornell University Press.

Redfield, Robert 1955: Societies and cultures as natural systems, *Journal of the Royal Anthropological Institute 85*, pp. 19–32.

Redfield, Robert 1956: *Peasant Society and Culture: An Anthropological Approach to Civilization*. Chicago: University of Chicago Press. [References are to pagination of hard-cover edition].

Redfield, Robert 1967: *The Little Community*. Chicago: University of Chicago Press.

Redfield, R. & Milton B. Singer 1954: The cultural role of cities, *Economic Development and Culture Change 3* (1), pp. 53–73.

Riesman, David 1950: *The Lonely Crowd*. New Haven, Conn.: Yale University Press.

Rothman, David J. 1971: *The Discovery of the Asylum*. Boston: Little, Brown.

Rowe, William L. 1964: Caste, kinship and association in urban India, paper prepared for Burg Wartenstein Symposium No. 26: Cross-Cultural Similarities in the Urbanization Process, Aug. 27–Sept. 8, 1964.

Rudolph, R. & S. Rudolph 1960: The political role of India's caste associations, *Pacific Affairs 33* (March, 1960), pp. 5–22.

Rudolph, R. & S. Ruldolph 1967: *The Modernity of Tradition: Political Development in India*, Calcutta.

Rule, James B. 1973: *Private Lives and Public Surveillance*. London: Allen Lane.

Sahlins, Marshall 1965: On the sociology of primitive exchange, pp. 139–236 in M. Banton, ed: *The Relevance of Models for Social Anthropology*. New York: Praeger.

Sahlins, Marshall 1968: *Tribesmen*. Engelwood Cliffs, N.J.: Prentice-Hall.

Sapir, Edward 1949: Culture, genuine and spurious, pp. 308–331 in D. Mandelbaum, ed: *Selected Writings of Edward Sapir*. Berkeley: University of California Press.

Saraswati, B. 1971: *Contributions to the Understanding of Indian Civilization*, Dharwar.

Saraswati, B. & Surajit Sinha 1970: *Organization of Ascetics in Kasi*. (Unpublished Report, Anthropological Survey of India).

Schmalenbach, Herman 1961: The sociological category of communion, in T. Parsons et al., eds: *Theories of Society*, Vol. I. Glencoe, Illinois: Free Press.

Schutz, Alfred 1962: *Collected Papers I: The Problem of Social Reality*. (M. Natanson, ed.) The Hague: Martinus Nijhoff.

Schwartz, Theodore & M. Mead 1961: Micro- and macro-cultural models for cultural evolution, *Anthropological Linguistics 3* (1), pp. 1–7. Reprinted in M. Mead, *Continuities in Cultural Evolution*.

Schwartz, Theodore 1962: The Paliau movement in the Admiralty Islands, 1946–1954, *Anthropological Papers of the American Museum of Natural History, New York. Vol. 49, pt. 2*, pp. 207–421.

Schwartz, Theodore 1963: Systems of areal integration: some considerations based on the Admiralty Islands of Northern Melanesia. *Anthropological Forum, 1*, (1), pp. 56–97.

Schwartz, Theodore 1968: Beyond cybernetics: constructs, expectations, and goals in human adaptation. Paper presented at Burg Wartenstein Symposium No. 40, Wenner-Gren Foundation for Anthropological Research.

Schwartz, Theodore 1973: Cult and context: the paranoid ethos in Melanesia, *Ethos 1* (2), pp. 153–174.

Schwartz, Theodore 1975a: Cultural totemism: ethnic identity, primitive and modern, pp. 106–131, in George DeVos & Lola Romanucci-Ross, eds: *Ethnic Identity: Cultural Continuities and Change*, Palo Alto, California: Mayfield.

Schwartz, Theodore 1975b: Relations among generations in time-limited cultures, *Ethos 3* (2), pp. 309–322. (Special issue dedicted to Margaret Mead, edited and with introduction by Theodore Schwartz, to appear in book form as *Socialization as Cultural Communication*, University of California Press: Berkeley.

Schwartz, Theodore 1975c: Cargo cult: A Melanesian type-response to culture contact. in George DeVos, ed: *Responses to Change*, New York: Van Nostrand.

Schwartz, Theodore in press: Where is the culture? in G. Spindler, ed: *The Making of Psychological Anthropology*, Berkeley: University of California Press.

Scott, John Finley 1971: *Internalization of Norms*. Englewood Cliffs, N.J.: Prentice-Hall.

Scudder, T. 1962: *The Ecology of the Gwembe Tonga*. Manchester: Manchester University Press

Service, Elman R. 1966: *The Hunters*.

Englewood Cliffs, N.J.: Prentice-Hall.

Shanin, Teodor 1966: The peasantry as a political factor, *Sociological Review n.s. 14*, pp. 5–27.

Shanin, Teodor 1971: Peasantry: delineation of a concept and a field of study, *European Journal of Sociology 12*, pp. 289–300.

Shanin, Teodor 1972: Yankee intuition, *Peasant Studies Newsletter 1*, pp. 158–160.

Shanin, Teodor 1973: The nature and change of peasant economies. *Sociologia Ruralis 13*, pp. 141–171.

Simmel, Georg 1950: The metropolis and mental life, pp. 409–424 in *The Sociology of Georg Simmel* (K. Wolff, trans. and ed.) Glencoe, Illinois: Free Press. [First published, in German, 1903].

Simmel, George 1950: *The Sociology of George Simmel*. Part II, Quantitative Aspects of the Group. pp. 87–174. New York: Free Press.

Simmel, George 1971: The stranger, in Donald Levine, ed: *On Individuality and Social Forms*. Chicago: University of Chicago Press. [original, 1908]

Singer, Milton B. 1958: The Great Tradition in a metropolitan center: Madras. *Journal of American Folklore 71* pp. 347–388.

Singer, Milton B. 1968: The Indian joint family in modern industry, pp. 423–454 in Singer & Cohn eds: *Structure and Change in Indian Society*. Chicago: Aldine Publishing Co.

Singh, Rudra Datt 1956: The unity of an Indian village, *Journal of Asian Studies 16*, pp. 10–19.

Sinha, Surajit 1958: Tribal cultures of peninsular India as a dimension of little traditions in the study of Indian civilization: a preliminary statement, *Journal of American Folklore 71*, pp. 504–518.

Sinha, Surajit 1962: State formation and Rajput myth in tribal Central India, *Man in India 42*, pp. 35–80.

Sinha, Surajit 1965: Tribe-caste and tribe-peasant continua in Central India, *Man in India 45*, pp. 57–83.

Sinha, Surajit 1967: Caste in India: its essential pattern of socio-cultural integration pp. 92–105 in A. de Reuck & J. Knight, eds: *Caste and Race: Comparative Approaches*, London: J. & A. Churchill Ltd.

Sinha, Surajit 1968: Urgent problems for research in social and cultural anthropology: perspective and suggestions, pp. 162–169 in *Urgent Research in Social Anthropology*, Simla.

Sinha, Surajit 1970: *Science, Technology and Culture: A Study of Cultural Traditions and Institutions of India and Ceylon in Relation to Science and Technology*. New Delhi.

Sinha, Surajit 1972: Kali Temple at Kalighat and the City of Calcutta, pp. 61–72 in Surajit Sinha ed: *Cultural Profile of Calcutta*.

Sinha, Surajit et al. 1966: *Ethnic Groups, Villages and Towns of Pargana Barabhum: Report of a Survey*. Anthropological Survey of India, Memoir No. 14.

Sjoberg, Gideon 1960: *The Preindustrial City*. Glencoe, Illinois: Free Press.

Slater, Philip 1970: *The Pursuit of Loneliness: American Culture at the Breaking Point*. Boston: Beacon Press.

Smith, A. D. 1971: *Theories of Nationalism*. London: Duckworth.

Smithies, B. & P. Fiddick 1969: *Enoch Powell on Immigration*. London: Sphere.

Spencer, Baldwin & F. J. Gillin 1899: *The Native Tribes of Central Australia*. London: Macmillan.

Srinivas, M. N. 1966: *Social Change in Modern India*. Berkeley: University of California Press.

Steen, Lynn Arthur 1976: Computational unsolvability, *Science News 109* (19), May 8, 1976, pp. 298–301.

Stevens, Stanley Smith 1946: On the theory of scales of measurement, *Science 103*, pp. 677–680.

Steward, Julian 1955: *Theory of Culture Change*. Urbana: University of Illinois Press.

Stouffer, Samuel Andrew, et al. 1950: Measurement and prediction. Princeton, N.J.: Princeton University Press. (*Studies in Social Psychology in World War II*, vol. IV.)

Sturt, George *see* Bourne, George (pseudonym).

Suttles, Gerald 1972: *The Social Construction of Communities*. Chicago: University of Chicago Press.

Swartz, M. J. 1968: *Local-Level Politics*. Chicago: Aldine.

Tambiah, Stanley Jeyaraj 1955: An examination and critique of Robert Redfield's folk-urban continuum, *University of Ceylon Review 13*, pp. 29–49.

Thompson, D'Arcy 1917: *On Growth and Form*. Cambridge University Press.

Tönnies, Ferdinand 1940: *Fundamental Concepts in Society*. (C. Loomis, trans. and ed.) New York: American Book Co.

Torgerson, Warren Stanley 1958: *Theory and Methods of Scaling*. New York: Wiley.

Toynbee, Arnold J. 1947: *A Study of History* (abridged by D. C. Somervell). New York: Oxford University Press.

Travers, J. & S. Milgram 1969: An experimental study of the small world problem, *Sociometry 32*, pp. 425–443.

Turner, Ralph 1956: Role-taking, role standpoint, and reference-group behavior. *American Journal of Sociology 61*, pp. 316–328.

Turner, Roy (ed.) 1974: *Ethnomethodology: Selected Readings*. Harmondsworth: Penguin Education.

Turner, Victor W. 1969: *The Ritual Process: Structure and Anti-Structure*. Chicago: Aldine.

Turner, Victor W. 1972: *Mukanda: The Politics of a Non-Political Ritual*, in Swartz 1968.

Uberoi, J. P. S. 1962: *Politics of the Kula King*. Manchester: Manchester University Press.

Valen-Sendstad, Olav 1952: *Moskva og Rom: fjorten epistler om verdenspolitikken og det 20. århundres motrevolusjon*. Bergen: Dagens rotasjontr.

Vatuk, Sylvia 1969: Reference, address and fictive kinship in urban North India. *Ethnology 8*, pp. 255–272.

Vatuk, Sylvia 1972: *Kinship and Urbanization: White-Collar Migrants in North India*. Berkeley: University of California Press.

Wadel, Cato 1971: Capitalization and ownership: the persistence of fishermen–ownership in the Norwegian herring fishery, pp. 104–119 in Raoul Anderson & Cato Wadel, eds: *North Atlantic Fishermen: Anthropological Essays on Modern Fishing*. St. John's, Newfoundland; *Newfoundland Social and Economic Papers no. 5.*

Wallace, Anthony F. C. 1961: *Culture and Personality*. New York: Random House.

Weber, Max 1958: *The City*. (D. Martindale & G. Neuwirth, trans. and eds.) Glencoe, Illinois: Free Press [First published, 1921].

White, Leslie 1959: *The Evolution of Culture*. New York: McGraw-Hill.

White, Leslie 1975: *The Concept of Cultural Systems*. New York: Columbia University Press.

Wilson, Godfrey & Monica Wilson 1945: *The Analysis of Social Change*. Cambridge: Cambridge University Press.

Wilson, Monica 1971: *Religion and the Transformation of Society*. Cambridge: Cambridge University Press.

Wirth, Louis 1938: Urbanism as a way of life, *American Journal of Sociology 44*, pp. 1–24. (Reprinted, pp. 60–84 in *On Cities and Social Life* (ed. A. J. Reiss, Jr.). Chicago: University of Chicago Press. 1964.)

Wittfogel, K. A. 1967: *Oriental Despotism*. New Haven Conn.: Yale University Press.

Wolf, Eric Robert 1955: Types of Latin American peasantry: a preliminary discussion, *American Anthropologist 57*, pp. 452–471.

Wolf, Eric Robert 1966: *Peasants*. Englewood Cliffs, N.J.: Prentice-Hall.

Yinger, J. Milton 1960: Contraculture and subculture, *American Sociological Review 25*, pp. 625–635.

Notes

INTRODUCTION

1 Participants in the meetings in Burg Wartenstein were F. G. Bailey, John A. Barnes, Fredrik Barth, Burton Benedict, Gerald D. Berreman, Jan-Petter Blom, Ralph N. Bulmer, Abner Cohen, Elizabeth Colson, Ronald Frankenberg, Ernest Gellner, Reidar Grønhaug, David Jacobson, Robert Paine, Theodore Schwartz, and Surajit Sinha. We are grateful to all participants for their contributions in writing and discussion, and to the staff of the Wenner-Gren Foundation for assisting us through the meetings.

SCALE AS A VARIABLE IN ANALYSIS

1 This paper is a revised version of one submitted to the Burg Wartenstein symposium no. 55 in 1972. I thank the Wenner-Gren Foundation for the grants to my Herat fieldwork and participation at Burg Wartenstein. I have benefitted especially from the symposium papers submitted by Surajit Sinha and Theodore Schwartz. I found the ten discussion sessions very rich and have gained much from studying the debate as reported in 'Extracts from discussions . . .' edited by Jan-Petter Blom. For remarks helping me to clarify my own paper I thank especially Fredrik Bailey, John Barnes, Fredrik Barth, Ernst Gellner, David Jacobsen, Robert Paine, Sinha, and Schwartz. I also acknowledge my debt to colleagues and students in Bergen for seminar discussions of my theme, and to Robert Minnich for help with the final editing of this article.

2 The usefulness of distinguishing numerical scale from structural complexity was in different ways suggested by several of the symposium participants, e.g. in the papers of Barth, Benedict, Colson, and Schwartz. John Barnes took up the point as an introductory problem for our discussions suggesting a 3×3 table with the two dimensions of size and complexity.

3 Fieldwork in Antalya lasted 12 months 1966–67 and 1969, and in Herat 5 months 1971–72. Some of my earlier work with these procedural and empirical themes is presented in Grönhaug 1971, 1971a, 1972, and in press.

4 For views relating the formation of social persons to aggregate social organization, I refer to Nadel on 'role allocation' (1965), Barth's comparative discussion (1972) Eidheim on Lappish identity management within the Scandinavian majority-minority context (1971), and my 'Micro-macro relations . . .', (in press).

5 The way I think of 'fields' relates to diverse applications of 'field', 'domain', 'level of integration' and similar terms in anthropology (cf. e.g. Redfield 1942, 1967b, Fortes 1969 and earlier works, Hanssen 1953, Barnes 1954, Steward 1972, Firth 1951, Gluckman 1964, Benedict 1966, Bailey 1970, Swartz 1972, Turner 1972, Cohen 1972). For a broader empirical and theoretical exposition of my multi-field analysis, cf. Grönhaug in press.

6 The little community's weakness in mobilizing effectively for a common community interest is a well-known theme in the literature on stratified agrarian societies. From my experience in Antalya I was surprised by the

287

pattern in Herat. The average Antalya village is much more of a veritable political corporation than is its Herat parallel. The Antalya village does in fact mobilize itself for quite extensive community tasks. Villagers pool labour and money for roads, water pipes, schools, and mosques. They display discipline and coordination, and the village headmanship is frequently an important position subject to much competition involving factions and alliances (cf. Grönhaug 1971). Antalya villages also have more stable populations than their Herati counterparts. Although the most drastic versions of Middle Eastern feuding are alien to Antalya people, the patterns of grouping within the village are clearly related to issues of honour and shame.

7 At this point I am especially thankful to Gellner, Paine, Schwartz, and Sinha for critical remarks underlining the necessity of showing more clearly the hierarchy of levels of religious organization in Herat, in analogy for example to the different levels of scale within economic organization (cf. Blom 1972, session 3, pp. 6–13).

8 Radcliffe-Brown, Gluckman, Fortes, Barth, and others provide the background for this view. 'The basic notion of course has long been familiar. It has been elaborated in a variety of contexts by theoretical sociologists from Simmel . . . to Parsons. . . . Karl Marx's often quoted dictum that "the human essence is no abstraction inherent in each single individual. In its reality it is the ensemble of the social relations" . . . (6th Thesis on Feuerbach) pithily sums up the proposition' (Fortes 1969:96).

9 While employing the characteristic techniques and concepts of social anthropology in the study of large-scale fields dominated by single-stranded relationships, I think I have shown that I thereby do not trespass the boundaries of my 'competence' as an anthropologist (cf. Grönhaug, in press). My methodological emphasis thus differs from that recommended in *Closed systems and open minds* (Gluckman 1964, e.g. on pp. 14, 188, 212, 257–8).

10 I regard the proper dynamics essentially as a structure of events in space-time, and the question of dominance pertains to the relationship of such structures to each other (see also Grönhaug, in press). My approach differs from the formulations on structural dominance put forth by M. Godelier (e.g. in 1973). I find many of his insights stimulating, but sometimes have difficulties in following his discovery steps connecting the 'hidden logic' of a structure with events in space-time and specifically the process of determination whereby a structure is effective in the social production of the human beings themselves.

11 '. . . The main point that we are dealing with is multiple levels of scale and multiple level of system, something of this sort, . . ., and the coexistence in multiple domains, each on a different scale. It seems that almost any two domains that we define are going to be defined on dimensions having different sizes . . . The individual's participation is on a number of points at once . . . He is at all levels at once, but his degree of participation on any given level may be relatively slight participation in terms of his effects on that level and also in terms of how much he is effected by it' (Schwartz, in Blom 1972, 'Final comments', session 10, p. 8).

SCALE AND SOCIAL CONTROL

1 The following view of social control mechanisms is drawn from a re(atively large and amorphous literature; the most useful items include Beccaria 1819), Krislov (1972), Rule (1973), and Scott (1971).

2 See Colson's 'A Redundancy of Actors'.

3 These may also be described as 'personal networks', 'personal communities', or 'small worlds'. For references to circles, see, among others, Evans-Pritchard

1940:114–117, 226; Sahlins 1965:151–152; Boissevain 1968:546–547; Bailey 1971:17; Suttles 1972:21.

5 Sally Merry conducted this field research as part of her graduate training in the Department of Anthropology, Brandeis University.

7 Henslin's study (1968) of cab-drivers and their passengers further illustrates the way in which control is secured in uniplex relations. In his analysis of this typically 'fleeting' relationship, Henslin describes the way in which 'strangers' seek to locate one another in a social network, in order to gain control over the relationship. Henslin describes the process of thus locating an individual in terms of his 'trackability'. Drivers assume greater trackability on the part of a potential passenger when he calls from a residentially stable neighborhood, in the belief that there is a link between the caller and others residing at his point of departure. A passenger, on the other hand, assumes greater trackability on the part of a potential driver when he works for a well-known and reliable cab company. Even the Wilsons note that social pressure could be applied to (and by) 'strangers', if they were linked to someone else who was known and accountable (1945:35).

TERTIUS GAUDENS AUT TERTIUM NUMEN

1 In addition to those who attended the conference, I wish to thank my colleagues Mel Spiro and Marc Swartz for their comments.

2 Another common meaning of *tertius gaudens* is different. Sometimes when there are two equally strong claimants to office, a third, possibly less qualified claimant, is selected. Nehru's successor, Shastri, was said to have benefitted in this way. Certainly, there is an element of *gaudens* in such situations; but there is also an element of *numen*, since in effect the two stronger candidates willy-nilly resign their claim in the interests of the collectivity to which they both belong and which the chosen candidate comes to serve and represent.

3 Five Latin words are enough for a title, so I left out a third variety of third person. This is *tertius dolens* [lit. the third man grieving]. The literature amply documents occasions on which the third person has cause for grief. The headman in British Central Africa could find himself pulled one way by his people and the opposite way by the Administration. He was required to interpret between two idioms of social life, which were such that translation was impossible (Fallers 1956; Gluckman, Mitchell & Barnes 1949). Each side sees him at best as incompetent and more often as a traitor: in fact, as *tertius gaudens*, when he should be *tertium numen*. The foreman in industry, caught between the millstones of management above and shop stewards below, finds himself abraded by being required to reconcile irreconcileable interests. Frankenberg's (1957) villagers invite an outsider to mediate their disputes, thus giving themselves the opportunity to blame him for anything unfortunate which may emerge from the settlement. In certain circumstances, in short, the fate of the peacekeeper is to be shot at by both sides. The role of *tertium numen* winds up as *tertius dolens*. In fact, although the distinction has tactical importance for those concerned, we need not involve it further in our analysis. *Numen* and *dolens* bracket together against *gaudens*.

4 The terms 'collectivity' and 'transcending value' require one another. The collectivity is defined as those who possess some common value: a value exists only insofar as it is held by one or more collectivities. Nevertheless, the concepts are not identical: later I will argue that as the collectivity increases in size, values may be at first enhanced and later diminished.

5 Do societies which maintain descent through women have myths of virgin birth?

6 We began by taking into account three actors: two contestants and a third

289

person claiming the moral right to intervene. As soon as this is redefined to focus upon claims to define the situation, the model requires only the two actors represented as T and A. Any proposition which we make need not apply only to contest situations in which there is intervention by a third person, but to any situation in which the moral right of one person to behave as *numen* is questioned. To behave as *numen* is to claim the right to be, in one form or another, a leader. Our problem has become generalized into asking what is the connection between scale and the moral basis of leadership.

This modification dispenses with the need for a literal third person. We can consider the not uncommon situation in which, of two contestants, one claims the right to settle the affair on the basis of moral superiority.

A similar simplification can be made in the other direction. The intention of a debater is to convert someone else to his own definition of the situation. This other person may be an opponent in the debate; it may be an audience: or it may be both these. Actual situations get complicated because it is sometimes effective to try to pretend to try to convince an opponent, whereas the message is really directed at an audience: sometimes the reverse is true, as when a display of conspicuous power, ostensibly addressed to no one in particular, is in fact a warning to a particular opponent.

But once we have reduced the situation to T and A, we need no longer take account of the possible combinations of different kinds of audience and opponent. For example, if one way to convince an opponent is by showing that the means which you propose serve an end which he accepts, while the plans which he puts forward do not, this applies whether A stands for the opponent or for the audience listening in.

Of course, there are situations in which it pays to keep distinct the opponent and the audience. Such situations are not considered, except incidentally, in this essay.

7 Indeed, the mask may be put in the way. Mr. Nixon's vain efforts to use the 'Presidency' and 'Executive privilege' are an excellent example.

THE SIZE AND SHAPE OF A CULTURE

1 Only a brief indication of this distributive model of culture will be included here. A more detailed discussion with references to other models is in Schwartz, 'Where Is the Culture?' (in press), which was developed from an excerpt of the original version of this paper. See also Schwartz 1958, 1962, 1963, and 1968.

2 Note the implication for the concept of 'personality'. Culture is no more that which is shared by all members of a society than personality is confined to that which is unique to individuals. 'Personality' is defined as an individual's total set of derivatives from experience, including those unique to him as well as those held in common with some social subset of individuals, including the possibility of some constructs that may be held in common with all other members of that society. Schwartz, 'Where Is the Culture?' (in press).

3 I would suggest the term 'sociates' for the hierarchic and coordinate component societies of larger social integrations.

4 These terms roughly correspond to 'primary and secondary relations' derived from Charles Cooley.

5 Peter Black reports on the effects of drastic population reduction on Tobi Atoll on social structure and status qualifications (dissertation in preparation, UCSD).

6 For a fuller discussion of time-limited or generational cultures, see Schwartz 1975b.

7 'The Metropolis and Mental Life', in Simmel 1950.

8 See Schwartz, 1963, on 'dispersed' versus 'oriented' networks.
9 Gallant & Prothero 1972: 382. They also review interesting organizational consequences of escalation not covered here.
10 Haudricourt 1961. The above is my argument; Haudricourt's is based on complexity through additive bilingualism.
11 See Schwartz 1968, and references therein for further discussion of control mechanisms.
12 See Schwartz, 1963, 1975c, on warfare.
13 Simmel, 'The Stranger', [1908], in Levine 1971.
14 Another instance of the *tertius numen*, Bailey, this volume.
15 See Schwartz 1975b, on relations among generations.

CONCLUSIONS

1 My previous explication of this system (Barth 1961) although done without benefit of an explicit concept of scale, contains the main structure of this argument. Unfortunately, this attempt at analyzing a rather interesting paradigm case of politics in plural situations has been misinterpreted as a functionalist search for justification of the tribal authority system, and criticized as an inappropriate application of the market model (Asad 1972:136 ff). Of course the chief's potential mobilization in such a conflict no more 'justifies' the particular authority structure so mobilized than does the mobilization of the landowner patron 'justify' his land rights. Nor does a market model serve to elucidate these events: to my understanding, the institutional framework of a market is, quite to the contrary, one that facilitates the participation of small actors in a large-scale system without the mobilization of complex collectivities. What we see, hopefully, in the present case are processes which quite conversely involve a diversity of persons and collectivities with highly differing purposes, interests, and degrees of concern for events of very uncertain outcome. A functionalist perspective, whether openly embraced or obliquely entailed in a critique, distorts these processes beyond recognition.

2 Again (see Note 1 above), it is not question of showing the function (and thus, supposedly, the justification) of parts in contributing to sustaining the whole: we are making no assumptions about the necessity or desirability of the whole in seeking to specify its system properties.